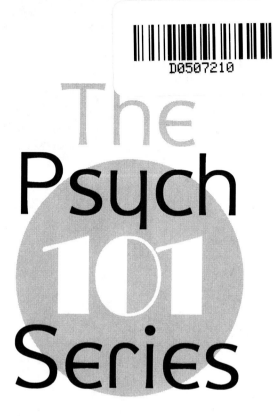

The
Psych
101
Series

James C. Kaufman, PhD, Series Editor
Department of Educational Psychology
University of Connecticut

C. Emily Durbin, PhD, is an associate professor of psychology at Michigan State University in East Lansing, Michigan. She received her PhD from Stony Brook University, Stony Brook, New York, in 2002. Her laboratory focuses on describing and understanding the origins of temperamental risk factors for depressive disorders and their trajectory across development.

Depression 101

C. Emily Durbin, PhD

SPRINGER PUBLISHING COMPANY
NEW YORK

Springer Publishing Company, LLC
11 West 42nd Street
New York, NY 10036
www.springerpub.com

Acquisitions Editor: Nancy S. Hale
Composition: Amnet Systems

ISBN: 978-0-8261-7106-1
e-book ISBN: 978-0-8261-7107-8

13 14 15 16 / 5 4 3 2 1

The author and the publisher of this Work have made every effort to use sources believed
to be reliable to provide information that is accurate and compatible with the standards
generally accepted at the time of publication. The author and publisher shall not be
liable for any special, consequential, or exemplary damages resulting, in whole or in
part, from the readers' use of, or reliance on, the information contained in this book.
The publisher has no responsibility for the persistence or accuracy of URLs for external
or third-party Internet websites referred to in this publication and does not guarantee
that any content on such websites is, or will remain, accurate or appropriate.

Library of Congress Cataloging-in-Publication Data

Durbin, C. Emily, author.
  Depression 101 / C. Emily Durbin, PhD.
    pages cm. — (Psych 101 series)
  ISBN 978-0-8261-7106-1 (print : alk. paper)—ISBN 978-0-8261-7107-8
(e-book) 1. Depression, Mental. I. Title. II. Title: Depression one
hundred one. III. Title: Depression one hundred and one.
  RC537.D87 2014
  616.85'27—dc23

                                                                    2013033879

Special discounts on bulk quantities of our books are available to corporations,
professional associations, pharmaceutical companies, health care organizations, and
other qualifying groups. If you are interested in a custom book, including chapters
from more than one of our titles, we can provide that service as well.

For details, please contact:
Special Sales Department, Springer Publishing Company, LLC
11 West 42nd Street, 15th Floor, New York, NY 10036-8002
Phone: 877-687-7476 or 212-431-4370; Fax: 212-941-7842
E-mail: sales@springerpub.com

Printed in the United States of America by Gasch Printing.

Contents

CONTENTS

Preface

epression 101 provides a comprehensive overview of all aspects of unipolar and bipolar depressive disorders, including their presentation, course, impact on functioning, etiology, and treatment. It integrates recent research on risk factors for these conditions and biological underpinnings of depression and mania alongside well-established observations regarding the phenomenology and correlates of these conditions.

Creativity 101
James C. Kaufman, PhD

Genius 101
Dean Keith Simonton, PhD

IQ Testing 101
Alan S. Kaufman, PhD

Leadership 101
Michael D. Mumford, PhD

Anxiety 101
Moshe Zeidner, PhD
Gerald Matthews, PhD

Psycholinguistics 101
H. Wind Cowles, PhD

Humor 101
Mitch Earleywine, PhD

Obesity 101
Lauren Rossen, PhD
Eric Rossen, PhD

Emotional Intelligence 101
Gerald Matthews, PhD
Moshe Zeidner, PhD
Richard D. Roberts, PhD

Personality 101
Gorkan Ahmetoglu, PhD
Tomas Chamorro-Premuzic, PhD

Giftedness 101
Linda Kreger Silverman, PhD

Evolutionary Psychology 101
Glenn Geher, PhD

Psychology of Love 101
Karin Sternberg, PhD

Intelligence 101
Jonathan A. Plucker, PhD
Amber Esping, PhD

Depression 101
C. Emily Durbin, PhD

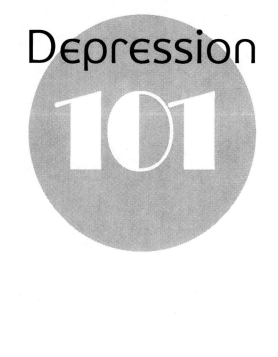

Depression
101

What Is Depression?

epression is a rich, multifarious concept; it encompasses a broad range of human experiences from the momentary to the characterological. The challenges of naming, capturing, and ultimately understanding this vexing construct have inspired great art, religious and spiritual explorations, personal disclosures, and scientific study. The suffering created by depression and the gravity of its frequent consequences (including relationship dissolution, ill health, and suicidality) give a sense of urgency to the mission of learning how to most effectively understand, treat, and prevent it. The aim of this book is to highlight and clarify the particular ways in which scientific disciplines have approached understanding the variety of experiences we call depression, and to demonstrate how the knowledge generated by science has shed light on our human understanding of depression and resulted in improved identification and treatment of these conditions.

In everyday discussions, the terms "depressed" or "depression" can refer colloquially to the kinds of mundane, momentary, negative reactions that are tightly bound to our experience of particular stress-ors or disappointments, or to more diffuse, short-lived periods (e.g., days) of malaise and unhappiness after which we rebound to a more positive (or at least, less depressed) mood state. These experiences are a ubiquitous part of being a human, living in a complex world characterized by unavoidable challenges, setbacks, and fluctuating goals. Most of us find these experiences readily understandable and manageable, albeit unpleasant, to endure. However, depression can also refer to much more elaborate, complex manifestations of these problems that are troubling in their length, their lack of transparent connection to environmental precipitants, imperviousness to mood repair techniques, or their impact on our ability to function in rela-tionship to self, work, or others. Consider the following observation by the novelist William Styron (1990), who suffered from a serious depressive disorder and described it as follows in his memoir *Dark-ness Visible: A Memoir of Madness*:

> That the word "indescribable" should present itself is not fortuitous, since it has to be emphasized that if the pain were readily describ-able most of the countless sufferers from this ancient affliction would have been able to confidently depict for their friends and loved ones (even their physician) some of the actual dimensions of their tor-ment, and perhaps elicit a comprehension that has been generally lacking; such incomprehension has usually been due not to a failure of sympathy but to the basic inability of healthy people to imagine a form of torment so alien to everyday experience. (pp. 16–17)

This book focuses primarily on understanding the meaning of depression, an experience that is neither ubiquitous nor eas-ily understandable to everyone, but which nonetheless affects a significant number of people in profound ways. This meaning is sometimes referred to by the global phrase "clinical depression," or more formally (and precisely) in the scientific literature by one of the psychiatric diagnostic labels that include these and related symptoms. The diagnostic manuals in use in the United States and internationally—the *Diagnostic and Statistical Manual of Mental Disorders* (*DSM-5*) and the *International Classification of*

Diseases (*ICD-10*)—recognize several formal diagnostic labels in the family of depressive disorders, three of which are the primary focus of this book: Major Depressive Disorder (MDD), Dysthymic Disorder (DD), and Bipolar Disorder (BD). The current definitions of these labels were constructed based on theory and empirical research so as to distinguish them in valid ways from colloquial or lay meanings of the term depression.

Diagnoses of depressive disorders differ from colloquial meanings of the term depression—often used to refer to more temporary reactions—to those more troubling manifestations of the concept that are the province of psychopathological research. One important difference is that diagnoses fit the concept of a syndrome. A syndrome is a set of signs and symptoms that appear together in time in a coherent pattern. In the case of psychiatric disorders such as depression, symptoms are those problems that can be described by someone experiencing them but that are not readily observable by others, such as thoughts of hopelessness. In contrast, a sign is an objectively identifiable indicator exhibited by the person that can be noticed by others, such as tearfulness or decreased speech. When we describe depressive disorders as syndromes, we mean that they identify periods in which a person is simultaneously experiencing multiple signs and symptoms that represent a change from the individual's usual functioning or experience, which appear (or onset) at roughly the same period in time, last for a significant length of time, and may intensify in their presentation at the same time or rate. A syndrome includes multiple co-occurring signs and symptoms that involve more than one psychological system, as opposed to fleeting reactions to stressors that may be characterized by a circumscribed reaction—such as sadness and temporary insomnia. For example, a person may feel depressed, socially withdrawn, amotivated, sleep much less than usual, and engage in more self-critical thinking for a period of several months. Inherent in the notion of a syndrome is the assumption that the separate indicators (e.g., depressed mood, social withdrawal, amotivation, and so on) co-occur in time and wax and wane together in their intensity because they are caused by the same underlying process or processes. This is in contrast to an experience in which an individual simultaneously feels sadness over the loss of a friend and difficulty sleeping due to noisy nighttime construction work outside of the individual's home; in this case, the two signs/symptoms are not caused by the same process and thus would not be expected to relate to one another over time.

Descriptive psychopathology focuses on identifying the most defining, distinctive, and troubling/impairing symptoms and signs of various psychiatric syndromes, as well as detailing their temporal boundaries (i.e., their required duration). Careful description of signs and symptoms allows for more precise assessment of the condition of interest and suggests features that could be targeted for treatment of individuals suffering from the syndrome. It also facilitates precise measurement of the syndrome for use in other forms of research. The exact nature of these signs and symptoms, however, may or may not point to obvious candidates for the processes that initially caused the syndrome to occur or those that may cause them to remit over time. Etiological research goes beyond descriptive psychopathology to focus on identifying and understanding the factors that cause a person to develop the syndrome. The initial focus here is on describing the content of depressive disorder categories (i.e., their signs and symptoms) before turning to an understanding of their causes.

CLASSIFICATION OF DEPRESSIVE DISORDERS: *DSM-IV-TR* AND *DSM-5*

The classification systems used to delineate depressive syndromes for modern research and clinical practice, the *Diagnostic and Statistical Manual of Mental Disorders* (issued in its 5th revision in 2013 by the American Psychiatric Association) and the *International Classification of Diseases* (*ICD-10* [World Health Organization, 2008], soon to be issued in its 11th edition), define several syndromes whose primary manifestation is an alteration of mood. *Depression 101* focuses on three of the most important and well studied of these conditions: Major Depressive Disorder (MDD), Dysthymic Disorder (DD), and Bipolar Disorder (BD).

The *DSM* and *ICD* systems both employ a categorical model for the classification of psychopathologies, including depressive disorders. In such a system, individuals are presumed to either have or not have a particular psychiatric condition; each condition is defined by a set of inclusion (things that must be present) and exclusion (signs/symptoms that must not be present) criteria that identify the presence of the condition. These criteria refer to symptoms, signs, and their frequency and/or duration, and set a threshold above which an individual's presentation must exceed in order to receive the diagnostic label. The advantages of systems of this type are that categories provide a clean fit to the kinds of clinical decisions that are necessarily dichotomous in nature, such as whether or not to treat a particular case, and they are simpler for purposes of communication (information is conveyed by a single label, rather than a list of symptoms or characteristics). Some obvious disadvantages are: (a) we do not have good evidence that the particular thresholds as currently laid out in our diagnostic systems cleanly differentiate separate groups of people who differ in qualitatively distinct ways, as would be expected if the world comprised people with and people without MDD, for example; (b) among all those who do meet diagnostic criteria for a particular depressive disorder, such as BD, there will still be considerable variability in the particular pattern and in the severity of the symptomatology they experience, such that there may be fewer commonalities among all those meeting diagnostic criteria than one would expect; and (c) some people who do not meet diagnostic criteria for a particular depressive disorder may nonetheless experience suffering or seek treatment for their symptoms. The relative superiority of categorical classification systems as opposed to other models—such as those in which individuals are seen as varying along a continuum of depressive severity ranging from not at all depressed to very depressed—has long been a topic of scientific contention. The chapters that follow review some of the evidence and arguments that are a part of this debate as they bear on the measurement of depression and understanding of its nature and etiology. For now, the focus is on understanding the content of the current classification models, as they have defined the individuals and variables that make up much of the modern science on depressive disorders.

All the depressive disorders identified in the *DSM* and *ICD* are composed of one or more discrete time periods of symptoms, the most central of which are alterations in mood state that vary in their intensity and duration. Current diagnostic systems set out the minimum duration and number and intensity of symptoms required to meet the diagnosis, and limit the diagnosis to those whose mood symptoms are not better explained by some other process whose effect on the brain mimics that of depressive disorders (i.e., exclusion criteria). These criteria sets thus lay out a threshold above which an individual is considered depressed; however, they do not guarantee that all such individuals are homogeneous in their symptomatic expression, functioning, or even the cause of their disorder. Thus, there is no strong presumption in the classification system that individuals with the same diagnosis will be similar on all (or even many) characteristics that often accompany depressive disorders or on the factors that may have caused the condition. Understanding any particular case of a depressive disorder thus still requires a careful picture of the individual. In particular, diagnosing a depressive disorder requires consideration of the person's typical mood state and functional capacities because depressive disorders are defined by symptoms that represent changes from an individual's prior functioning. Careful assessment of prior and current functioning allows for more precision in diagnosis and for more accurate measurement of the effectiveness of interventions for returning the person to a typical level of functioning.

Major Depressive Disorder

MDD is defined by the presence of at least one discrete and distressing/impairing period of depression, formally referred to as a major depressive episode (MDE). In an MDE, a person experiences at least five symptoms of depression that are a clear change from the individual's prior psychological state and functioning, all co-occurring during the same 2-week period. Each symptom must be present nearly every day during that 2-week period, wherein "nearly every day" is often operationalized as 5 days of the 7 days of the week, although the DSM does not stipulate this particular definition. At least one of these five symptoms is a primary disturbance of mood, either (a) depressed mood (in children and adolescents, irritable mood can substitute for depressed mood) or (b) anhedonia. The symptom of depressed mood refers to internally experienced feelings of sadness, depression, or emptiness, or indicators of such that can be observed by others (e.g., tearfulness); these mood disturbances must be evident most of the day, nearly every day.

The second mood disturbance, anhedonia, may be experienced instead of or in addition to depressed mood. Anhedonia refers to a near complete loss of or a serious decrease in feelings of pleasure derived from one's activities or a significant decrease in interest in those activities. This loss of pleasure or interest may be noticed by others in the form of a lack of engagement or a failure to respond positively to normally enjoyed events, or only experienced subjectively. For a person to meet this criterion, the anhedonia must be related to all or almost all of the activities the person previously enjoyed, and be evident most of the day, nearly every day. Activities that may be affected can include hobbies and leisure pursuits, work tasks, or social events. It can impact the motivation to engage in highly complex and coordinated behaviors that require sustained attention and effort, or even simple activities typically associated with easy pleasures, such as eating one's favorite meal or enjoying a walk. Individuals suffering from anhedonia may exhibit reduced self-care, such as taking much less effort to maintain their appearance, neglecting their hygiene, or failing to clean their homes. Anhedonia can impact these basic behaviors or those that were previously a source of great joy and pride. This is often one of the most devastating features of depression for those living with it. The novelist David Foster Wallace (1996), who suffered from recurrent bouts of depression, described it as follows in his novel *Infinite Jest*:

> a kind of radical abstracting of everything, a hollowing out of stuff that used to have affective content. Terms the undepressed toss around and take for granted as full and fleshy—happiness, joie de vivre, preference, love—are stripped to their skeletons and reduced to abstract ideas. They have, as it were, denotation but not connotation. . . . Everything becomes an outline of the thing. Objects become schemata. The world becomes a map of the world. An anhedonic can navigate, but has no location. I.e, the anhedonic becomes, in the lingo of Boston AA, Unable to Identify. (p. 693)

In addition to depressed mood and/or anhedonia, an MDE is defined by symptoms concerning basic circadian and biological rhythms, energy, and particular kinds of negative cognitions. An MDE can include weight changes, ranging from the less severe (a significant decrease or increase in appetite, experienced nearly every day) to the more severe (significant weight loss or gain, defined as a change of more than 5% of body weight in a month). Weight changes cannot be attributable to purposeful dieting. Most experiencing weight loss report a loss of interest in eating and food, and may merely go through the motions of eating more out of habit or encouragement by others than by any strong desire for particular foods, feelings of hunger, or pleasure experienced by eating. Changes in sleep may also be apparent, and are considered present if they occur nearly every day. These can take the form of insomnia (loss of sleep) or hypersomnia (a significant increase in sleep). These must be in contrast to a person's typical sleep routine when not depressed. One commonly applied rule of thumb is that insomnia refers to sleeping at least 1 hour less per night (and hypersomnia 1 hour more). Insomnia can take the form of initial difficulty falling asleep, trouble staying asleep, or awakening earlier than intended or desired. Individuals with hypersomnia may increase their sleep by sleeping more hours during the night or by napping more during the day. This symptom is often one of the most distressing for individuals experiencing an MDE because sleep disturbances can worsen other troubles that often accompany depression, such as anxiety, may make it more challenging to cope with other symptoms of depression, or may create conflict with significant others (e.g., hypersomnia may make it difficult for a parent to take care of many parenting responsibilities or restless sleep may disturb a partner's sleep patterns). A third additional symptom of an MDE is fatigue or loss of energy, experienced nearly every day. Unsurprisingly, this symptom is common among those who are experiencing insomnia. However, it is important to note that this symptom can occur in the absence of sleep difficulties; someone experiencing depression may feel completely fatigued and drained of energy despite sleeping what the person would typically consider to be an adequate number of hours per night. This symptom may be experienced as a bodily sensation of tiredness or languor or more psychologically as a failure to generate the steam to engage in many activities (and is thus often related to the experience of anhedonia). A final symptom of this type is psychomotor agitation or retardation, experienced nearly every day and of significant presence that it is noticeable to others in the individual's environment. Psychomotor agitation refers to restlessness and physical edginess; the person may pace, fidget, or be incapable of relaxing. Psychomotor retardation is characterized by a general slowing of motor processes, including speech. Others may observe the person taking much longer than normal to accomplish simple motor tasks. Some who have experienced this symptom describe it as "moving through sludge" or "being in quicksand."

The final three symptoms of an MDE are cognitive in nature. First, the person may experience a general blocking, slowing, or stymieing of thought. This may take the form of difficulty maintaining attention or concentration on a task, trouble with higher-order cognitions such as planning or evaluating options, or as trouble making everyday decisions (such as what to wear or to eat for lunch). These must be experienced nearly every day to be considered evidence of an MDE. For some, the dysfunction may be so apparent behaviorally that it is obvious to outsiders; whereas for others, they may be subjectively aware of such problems without other people noticing their impact. The final two symptoms concern the content of the person's cognitions. First, some individuals with depression experience a deterioration of their self-concept, ruminating about feelings of worthlessness or guilt that is excessive or inappropriate in nature. These thoughts must occur nearly every day, cannot be limited to guilt or self-criticism about being depressed, and should be considerably more severe than more normative levels of low self-esteem. Worthlessness often takes the form of pervasive self-criticism, feelings of insurmountable inadequacy, or judgments that one contributes nothing to others or to the world in general. If the person tends to be self-critical typically, the pervasiveness and negativity of self-judgment tend to become even more inflated during an MDE. Guilt is characterized as excessive if the person accurately identifies an action that could be regretted but overestimates the severity of the transgression or its impact or remains guilty about it despite being forgiven by the aggrieved parties. Inappropriate guilt refers to self-recrimination about actions (or perhaps thoughts) for which the person was either not in error or for which they cannot reasonably be held responsible; for example, a depressed mother may feel convinced that her child developed cancer because she did not provide sufficiently nutritious meals for her family. In some MDEs, the level of guilt or worthlessness can have a delusional aspect (e.g., taking guilty responsibility for acts that one did not commit). Finally, MDEs are often characterized by suicidality, ranging in severity from recurrent thoughts concerning one's own death (sometimes taking the form of picturing the responses of loved ones or others upon one's death); recurrent thoughts or images concerning committing suicide (which may be experienced as brief impulses to engage in a suicidal act without intent to do so); or devising a specific plan for committing suicide or attempting to do so.

In addition to meeting the diagnostic threshold for the total number and duration of these symptoms, there must not be any obvious medical condition or consumption of a psychoactive substance that could account for the appearance of the symptoms. The *DSM-IV* also included an exclusion for some cases with particular symptom presentations in which the syndrome appeared after the loss of a loved one (referred to as bereavement); this criterion was eliminated in *DSM-5*, and the rationale for this decision is discussed further in Chapter 8. Finally and critically, the person's symptoms must cause significant distress to the individual or be expressed as or have the consequence of creating impairment (difficulty in functioning) in some important area of functioning, including social relationships, occupational functioning, or self-care. The kinds of functioning impairments associated with depressive disorders are more fully identified in Chapter 4; however, suffice it to say that the degree of impairment for those meeting symptom criteria can range in severity. Some people may endorse enough symptoms to meet the criteria for a depressive disorder, but not indicate that they are noticeably impacting their functioning. Others may experience significant and pervasive inability to meet most or any of the demands of their lives (e.g., they may be unable to work, engage in basic self-care, or have profound difficulties in their relationships as a result of their symptoms). Significant distress is often assumed if the person seeks treatment to ameliorate the symptoms or reports a desire for them to end.

MDD is defined by the presence of at least one MDE, although in fact many individuals experience more than one MDE during their lifetimes (referred to as recurrent MDD, recognized as a subtype or specifier of MDD). The *DSM-IV* also recognized another subtype referring to the course of depression, a Chronic MDE. A Chronic MDE is one that lasts at least 2 years. These and other subtypes are discussed in more detail in Chapter 2.

Dysthymic Disorder

DD is a chronic mood disorder. Its principal criterion is the presence of depressed mood, occurring most of the day for more days than not for a duration of 2 years (for children and adolescents, only 1 year of duration is required). The depressed mood may be subjectively reported or noticeable to others. "More days than not" is often operationalized as meaning 4 days of the 7 days of the week, although this is not explicit in the *DSM*. In addition to depressed mood, the person must also experience at least two of the following symptoms: appetite problems (overeating or poor appetite), sleep difficulties (insomnia or hypersomnia), low energy or fatigue, low self-esteem, cognitive problems (difficulty making decisions or with concentration), and feelings of hopelessness. Thus, five of these symptoms are either the same or less intense versions of symptoms of an MDE. The final criterion is unique to DD. This disorder requires fewer symptoms, with less within-week frequency, than an MDE but for a much longer overall duration (2 weeks vs. 2 years). The symptoms of DD must be pervasive across the total 2-year period, with no longer than a 2-month interval without these symptoms. Finally, to distinguish DD from an MDE, DD is not diagnosed if the person experienced an MDE at any time during the first 2 years during which the individual met criteria for DD (such a person would instead receive a diagnosis of a chronic MDE). Individuals who have ever experienced episodes indicative of a bipolar disorder (described in the following) cannot be diagnosed with DD. As for MDD, the symptoms cannot be accounted for by the effects of substance use or a medical condition. Finally, the symptoms must result in significant distress or impairment. *DSM-5* combined the categories of DD and chronic MDE into a new disorder, Persistent Depressive Disorder. The logic for this combination of categories is discussed further in Chapter 2.

Bipolar Disorder

BD is defined by the presence of a manic episode (ME). Individuals with BD must have at least one ME and may or may not also experience one or more MDEs. The first, and defining, criterion of an ME is a discrete period in which the person exhibits persistently elevated, expansive, or irritable mood (much different from the individual's typical mood state), lasting at least 1 week. Abnormally positive mood (feeling excited, elated, or expansive) is considered a classic presentation of mania. Irritable presentations are less prototypical, although this variant has received increasing research attention in the last decade or so. If the person's presentation is so serious that hospitalization is required, then the abnormal mood can be of any duration. In addition to the mood abnormality, the person must experience at least three additional symptoms if the mood state is abnormally positive, or at least four additional symptoms if the mood is only irritable. Some of these symptoms involve an alteration of activity and motivation. First, the person may exhibit a decreased need for sleep; this is typically operationalized as objectively sleeping only a few hours per night (e.g., 3 hours) and yet still feeling rested and energized. Second, the person may have a marked change in the extent and enthusiasm for engagement in goal-directed activities, which can include socializing, work or school tasks, sexual behaviors, or psychomotor agitation. This may be reflected in an increase in time spent on one's usual activities, such as seeking out social interactions, engaging in novel activities that are not part of one's typical behavioral repertoire (e.g., taking on many new hobbies), or an increase in restless energy (agitation) expended on any number of tasks (cleaning, organizing, and so on). Many times, the content of these new activities is unconnected to the person's prior goals (e.g., a man with no prior interest or expertise in cars begins rebuilding a clunker in his garage until the wee hours of the morning), or the interests are bizarre or delusional in nature (e.g., writing a treatise on a new language used to communicate with insects). Finally, the person may exhibit problematic involvement in activities that are highly reinforcing but likely to result in negative consequences, such as risky sexual behavior, unwise spending sprees, and so on. Four more symptoms chiefly concern cognitive manifestations of mania. First, the person expresses or conveys a grossly inflated sense of self-worth or grandiosity; this may range from excessively positive views of one's objective characteristics to more delusional presentations (e.g., believing one has the ability to influence national foreign policy or to attract the attention and love of a celebrity). Second, the individual has an internal sense of thoughts racing quickly from one topic or idea to the next; in many cases, this is obvious to others because of its impact on the person's speech. Third, the subject may engage in more verbal behavior than usual or feel a great pressure to continue speaking; often, others have difficulty getting a word in edgewise with an acutely manic person. Finally, the individual may be highly distractible, such that attention persistence is weakened to the point where focus can be easily captured by extraneous, unimportant stimuli, either in the environment or in thoughts. These cognitive manifestations can be sufficiently severe to produce an extremely disorganized presentation in which others may find the person's thoughts, speech, and manner bizarre, upsetting, and incomprehensible. Taken together, the symptom presentation cannot be attributable to a medical condition or the effects of ingesting a substance, and they must result in notable impairment—as evidenced by difficulty functioning in one or more life domains, necessitation of hospitalization to prevent harm to self or others, or the presence of psychotic features (e.g., delusions or hallucinations). The psychotic features that occur during MEs can be extreme. For example, the actress Margot Kidder suffered a serious ME while working on her autobiography. As she described to *People* magazine (September 23, 1996), she worked on her book 10 to 12 hours per day; after losing her draft to a computer malfunction, her mania escalated into paranoia, described as follows:

> Kidder came to the conclusion that her first husband, novelist Thomas McGuane, "was trying to kill me." She had divorced McGuane . . . in 1977 after several turbulent years. Disoriented and terrified, she returned to the L.A. airport on Saturday afternoon, April 20. Kidder was fixated on the idea that McGuane and the CIA were plotting to kill her because her book was powerful enough to change the world. . . . Kidder saw agents and assassins everywhere. "I know you're looking at me!" she shouted at passersby at the airport. . . . Kidder had thrown away her purse because she thought there was a bomb in it. In the early hours of April 21, she tried to take a taxi but didn't have enough money for the trip. She tried to use her ATM card outside the airport but thought the cash machine was about to explode. "I took off running," Kidder recalls.

Some individuals with BD can experience an alternative manifestation, referred to as a mixed episode. A mixed episode is a period of at least 1 week in which the diagnostic criteria for both an ME and an MDE are met nearly every day. Bipolar II disorder (defined more fully in Chapter 2) is defined by the presence of one or more MDEs and subthreshold manic episodes called hypomanic episodes. Thus, as noted above, the presence of MDEs does not distinguish between BD versus MDD and DD. Rather, it is the presence of mania (regardless of the presence or absence of an MDE) that differentiates among these disorders, with any evidence of mania suggesting the presence of BD.

OVERVIEW OF THIS BOOK

In the chapters that follow, a number of important topics in depressive disorders are addressed: the theoretical distinction between BD and the unipolar mood disorders (MDD and DD)

(Chapter 2); the spectrum of depressive presentations (Chapter 2); who is most likely to experience depression and what this tells us about potential causes of these disorders (Chapter 3); the extent and nature of depression's impact on a variety of forms of functioning (Chapter 4); theoretical models of why depression exists (Chapter 5); and how it might be caused (Chapter 6). The remainder of the book focuses on theory and evidence regarding a number of possible causal pathways to depression (Chapters 7, 8, and 9); treatment of depression (Chapter 10); and a description of exciting new research avenues that may shed fresh light on depressive disorders and potentially impact our ability to treat them effectively (Chapter 11).

How Does Depression Manifest?

Depression is not a unitary construct, as noted in Chapter 1. Rather, it refers to a variety of experiences and is the primary feature defining multiple psychiatric disorders recognized in the current classification systems. Both the *DSM* (*Diagnostic and Statistical Manual of Mental Disorders*) and *ICD* (*International Classification of Diseases*) recognize a family of disorders collectively referred to as mood or depressive disorders. This chapter focuses on (a) identifying those features that appear to be common across all or several of these disorders, as well as those that differentiate them from each another; and (b) describing the continuum of severity that can exist within any one of these disorders. Understanding the full spectrum of presentation of depressive disorders is useful for identifying features that may explain variability in functioning and outcome over time across individuals with the same disorder. It may potentially point to targets for understanding the etiology of these conditions. If we can properly identify the central variables that explain variation in depression severity, these may identify different etiological pathways to these conditions.

BIPOLAR VERSUS UNIPOLAR DEPRESSIVE DISORDERS

One of the most important distinctions made in psychiatric classification systems and in the scientific literature on depressive disorders is between Bipolar Disorders (BDs) (characterized by the presence of manic symptoms) and the unipolar mood disorders (all those that do not involve manic symptoms, including Major Depressive Disorder [MDD] and Dysthymic Disorder [DD]). In fact, the decision to view these as distinct conditions is one of the most important in the history of psychiatric classification and descriptive psychopathology. Many major figures in scientific psychiatry—beginning with Emil Kraepelin, often referred to as the "father of psychiatric nosology"—contributed to our understanding of unipolar and bipolar depressive disorders as reflecting different disease processes. Kraepelin is lionized for his detailed and insightful descriptions of his patients' psychiatric presentations. His approach, which now seems surprisingly modern for someone working in the late 1800s, was to focus on careful and detailed observation of patients over time, rather than focusing on a mere snapshot of their symptoms at a single time point. This approach is echoed in current proposals regarding the spectrum of depressive disorders that emphasizes the importance of course for distinguishing cases on the basis of their outcome, severity, and etiology (e.g., Klein, 2008). Kraepelin described the presentation of his patients over several hospitalizations, detailing similarities and differences in their symptoms across varying episodes. He was responsible for coining the term *manic depression* and made the critical observation that some patients exhibit a recurrent course of mood symptoms characterized by patterns of remission (i.e., abatement of symptoms), relapse, and exacerbation of symptoms. Patients with this type of course can be distinguished from those who do not experience repeated episodes of mood symptoms over time. Thus, Kraepelin's observations were critical to our understanding of course (i.e., the pattern, persistence, stability, and change in symptoms and functioning over time) as a critical feature of the bipolar presentation; however, he did not propose that courses including manic episodes, as opposed to those that do not, reflect a different disease process.

The first clearly articulated distinctions between unipolar and bipolar depressive disorders were made in the mid-20th century by the German Karl Leonhard, and later expanded upon by Angst, Perris, and Winokur in the late 1960s. These scientists demonstrated in a series of independent studies that people with and without mania differ systematically in their clinical characteristics, their familial history of psychopathology, and their course over time. Taken together, these lines of evidence suggest that bipolar and unipolar depression reflect separate disease processes. An explosion of research followed, further validating this distinction between manic and nonmanic forms of depression. Ultimately, this culminated in the incorporation of the distinction between unipolar and bipolar disorders in psychiatric classification systems. This view was first instantiated in the 3rd edition of the *DSM* (*DSM-III*), and has remained ever since.

The idea that manic episodes reflect a unique etiological pathway and have different implications for functioning and outcome—compared to unipolar depressive disorders—has received considerable empirical support. First, there is specificity of the familial transmission of these disorders. Rates of bipolar disorders are elevated (compared to population base rates) among the family members of people with BD, and are higher than the rate of BD among family members of people with unipolar depressive disorders (e.g., Winokur, Coryell, Endicott, & Akiskal, 1993). This suggests that there may be genetic pathways to the development of BD that are separate from those that lead to unipolar depressive disorders. Second, BD tends to have a more severe course than unipolar mood disorders (e.g., Angst & Preisig, 1995). This indicates that one advantage of having separate categories for bipolar and unipolar depressive disorders is that it may facilitate our ability to predict the long-term prognosis for a particular case, and to intervene in ways that take this poorer prognosis into account.

DISTINGUISHING UNIPOLAR AND BIPOLAR DEPRESSIVE DISORDERS OVER TIME

As noted in Chapter 1, an individual with BD may or may not experience major depressive episodes (MDEs), but must have had at least one manic episode. The majority of those who ever experience a manic episode do in fact have MDEs at some point during the course of their illness. Thus, practically speaking, any patient with a current MDE may or may not have BD. One must know whether or not the person has ever had a manic episode in order to distinguish between BD and unipolar depressive disorders. Furthermore, even for patients who have only had depressive episodes to date, some will eventually experience a manic episode. Accordingly, their diagnosis would change from MDD to BD; this phenomenon is typically referred to as "switching." Thus, Kraepelin's insight regarding the importance of taking a longitudinal view of a patient's presentation is critical for understanding the difference between BD and the unipolar depressive disorders. Predicting which person presenting with an MDE but no history of mania will ultimately develop a manic episode (and thus, BD) is challenging. First, the number of people who will ultimately switch represents only a small proportion of people who present with an MDE, complicating efforts to predict this unlikely outcome. Data indicate that about 1% of those presenting with an MDE will develop a hypomanic or manic episode within 1 year (Angst & Preisig, 1995; Coryell et al., 1995; Kinkelin, 1954). In a large longitudinal study of depressed people, the National Institute of Mental Health (NIMH) Collaborative Study of Depression, 8.6% of those with an MDE switched to Bipolar II (i.e., developed a hypomanic episode) over the 11-year follow-up period. Predictors of this switch were early age of onset of the first MDE, recurrent depression (Roy-Byrne, Post, Uhde, Porcu, & Davis, 1985), and several markers of psychosocial dysfunction, such as divorce or separation, work and school problems, and drug abuse (Akiskal et al., 1995). Similarly, Goldberg and colleagues (2001) reported that over a 15-year follow-up, approximately one fourth of those who were hospitalized for MDD developed at least one episode of hypomania, and 19% had at least one manic episode.

This suggests that many with BD can have an extended course of depressive symptomatology before ever exhibiting signs of mania, and that greater psychosocial maladjustment may either identify a more severely impaired group that is ultimately destined to manifest mania, or that this maladjustment may be causally implicated in the development of mania and/or hypomania. Switching can also be predicted by the presence of lower grade manifestations of manic symptoms that do not meet the threshold for a manic episode. There is good evidence for the prognostic significance of Bipolar II and other subthreshold BD presentations for predicting the ultimate development of Bipolar I Disorder. A significant minority (approximately 10%) of those who meet criteria for these conditions do eventually develop a full manic or a mixed episode, thus transitioning to a Bipolar I diagnosis. Thus, longitudinal assessments are critical for accurately differentiating between unipolar and bipolar depressive disorders, and bipolar presentations may be presaged by earlier indicators of subthreshold manic symptoms, as well as greater severity of depression (i.e., recurrent MDEs) or greater psychiatric problems (e.g., comorbidity with substance use problems or dysfunction in major life domains, including work and social functioning).

COMMON MISCONCEPTIONS REGARDING BIPOLAR DISORDER

A common lay conception of BD is that its course is defined by swinging between mania and depression, and that the experience of the disorder is one of wild vacillations between extremes of reckless elation and utter depression. Media depictions of the disorder have often contributed to these inaccuracies; and, given the rarity of the disorder in the population, most people do not know anyone who has BD. As a result, misunderstanding about the disorder abounds. Contrary to some depictions of the disorder, most individuals with BD have considerable well periods in which they do not experience significant symptoms of either depression or mania. They may be indistinguishable from their nonbipolar peers in terms of their functioning during these well periods, or may exhibit difficulties that are less grave than during an episode but that still pose a challenge. These functioning difficulties that occur during asymptomatic periods may be attributable to the lingering problems created by prior manic episodes (e.g., the need to rebuild relationships severed or impaired due to the person's earlier behavior, or to stabilize work performance following hospitalization), or they may be driven by the presence of subthreshold symptoms of either depression or mania or personality traits correlated with the disorder that may have a negative impact on functioning. Thus, a more nuanced view is that some people with BD may have only sporadic difficulty stemming from the illness and may function well if not actively symptomatic, such that their lives are not dominated by recurrent experiences of highs and lows. Furthermore, although most people who have BD will experience an MDE at some point in their lives, a substantial minority (around one fourth to one third) will never have an MDE (Depue & Monroe, 1978; Kessler, Rubinow, Holmes, Abelson, & Zhao, 1997). These mania-only courses of BD are more common among community samples than those recruited from treatment-seeking populations because those who also suffer from MDEs may be more likely to seek treatment compared to those who experience mania only. There is not an equal balance among those who have both manic and depressive episodes (course details of these disorders are discussed more fully in Chapter 3). Thus, very few people with BD fit the stereotype of someone moving back and forth sequentially between mania and depression. Finally, symptoms of depression and mania can co-occur at the same time; these mixed episodes, characterized by concurrent demonstrations of both manic and depressive episodes, are rather common among those with BD (e.g., Kessing, 2008). In addition, many individuals with mania have subthreshold depressive episodes (i.e., three or fewer depressive symptoms) during the course of their manic episodes. Therefore, it does not appear to be the case that depression and mania are opposing and incompatible ends of a pendulum. They can occur at the same time; experiencing one does not imply that a person will necessarily experience the other; and one type of episode does not reliably follow the other over time.

Another common idea about BD that has penetrated into public consciousness is that it differs from unipolar depressive disorder by virtue of being more attributable to biological/genetic factors and less influenced by environmental contributors than unipolar depressive disorders. This proposition is frequently made in the research literature as well. Consistent with this claim, there is in fact evidence from twin studies that BD has high heritability (Akiskal, 1983; Cardno et al., 1999; Kendler, Pedersen, Johnson, Neale, & Mathe, 1993). Estimates of the degree of variance in BD explained by genetic factors are higher than those reported for MDD. However, the overall number of twin studies underlying this conclusion is rather small, and no studies have directly compared the heritability of MDD to that of BD within the same sample. Thus, evidence supporting the greater genetic basis for BD compared to unipolar depressive disorders is somewhat indirect. Moreover, in a large twin study conducted by McGuffin and colleagues (2003), the authors found that the genetic contributions to mania and depression were correlates, suggesting similar genes are implicated in both poles. They also tested a model wherein BD and MDD share a genetic liability; however, bipolar is a more severe variant of this shared liability (i.e., the same genes are involved in both, but more of these genes are required to develop BD than to develop MDD). This model was not supported. Furthermore, evidence from molecular genetic studies suggests that some genetic polymorphisms are associated with both BD and recurrent forms of MDD, as well as psychotic disorders (e.g., Green et al., 2010). Thus, the relative importance of genes to each set of disorders and the nature of this genetic contribution (i.e., whether the genes involved in mania and depression are similar or unique) remain unresolved. The safest conclusion that can be drawn is that the distinction between unipolar and bipolar disorders does not translate directly into unique genetic pathways to either disorder, and that more serious forms of depressive disorders (i.e., recurrent depression, mania) may be caused by some of the same genes that are involved in other highly impairing psychiatric conditions.

Another idea commonly espoused is that major depressive episodes (MDEs) occurring within unipolar depressive disorders have a different etiology than those occurring among people with BD. Given the view that BD differs from unipolar disorders, it follows that the depressive episodes may be dissimilar across these two conditions. It is sometimes presumed that MDEs occurring in unipolar depression are reactions to life stressors, whereas those in BD emerge from an ongoing disease process that is fundamentally biological in nature and therefore less tied to environmental stressors. However, there is now convincing evidence showing stressors are critically involved in the course of both manic and depressive episodes of BD (Johnson, 2005; Johnson & Miller, 1997; Post & Leverich, 2006). (The role of stress in both unipolar and bipolar depressive disorders is covered more completely in Chapter 8.) This suggests that models depicting bipolar conditions as being principally driven by inherited, biological mechanisms, and unipolar conditions as more intimately wrapped up with the person's environmental context are not entirely accurate. Moreover, a broad review of psychosocial, cognitive, and biological correlates of depressive episodes and symptoms within bipolar and unipolar depressive disorders revealed that, in general, they are more alike than dissimilar (Cuellar, Johnson, & Winters, 2005). One potentially important distinction, however, is that MDEs among those with BD may be somewhat more severe in terms of their symptomatic level and impact on functioning. For example, in the National Comorbidity Study-Replication (NCS-R) (Kessler, Merikangas, & Wang, 2007), MDEs occurring in the prior 12 months among those with lifetime Bipolar I Disorder or subthreshold BD were more likely to be rated as serious in their level of severity than those MDEs occurring among individuals with MDD. Thus, the bipolar spectrum is associated with worse depressive episodes; however, their occurrence does not appear to be predicted by variables different from those for unipolar depressive disorders.

Some assumptions about the scope to which the distinction between unipolar and bipolar depressive disorders extends beyond their phenomenology and course to their causes have not met with empirical validation. Taken together, the lines of evidence presented above regarding distinctions between unipolar and bipolar disorders in terms of their etiology and outcome suggest a complicated picture of this traditional diagnostic distinction. The clinical picture of the two forms of depressive disorder is different, and those who experience threshold or subthreshold manic episodes appear to have somewhat worse prognosis over time, compared to those who only experience MDEs. However, there do not appear to be distinct etiological pathways that typify bipolar disorders and differentiate them from unipolar depression. As a result, some psychopathologists have proposed that rather than thinking of the critical distinction as being between unipolar depressive disorders and bipolar disorders, the appropriate one is between depression and mania, with the presence of manic/hypomanic symptoms serving as a marker of increased psychiatric severity (e.g., Cassano et al., 2004). For example, dimensional measures of lifetime manic symptoms are associated with elevated suicidality and psychotic symptoms (such as auditory hallucinations and paranoia), both in those with Bipolar I as well as in those with recurrent MDD (Cassono et al., 2004). Thus, the degree of manic or hypomanic symptoms (even those below the diagnostic threshold) is predictive of important phenomena, even when occurring in the context of a unipolar depressive disorder.

One implication of these findings is that BD might be thought of as a confluence of two disease processes, one leading to depression and the other to mania, rather than a single, unique disease process that produces both depressive and manic episodes. If this viewpoint were to be supported by additional evidence, it would represent a major change in our thinking about unipolar and bipolar depressive disorders and have important implications for how we study the etiology of these conditions. Traditional research designs focusing on diagnostic groups tend to compare groups of individuals with Condition A to Condition B or to a control group without the condition of interest. The bulk of the research on the impact and etiology of depressive disorders focuses on a single depressive disorder (e.g., Bipolar I, MDD), with fewer studies comparing bipolar and unipolar conditions to one another, and even fewer exploring shared and unique predictors of manic and depressive episodes (collapsing across diagnostic categories). Such designs will be necessary for furthering our understanding of the nature of these conditions and their causes. Taking to heart the Kraepelinian tradition of viewing course as a critical factor in parsing different etiological pathways and disease states, it may prove important to consider recurrent forms of mania and depression—as well as other indicators of the chronicity of these conditions—as the phenotypes to be explained by possible etiological factors, rather than the separate diagnostic categories of unipolar and bipolar disorders.

BEYOND BIPOLAR I AND MAJOR DEPRESSIVE DISORDER: THE "SOFT" SPECTRUM OF DEPRESSIVE DISORDERS

As the research base on depressive (unipolar and bipolar) disorders has grown, there has been a proliferation of categories in the psychiatric diagnostic systems (i.e., *DSM* and *ICD*) meant to tap the varying presentations that can be observed among

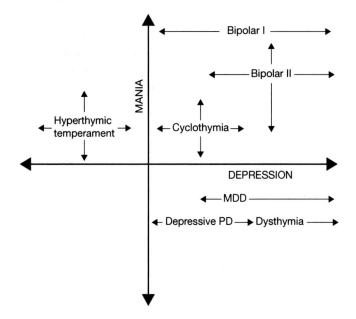

FIGURE 2.1 The spectrum of depressive disorders; manic and depressive continuum.

individuals prone to depression. Most of this proliferation has consisted of the addition of categories capturing less severe manifestations of depressive disorders, although some have proposed subtypes within particular diagnostic categories. See Figure 2.1 for a depiction of these manifestations of depressive disorders.

Bipolar II

This diagnosis is given to individuals with a history of at least one MDE and at least one hypomanic episode, but who have never had a full threshold manic or mixed episode. In the *DSM-5*, a hypomanic episode consists of the following criteria: a period of mood disturbance (i.e., elevated, expansive, or irritable mood) that lasts at least 4 days (most of the day), accompanied by three or more of the symptoms for a manic episode (four symptoms if the person's mood is only irritable). The behavior described by the criteria must represent a change from the person's typical functioning, and this change must be salient enough to be noticeable to others (i.e., not just subjectively felt by the individual). In contrast to a manic episode, however, hypomanic episodes do not cause marked impairment in functioning, there is no evidence of psychosis, and hospitalization is not required. The *DSM* definition of hypomania is essentially a subthreshold manifestation of the same presentation observed in those with a manic episode.

Akiskal and colleagues (2000) offered an alternative description of hypomania, including the presence of three or more of the following symptoms that represent a change from the person's baseline behavior, present for at least 2 days: cheerfulness, gregariousness, heightened sexual drive and sexual behavior, talkativeness, overconfidence and excessive optimism, disinhibited/carefree attitudes, reduced sleep, vitality, and involvement in new projects. This definition involves both a shorter required duration of symptoms, as well as descriptions of symptoms that are broader and less obviously dysfunctional. Broadening the definition in this way would be expected to produce higher prevalence rates of hypomania. Angst has noted that some of the manifestations of this condition may be reflected in greater motivation to seek out rewards of various kinds. For example, among community samples, those with hypomania report increasing their activities (such as working more hours); spending too much money; feeling less shy or inhibited; consuming more coffee, cigarettes, and alcohol; and making more jokes and puns (Angst, 1998).

Bipolar Disorder Not Otherwise Specified (NOS)

This diagnosis applies to all those who have some features of BD that are clinically significant or notable, but do not meet the diagnostic criteria for either bipolar I or II. For example, someone who exhibits full threshold manic and depressive symptoms that alternate over days but do not meet the duration criteria for a manic, major depressive, or hypomanic episode would receive a diagnosis of Bipolar Disorder NOS.

Cyclothymic Disorder

This condition is a chronic, low-grade variant of BD. The first criterion: over a 2-year time span, the person experiences numerous periods of hypomanic and depressive symptoms, none of which meet criteria for an MDE. The individual must have never met the criteria for a manic episode. There are no symptom-free periods lasting longer than 2 months, and the symptoms (of depression or hypomania) are evident at least one half of the time. During the first 2 years of the disturbance, there is never an MDE, manic, or mixed episode (although these can be superimposed on the underlying cyclothymia after this first 2 years). Many view this category as reflecting a temperamental predisposition toward affective problems, which may be either predominately depressive/irritable or hyperthymic (i.e., trait hypomanic). Therefore, cyclothymia is not an episodic state but a chronic/pervasive pattern of affective problems. Consistent with their tendency to vary in their predominant mood state, people with cyclothymia may also exhibit inconsistent patterns of interpersonal behavior and self-concept, such as vacillating between overconfidence and poor self-esteem, talkativeness alternating with verbal withdrawal, or periods of self-absorption followed by periods of seeking out social interaction (Akiskal et al., 1998). As noted by Akiskal et al. (2000), many individuals meeting criteria for cyclothymia also meet diagnostic criteria for borderline personality disorder and related conditions. Validity of this category is supported by evidence that rates of cyclothymia are elevated in the offspring of those with BD (Klein, Depue, & Slater, 1986).

Premenstrual Dysphoric Disorder (PMDD)

This category appears in *DSM-5* and was first included in the appendix of *DSM-IV-TR* (which contains numerous categories "for further study" that are not part of the diagnostic nomenclature). PMDD refers to symptoms of depression that regularly occur during the last week of the luteal phase of the menstrual cycle, evident during most menstrual cycles in the prior year. The symptoms must disappear completely after the onset of menstruation, and a total of five symptoms must be present. The first required criterion is that the individual must have at least one of the following symptoms: feelings of sadness/hopelessness/self-deprecation; tension/anxiety; lability of mood with frequent tearfulness; and persistent irritability/anger/increased interpersonal conflict. Of note, the list of anchor symptoms is more expansive than that required for an MDE, with only two defined by sad/depressed mood and none involving anhedonia. A total of five symptoms must be evident among those listed above, and include at least one of the remaining: decreased interest in typical activities; concentration problems; lethargy or low energy; marked appetite changes (perhaps including binges or cravings for particular foods); sleep disturbance (insomnia or hypersomnia); feeling overwhelmed or out of control; and physical symptoms, such as bloating, headaches, and so on. Two of these symptoms are the same as those included in the criteria for an MDE; the remainder are unique to PMDD. The symptoms must be present in the week before onset of menses, improve within a few days of its onset, and disappear (or be minimal) in the week after menses. PMDD is not diagnosed if the symptoms represent a worsening of another disorder, such as MDD or a personality disorder.

Minor Depressive Disorder

This category was included in the appendix of *DSM-IV-TR*. It includes periods of depressive symptoms that last as long as those required for an MDE (i.e., 2 weeks); however, these periods are characterized by fewer symptoms than those required for an MDE (i.e., less than five symptoms), and they are associated with less impairment than in the case of an MDE.

Recurrent Brief Depressive Disorder

This category, a type of "other specified depressive disorder" in *DSM-5*, fits individuals who experience repeated periods of depressive symptoms, two or more of which fulfill the symptom threshold (i.e., five symptoms, including depressed mood or anhedonia) but not the duration threshold (i.e., 2 weeks) for an MDE. The episodes must last at least 2 days (but less than 2 weeks), and they must recur at least once per month for a period of 12 consecutive months, and must be associated with significant distress or impairment.

Rapid Cycling Bipolar Disorder

Rapid cycling is defined in the *DSM-5* as having a minimum of four manic/hypomanic and/or MDEs per year. During times in which individuals are cycling in this manner, they tend to have very few symptom-free periods. Clinicians have also reported seeing patients with "ultrarapid" cycling, defined as four or more episodes within a month, or ultradian cycling, defined by cycling within a day. Evidence suggests that ultracycling does not represent a distinct subgroup of individuals. Rather, most who ever exhibit a rapid-cycling pattern tend to return to a noncycling pattern over a follow-up period. Studies that have collected closely spaced repeated assessments of symptoms have found that among treatment-seeking samples, approximately one third exhibit rapid cycling, with a significant proportion of these meeting criteria for ultrarapid or ultradian cycling (e.g., Kupka et al., 2005).

RESEARCH CATEGORIES NOT RECOGNIZED IN DSM-IV OR DSM-5

Other researchers have suggested additional categories not currently represented in the *DSM* or *ICD*, arguing for the presence of a broader range of bipolarity, sometimes referred to as the "soft bipolar spectrum" (Akiskal & Mallya, 1987). This spectrum is described as including manic presentations, mixed manic/depressive presentations, those with rapid cycling, those who primarily experience recurrent depressive episode along with hypomania, those who develop mania or hypomania following treatment with antidepressant medications (Akiskal et al., 2000), and those with hypomanic episodes of briefer duration than those laid out in the *DSM* (less than 4 days; Angst, 1998).

Hyperthymic Temperament

Akiskal and colleagues (1998) described a range of temperamental styles indicating tendencies toward manic/hypomanic and depressive symptoms that may be evident in community populations. Hyperthymia consists of a pattern of behaviors suggesting elevated mood and energy, including exuberance and optimism, promiscuity or other forms of stimulus seeking, experiencing restless impulses and rash plans, being socially intrusive and overinvolved, and being self-assured or boastful.

Depressive Personality Disorder/ Depressive Temperament

The depressive temperament has been recognized since ancient times, and was also described by Kraepelin. Schneider (1958) described the following characteristics of the disorder: being reticent, passive, and nonassertive; having a gloomy and serious demeanor/seeming incapable of having fun; engaging in self-derogatory thoughts; expressing a skeptical and hypercritical attitude toward others; being overly conscientious and self-disciplined; brooding, worry, and preoccupation with negative events, personal shortcomings, and feelings of inadequacy. Importantly, depressive personality disorder is associated with impairment (Klein & Miller, 1993), can be distinguished from unipolar depressive disorders (e.g., dysthymia, MDD; Klein & Miller, 1993), and runs in the families of those with chronic forms of depression (Klein, 1999). It also predicts the long-term course of depressive conditions over time (Klein & Shih, 1998), as well as the development of mood disorders (Kwon et al., 2000; Rudolph & Klein, 2009). It is uncommon in the community, with prevalence rates of around 2% (Orstavik et al., 2007), but more prevalent in treatment-seeking populations, with a rate of around 25% (Klein, 1990).

THE SPECTRUM OF DEPRESSIVE DISORDER CATEGORIES

Both categories evident in the *DSM* and *ICD* systems, as well as those utilized by researchers to study the range of presentations of mood symptoms (e.g., depressive and hypomanic), demonstrate the variability in severity and course of presentation of these symptoms across the population, as well as the degree to which they can shade into personality styles defined by high levels of depressive or optimistic mood. The sheer number of categories available for labeling gradations of these problems belies their dimensionality, and suggests that pathological mood states exist in a subtle gradation of severity that varies in the type, chronicity, and extremity of these symptoms.

Early-Onset Bipolar Disorder

Since the mid-1990s, there has been a surge of interest in BD among youngsters. Although the typical onset age of these conditions is in late adolescence or early adulthood (see Chapter 3), several groups began reporting higher prevalence of these conditions than previously thought possible for younger children (e.g., Wozniak et al., 1995). Few researchers doubted that youngsters could exhibit BD because approximately one fourth to one third of adults with Bipolar I Disorder report an onset age in childhood, with most indicating that the first episode was depressive rather than manic (Joyce, 1984; Lish, Dime-Meenan, Whybrow, Price, & Hirschfeld, 1994). This suggests that BD may appear rather early in life, although it initially may be missed among those whose first episode is depressive. However, other researchers argued that many more children with manic episodes were in fact routinely being missed by mental health professionals because their presentation varied in developmentally specific ways from the typical symptom profile exhibited by adults. Lists of alternative manifestations and novel, developmentally specific diagnostic criteria appeared in the scientific literature, in literature written for the public (Papolos & Papolos, 1999), and in the popular press. For example, there were widely discussed proposals that pediatric BD be defined by irritable rather than grandiose mood; that temper tantrums or episodes of rage were indicative of the disorder; and that these conditions could onset as early as the toddler or preschool years.

The reach of these proposals was remarkable, as the transmission of these ideas across the mental health field was followed by a rapid increase in the prevalence of these diagnoses in the community. For example, Moreno et al. (2007) reported on national trends in the United States of utilization of outpatient services associated with bipolar disorder diagnoses in people under 20 years old. They found that the rates of these visits increased from 25 per 100,000 youths in 1994–1995 to 1,003 youths per 100,000 in 2002–2003. Moreover, this increase in outpatient visits for BD was much larger than that observed among adults. Evidence indicates that many of these diagnoses made in the community were not consistent with documentation from gold standard approaches. In one study (Pogge et al., 2001), adolescent inpatients who had received diagnoses of BD from community providers tended to receive diagnoses of unipolar depression or conduct disorder when reevaluated using gold standard assessments. Evidence such as this provoked considerable controversy regarding the validity of these diagnoses in the community and of propositions to alter the diagnostic criteria for children. Three issues generated the most discussion: the validity of definitions of mania that included only irritable mood (but not elevated mood); the boundary between pediatric BD and disruptive behavior disorders; and the likelihood that these pediatric cases will have typical presentations of BD in adulthood. These issues are explored in further detail in Chapter 3.

The newest version of the *DSM* (*DSM-5*) includes a new category called Disruptive Mood Dysregulation Disorder (DMDD). This category, based largely on research by Leibenluft and colleagues on a phenotype they termed *severe mood dysregulation*, is meant to represent part of the broader phenotype of conditions previously referred to as pediatric bipolar disorder. The impetus behind attempts to validate the new disorder of DMDD is to define and then test the scientific utility of a set of diagnostic criteria that tap those clinical presentations of extreme disturbances of mood and behavior in youngsters that spurred the original interest in pediatric bipolar disorder. Future research will focus on exploring whether DMDD is in fact a part of the BD phenotype. Leibenluft's description of this condition includes the following characteristics: (a) abnormal baseline mood (extreme irritability, anger, or sadness that is chronic and noticeable to others); (b) symptoms of hyperarousal (insomnia, physical restlessness, distractibility, racing thoughts/flight of ideas, pressured speech, social intrusiveness/impatience); and (c) increased reactivity to negative emotional stimuli (defined by temper outbursts, verbal rages, or aggression toward others or property) that occurs at least three times per week. The symptoms must be evident prior to 12 years of age, persist over the course of a year with no symptom-free periods longer than 2 months in duration, and be associated with impairment in at least two of three domains (home/family, school, peer relationships).

DMDD builds upon research on the broader bipolar phenotype that emphasizes the centrality of irritability, rather than elevated/expansive mood. In contrast to the criteria for a manic episode (required for a diagnosis of BD), DMDD consists of chronic (rather than episodic) negative mood/irritability. This is consistent with evidence from clinical samples demonstrating that children with BD tend to have relatively long episode durations (on average, lasting nearly a year), as well as daily cycling between different mood states (Birmaher et al., 2006; Geller, Tillman, Craney, & Bolhofner, 2004; Tilman & Geller, 2007). This contrasts, however, with classic descriptions of typical bipolar presentations in adults. However, Judd and colleagues (2002) have shown that even among adults with classic bipolar presentations, their course is often chronic, with these individuals exhibiting subthreshold manic and depressive symptoms (as well as full threshold presentations) for persistent periods over a substantial follow-up period. Stringaris and colleagues (2010) found that children who meet criteria for severe mood dysregulation had greater comorbidity with ADHD (Attention Deficit Hyperactivity Disorder) and ODD (Oppositional Defiant Disorder) than children who meet criteria for narrowly defined BD (i.e., using the traditional adult criteria). Bhangoo et al. (2003) showed that children with chronic irritability were less likely than those with episodic manic/hypomanic epsiodes to have MDEs, psychosis, suicide attempts, or parents with a history of BD. In an epidemiological sample, Brotman and colleagues (2006) found that the lifetime prevalence of severe mood dysregulation was 3.3%. This rate is consistent with those for other depressive disorders in childhood. Most of these children (68%) had an additional psychiatric disorder, typically ADHD (94%), conduct disorder, or ODD. At follow-up in young adulthood, those who met lifetime criteria for severe mood dysregulation in childhood/adolescence were more likely to experience a depressive disorder (MDD or DD) than those who never met criteria for severe mood dysregulation. However, the groups did not differ on their rates of bipolar spectrum disorders across the follow-up, suggesting this variant may not tap a developmentally early manifestation of the bipolar spectrum. Another study by Stringaris et al. (2010) replicated this finding, showing that children with severe mood dsyregulation did not tend to develop manic or hypomanic episodes over a substantial follow-up period. Taken together, these lines of evidence suggest that alternative manifestations of pediatric BD, defined by persistent negative moods rather than acute irritability or mania, may not lie on a continuum with classic BD, but rather that they reflect extreme variants of externalizing (i.e., behavioral/acting out) problems (Carlson, 2007).

There is evidence that youngsters can in fact exhibit the classic signs of BD, although the manifestations of this condition must be understood in light of developmental constraints and affordances that allow for the expression of certain kinds of behavior and make others unlikely. Geller and Luby (1997) gave several excellent examples of classic manifestations of Bipolar I Disorder among children and adolescents. For example, grandiosity may manifest as persistent intrusive comments directed at the teacher (e.g., telling the teacher how best to teach a subject) or an adolescent claiming (despite failing grades) future attainment of a high-status career requiring an advanced degree. Hypersexuality may be evident in the form of frequent masturbation, often conducted in insufficiently private ways. Even among those with these more classic presentations of manic episodes, the rates of comorbidity with externalizing problems are very high. The rate of comorbid ADHD in children with classic Bipolar I Disorder is around 90%, and that of conduct disorder is approximately 20% (Geller & Luby, 1997).

Geller and colleagues (2008) followed a sample of children diagnosed with their first episode of childhood-onset Bipolar I Disorder (using *DSM-IV* criteria for a manic episode) over several years. They found that the majority of these cases recovered from their index episode, and most had a subsequent relapse. Manic episodes in this sample of youngsters were lengthy (mean durations of 8 months to nearly 1 year) and frequently characterized by psychosis and daily cycling. Among those who were 18 years of age or older at the last follow-up, 44% had classic manic episodes, suggesting that those meeting more narrowband definitions of mania in childhood do in fact go on to exhibit classic manic presentations in adulthood. The presence of daily cycling was also evident in the follow-ups in adulthood, suggesting that this phenomenon may be more common than has been recognized in the evidence base from samples with more typical (i.e., later) onset ages. Thus, it seems that alternative conceptualizations of the bipolar spectrum that have been generated through descriptions of early-onset cases deviating from traditional criteria for mania are less clearly linked to valid indicators of bipolar proneness, including the ultimate development of traditionally defined BD. They do, however, seem to mark a group of children with serious psychiatric problems that span both internalizing and externalizing (i.e., behavioral/acting out) issues that may ultimately be shown to relate to the bipolar spectrum. However, further studies exploring these newer conceptualizations—following samples with these conditions up through the traditional age of risk for major psychopathologies, and directing comparison to youngsters who meet traditional criteria for BD—will all be important lines of evidence for resolving the many questions and controversies that surround the concept of pediatric BD.

Subtypes of Major Depressive Episodes and Manic Episodes

Subtypes are part of both the *DSM* and *ICD* categories for MDD. These have a long history in psychiatry; and although the precise definitions have changed somewhat over time, the central characteristics of many of these subtypes have been discussed by clinicians and researchers for many years. Historically, much of the focus in identifying subtypes of depressive disorders was aimed at distinguishing between presentations that varied in their etiology. Specifically, the first edition of the *DSM* distinguished between cases that were "organic" and those that were "reactive," with the former assumed to be biological in origin and the latter environmentally provoked. The second edition of the *DSM* continued this tradition, but favored the terms *psychotic* and *neurotic* as etiological subtypes. Theoretically, it was assumed that organic/psychotic cases had a poorer prognosis (i.e., were less responsive to psychotherapeutic interventions), whereas reactive/neurotic cases could resolve if the environmental cause were removed. The *DSM-III* eliminated all presumed etiological notions from the diagnostic nomenclature, setting out a list of standardized inclusion and exclusion criteria for psychiatric disorders, including depressive disorders. None of the categories in the *DSM-III* (or subsequent editions) carry with them a necessary presumption of the etiological basis of the disorder. However, researchers continue to explore whether patterns of observed clinical phenomena (i.e., different constellations of symptoms) can identify subgroups of depressed persons that vary meaningfully in their etiological pathway and/or their likelihood of responding to different therapeutic approaches.

Melancholia. One subtype with the longest history is the endogenous subtype now referred to as the melancholic subtype in the *DSM-IV-TR*. People with MDD meet the criteria for the melancholic subtype if they experience anhedonia, as well as three symptoms from among the following: diurnal variation of mood (mood is worse in the morning than in the afternoon or evening); considerable psychomotor agitation or retardation; early morning wakening (i.e., awakening hours before one's scheduled morning wakening and being unable to go back to sleep); significant appetite or weight loss; excessive or inappropriate guilt; and distinct quality of the depressed mood (i.e., experienced as qualitatively different from a normal feeling of grief or sadness that follows a loss). This subtype accounts for about one fourth of those with an MDE. Although the symptom criteria for melancholia focus primarily on somatic symptoms, melancholia is also associated with troublesome cognitions, including rumination about one's past failures, and anxious apprehension about a future that is perceived to be unlikely to hold any bright prospects (Gold & Chrousos, 1999).

The term *endogenous* has been used historically to differentiate cases of depression thought to have their origin in biological processes from reactive depressions that emerge in response to environmental precipitants (Kiloh & Garside, 1963). Thus, the endogenous subtype comes from a long tradition of interest in identifying a variant of MDD, initially only recognizable from symptom profile, that is more purely biological or genetic in etiology and therefore hypothesized to have a stronger relationship to biological markers. If true, then measurement of this subtype should hasten our understanding of the biological processes that give rise to depressive episodes because research could focus on characterizing individuals with this subtype on putative causal factors. However, it is possible that rather than identifying a distinct etiological subtype that is qualitatively different from other cases, melancholic/endogenous depression may instead simply mark more severe cases of depression. Consistent with the latter interpretation, Kendler (1997) found that female twins with a lifetime history of melancholic MDD had more lifetime episodes, higher symptom severity during their worst episodes, and greater impairment and help seeking associated with their depression, compared to those with a history of MDD (but no melancholia). They also had lower self-reported levels of the personality trait neuroticism than those with nonmelancholic MDD, perhaps suggesting this subtype is not associated with personality risk for unipolar depression. The melancholic and nonmelancholic groups did not differ on their age of onset or duration of their longest episodes. Melancholia in one twin was also associated with higher rates of MDD in the co-twin than in nonmelancholic MDD, and this effect could not be accounted for by overall severity. This finding suggests that melancholia may be an indicator of elevated genetic risk for depression, consistent with findings from a separate sample (McGuffin, Katz, Watkins, & Rutherford, 1996). Finally, there is also some evidence that melancholic depression is associated with markers of physiological hyperarousal, including elevated levels of the stress hormone cortisol (Gold & Chrousos, 2002). In summary, it appears that the melancholic subtype identifies individuals with a more severe history of depression, and it is associated with elevated genetic risk and some biological correlates of stress reactivity. However, the issue of whether melancholia is qualitatively distinct from other forms of depression has yet to be resolved.

Atypical. Like melancholia, atypical depression has also been the focus of a considerable research literature. Constructs similar to the *DSM-IV-TR* definition of an atypical subtype were first reported in the United Kingdom in the late 1950s, but its current manifestation was first articulated in the late 1960s (Parker et al., 2002). Atypical depression is defined by the anchor symptom of reactivity of the person's mood to positive stimuli (i.e., although depressed, the person responds with positive mood to reinforcing or pleasurable stimuli), as well as two of the following: weight or appetite increase, hypersomnia, leaden paralysis (feeling heavy or weighed down), and sensitivity to interpersonal rejection. Thus, some of the symptoms represent the opposite of what is commonly observed in classic depictions of an MDE (i.e., weight increase rather than loss, oversleeping rather than loss of sleep). The phenomenological sense of atypical depression is of a great lassitude, weariness, and disconnection, with fleeting moments of "brightening" to environmental circumstances. The rejection sensitivity characteristic of this subtype is believed to occur both when the person is in episode and also when not depressed, implying that this represents a trait characteristic of the individual. Much of the interest in this subtype was generated by reports that individuals with this constellation of symptoms were more likely to respond to a particular class of antidepressant medicines, the MAOIs (monoamine oxidase inhibitors), than to other types of antidepressants. There is evidence to support the validity of these observations (e.g., Liebowitz et al., 1988), although recent findings suggest these effects may be limited to a subset of patients with atypical depression who also have an early age of onset and chronic course (Thase, 2009). Research continues to explore the idea that people with atypical MDEs respond better to some classes of antidepressants than they do to other antidepressants.

Only about 15% to 30% of individuals with an MDE present with the atypical subtype (Gold & Chrousos, 2002), which may be more prevalent in women, those with comorbid anxiety disorders, and those with an earlier age of onset of depression

(Angst, Gamma, Sellaro, Zhang, & Merikangas, 2002; Matza, Revicki, Davidson, & Stewart., 2003; Novick et al., 2005). There is little evidence, however, that this subtype reflects a more chronic or severe variant of MDD (Kessler & Wang, 2009). Some have proposed that atypical depression is a marker for the soft bipolar spectrum because atypical MDEs are overrepresented within those with a history of hypomanic episodes (Perugi et al., 1998). However, the validity of this subtype has also been questioned because some data indicate very low intercorrelations among the symptoms of the atypical subtype, which is inconsistent with the idea that it represents a meaningful syndrome. Moreover, there is no evidence that mood reactivity is in fact a cardinal symptom of the typical subtype (Parker, 2002), further questioning the validity of atypical MDEs as a marker of the bipolar spectrum.

Catatonic Depression. Catatonia is a specifier that can be applied to an MDE, manic, or mixed episode occurring within MDD, or Bipolar I or II Disorder. It requires two of the following five symptoms: motoric immobility, excessive motor activity that appears to be purposeless, extreme negativism (defined by resistance to instructions, mutism, or maintenance of a rigid posture), peculiar movements, and echolalia or echopraxia (senseless repetition of a word or phrase spoken by someone else or imitation of others' movements). Catatonia is unusual, appearing mostly in inpatient settings. This subtype can be associated with depressive disorders, as well as psychotic or other disorders.

Psychotic Features. Depression with psychotic features is characterized by delusional thinking that may take the form of nihilistic or guilty delusions, or hallucinations. These delusions may be mood congruent, meaning they are characterized by morose, negativistic themes consistent with depressed mood, or mood incongruent, meaning their content is not centrally depressive. Some individuals with psychotic depression characterized by mood-incongruent features may exhibit signs/symptoms traditionally characterized as "first-rank" symptoms of psychotic disorders (e.g., schizophrenia). In population-based samples, MDEs with psychotic features are uncommon, accounting for only 14% of all MDEs in the representative Epidemiologic Catchment Area study (Johnson, Horwath, & Weissman, 1991). Psychotic features are more common in depressive episodes occurring to those with BD rather than those with MDD (Akiskal et al., 1983). Psychotic features seem to mark a group with more troubled course over time because they also have higher rates of suicidality, hospitalizations, comorbidity with other psychiatric conditions, and greater rates of relapse than those who have MDE without psychotic features, even after accounting for severity of depressive symptoms (Johnson et al., 1991). Furthermore, there is some evidence that those with mood-incongruent features have worse outcome, compared to those with mood-congruent psychotic features or no accompanying psychosis (Coryell & Tsuang, 1985). Leckman et al. (1984) conducted a family study of MDE subtypes, including melancholic/endogenous and psychotic depression. They found that subtypes characterized by delusions (e.g., psychotic depression) were associated with the highest rate of MDD in family members, and some evidence that delusional depression "breeds true," with approximately one third of the relatives of probands with delusional depression also meeting criteria for this subtype. This suggests that psychosis may represent a meaningful marker of a unique etiological process.

Postpartum Depression. Postpartum depression is defined in the *DSM-IV-TR* as an MDE in a woman that develops within 4 weeks after giving birth, although the research literature often defines it over a longer time span (e.g., within 1 year after childbirth). This presentation is relatively common among women in these circumstances, with prevalence estimates around 7% among new mothers (Gavin et al., 2005). It is distinguished from the less severe and more statistically normative "baby blues," characterized by mood lability, tearfulness, anxiety, insomnia, and interpersonal sensitivity occurring in the first week to week and one half after giving birth (O'Hara, 2009). The baby blues typically remit without any intervention or serious impairment. By contrast, MDEs occurring during the postpartum period can have serious consequences for mothers adjusting to their new role or addition to the family. In particular, postpartum cases associated with psychotic features can take the form of command hallucinations to harm the infant or delusions about the infant. Importantly, there is now evidence that the postpartum period is one of elevated risk for onset of first or new MDEs not only among mothers, but fathers as well (discussed in more detail in Chapter 3).

Premenstrual Dysphoric Disorder (PMDD). Another common variant typically discussed in the lay literature is PMDD (discussed earlier in this chapter), defined by depressive symptom changes that are linked to the phases of the menstrual cycle. In the *DSM-IV*, PMDD appeared as a variant of "depressive disorder not otherwise specified." This diagnosis is consistent with lay conceptions of premenstrual syndrome (PMS) and highly socialized attitudes about the role of hormonal differences in behavioral and emotional differences across genders. Formal diagnoses of PMDD require a clear pattern of depressive symptom onset and offset that is clearly linked to specific (late luteal) phases of the menstrual cycle. When symptom and menstrual cycle measures are taken repeatedly across the menstrual cycle, most women who attribute their depressive symptoms to the menstrual cycle do not actually demonstrate the required pattern (Kessler & Wang, 2009).

Seasonal Affective Disorder (SAD). Another variant of unipolar depressive disorders is seasonal affective disorder (SAD), defined by recurrent depressive episodes (meeting criteria for either major or minor depressive episodes) that exhibit a clear seasonal pattern, typically occurring in the fall or winter. The *DSM* requires that at least two thirds of the depressive episodes a person experiences follow a seasonal pattern. There is evidence that SAD may be common in regions of the planet farther from the Equator, and thus with longer winters and less exposure to sunlight. It may also be influenced by abnormal melatonin responses to light in patients (Wehr et al., 2001). This disorder is actually quite rare; although when looser definitions are applied, as many as 9% of the U.S. population report seasonal depression (Booker & Hellekson, 1992).

Validity of Subtypes

Subtypes are appealing to the extent that they are capable of identifying individuals who may respond differentially to particular treatments or who have different etiological pathways to the disorder. Thus, they could have considerable practical and research utility. However, the evidence for their validity as indicators of unique etiologically defined variants of unipolar disorders is mixed. For example, it does not appear that there is considerable longitudinal stability of subtypes, meaning that among individuals with multiple MDEs, the likelihood that they will exhibit the same subtype across different episodes is low, with the possible exception of psychotic depression (e.g., Coryell et al., 1994).

The existing subtypes of the *DSM-IV-TR* were generated largely through clinical observation and theory, rather than through empirical approaches. Unsurprisingly, these theoretically derived subtypes likely do not represent natural types that are recovered when empirical, statistical approaches are used to generate groups by summarizing the patterning of symptoms among depressed persons. For example, Sullivan, Prescott, and Kendler (2002) conducted exploratory analyses of symptoms of MDD in a large sample of individuals. They found seven classes (groups of individuals) that differed on their pattern of MDE symptoms. Only one of the classes was similar to an existing *DSM* subtype (atypical depression). Two of the classes had few depressive symptoms but had high levels of impairment, distress, and treatment seeking. However, most of the classes did not differ statistically from one another on important external criteria, including demographics and personality traits. This suggests that theoretically defined subtypes may not be the most accurate representation of how depressive symptoms tend to cluster in the population.

An alternative means of capturing the broad variability evident among those with depressive syndromes is to identify a smaller number of dimensions that capture this variability, rather than the addition of new categories. This dimensional approach views traditional depressive disorders as representing the extreme end of a continuum of depression, ranging from the low end (no symptoms of a depressive disorder) to subthreshold manifestations to less severe disorders to more severe and impairing disorders. The advantage of this model is its parsimony because a dimension of depression severity is simpler to consider and to evaluate with respect to its predictive validity for important criterion variables than are multiple diagnostic categories. An important question to consider is how to best define the composition of the dimension or dimensions underlying the clinical phenotypes. Can the clinical signs and symptoms that populate the current diagnostic categories be represented by one or more unitary dimensions?

Many researchers have proposed that symptoms of unipolar depression cluster into meaningful dimensions that should be considered as representing distinct constructs. However, structural analyses of existing self-report measures of depression suggest that most consist primarily of a general depression factor. Moreover, analyses of measures designed to broadly tap a range of dimensions of depression also find a prominent first factor defined primarily by symptoms of general distress (Watson, O'Hara, Simms, Kotov, & Chmielewski, 2007). However, smaller secondary factors can also be identified, including aspects of lassitude, suicidality, insomnia, and appetite problems (Watson, 2009).

One source of evidence for the usefulness of the dimensional approach is research on the correlates of subthreshold symptoms (i.e., mood symptoms that fall below the threshold required for receiving a categorical diagnosis of a depressive disorder). These studies typically show that subthreshold symptoms have some of the same correlates as depressive disorders, yielding support for the dimensional perspective. Several studies have shown that subthreshold unipolar depressive disorders are associated with problems in functioning and risk for future development of full-blown depressive disorders (Fergusson, Horwood, Ridder, & Beautrais, 2005; Gotlib, Lewinsohn, & Seeley, 1995; Harrington, Fudge, Rutter, Pickles, & Hill, 1990; Lewinsohn, Shankman, Gau, & Klein, 2004; Lewinsohn, Solomon, Seeley, & Zeiss, 2000; Nolen-Hoeksema, Girgus, & Seligman, 1992; Pine, Cohen, Cohen, & Brook, 1999), although most of this risk may be attributed to chronic or recurrent forms of subthreshold depression (Klein, Shankman, Lewinsohn, & Seeley, 2009). Moreover, subthreshold depressive conditions have a familial/genetic association with threshold diagnoses of depressive disorders (Kendler & Gardner, 1998; Lewinsohn, Klein, Durbin, Seeley, & Rohde, 2003). Therefore, one means of capturing an underlying dimension of severity may be to construct composites of the overall number of symptoms and/or severity of all symptoms expressed. Support from this model comes from several lines of evidence demonstrating that variations in symptom severity (from mild to severe) within a diagnostic category are predictive of treatment response, associated with genetic liability toward depressive disorders, and biological processes implicated in depression (Klein, 2008).

However, it is possible that symptom counts may not be the most valid means of deriving the key dimensions underlying depressive disorders. Symptom severity can be readily measured at any single time point using a variety of approaches, including interviews and self-report questionnaires. However, these approaches do not directly take into account the duration of symptoms or their patterning over time, which may be important factors to consider with respect to quantifying less to more severe presentations of depression. Klein (2008) proposed that the unipolar disorders can be captured by two dimensions: chronicity and severity (see Figure 2.2). The chronicity dimension takes into account the number of depressive episodes and

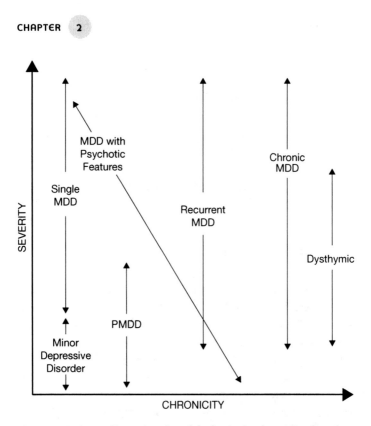

FIGURE 2.2 A two-dimensional model of unipolar depressive disorders.

duration of symptoms over an extended period of time. Adding a chronicity dimension has the additional advantage of cleaning up the multiple diagnostic categories that were added to the *DSM* to reflect different course parameters. Applying this single chronicity dimension eliminates awkward concepts such as "double depression," used to describe DD comorbid with an MDE; instead, one would simply describe this as a highly chronic form of depression, and the period of an MDE would be rated as higher in severity.

An important implication of this model is that conditions defined by apparently less severe symptoms (e.g., DD) can in fact reflect more serious depressive conditions than those with higher symptom thresholds (e.g., MDD), owing to the greater chronicity of the former. The validity of this dimension is supported by evidence indicating that disorders defined by greater chronicity differ significantly from those that are not chronic in a number of important respects. When comparing dysthymia to nonchronic MDD and chronic to nonchronic MDD, it is apparent that the chronic conditions are associated with greater comorbidity with other psychopathologies (including personality disorders), more extreme levels of personality traits, greater suicidality, greater impairment, more early adversity, and higher rates of depressive disorders in family members (reviewed by Klein, 2008). Chronicity has been less frequently proposed as a dimension; however, as noted by Klein (2008), variations in the duration of depressive symptoms are related to markers of overall psychiatric severity, including earlier onset, comorbidity, suicidality, and impairment. Greater chronicity is also associated with a number of important etiological factors, including elevated familial loading for depression, early adversity, differences in personality trait levels, and depressotypic cognitions. Moreover, chronicity also predicts poorer treatment response. Finally, there is specificity to the familial transmission of chronic mood disorders in that rates of chronic forms of depression are higher in the relatives of people with chronic depressions than in the relatives of people with nonchronic depressions, but do not differ across the relatives of healthy controls and those of people with nonchronic depressions.

CONCLUSIONS

In summary, there is considerable heterogeneity across individuals with depressive disorders and those prone to depression. A range of diagnostic labels has been offered to describe this variability in symptom severity, phenomenology, course, and developmental modifiers; and subtypes have been proposed to potentially capture etiologically different subgroups of individuals who meet criteria for the same diagnostic label. Alternatively, this heterogeneity can be captured with a smaller number of dimensions that are meaningfully related to etiology, course, and potentially to treatment (i.e., symptom severity and chronicity). In the following chapters, the possible causes of these dimensions are discussed as etiological models of depressive disorders are reviewed.

Who Is Likely to Experience Depression?

EPIDEMIOLOGY

Depression is sometimes referred to as the common cold of psychopathology. Consistent with this aphorism, epidemiological studies demonstrate that depressive disorders are indeed rather common across the life span. As one would expect, the rates vary depending on whether more or less stringent definitions of depression are used and whether one considers only the current time period and the recent past, or the entire life span. For example, the lowest population rates will be generated using the most stringent assessment approaches and definitions of depressive disorders, considering the smallest reasonable time window, and reporting on rates in a sample representative of the population. This system is used rather than drawing from groups wherein high rates of disorder are expected to be present—such as people seeking out treatment for psychological distress. Epidemiological studies utilize representative samples, and several have been conducted in the United States during the past several decades that employ structured interviews and describe the prevalence of disorders over clearly defined time intervals (i.e., the past year or the entire lifetime). Evidence from these studies indicates that the point prevalence, that is, the proportion of individuals who meet criteria for the disorder at any one point in time, is less than 10% over brief time intervals, with lower rates for more serious forms of depressive disorders. For example, the point prevalence for the past few months is approximately 2% to 4% of adults meet criteria for Major Depressive Disorder (MDD), compared to 6% of adolescents and less than 1% of children (reviewed by Kessler & Wang, 2009). By contrast, the point prevalence of Bipolar Disorder (BD) is considerably lower, with epidemiological studies indicating a lifetime rate of Bipolar I between 1% and 1.5% (Kessler, Rubinow, Holmes, Abelson, & Zhao, 1997; Merikangas et al., 2007; Regier et al., 1988; Weissman et al., 1996).

When less stringent measures are used, such as questionnaire screening scales that assess the severity of current depressive symptoms rather than diagnoses of disorders, it is evident that many more people experience subthreshold depression (i.e., below the diagnostic threshold), ranging from 20% in adults to 50% in youngsters (Kessler, Avenevoli, & Merikangas, 2001). If one considers those diagnoses that require fewer symptoms or shorter durations (e.g., minor depressive disorder, recurrent brief depression), then the rates are higher than those for MDD, but lower than the rates generated from screening instruments. For the bipolar spectrum, there is evidence that the prevalence of a broader definition (i.e., including Bipolar II, and subthreshold bipolar) is higher, with rates estimated at around 2% to 5% (e.g., Angst, 1998; Lewinsohn, Klein, & Seeley, 1995; Merikangas et al., 2007). This pattern of prevalence suggests a gradient of severity in which fewer individuals exhibit more severe and impairing forms of unipolar depression, whereas the least severe conditions are experienced by a relatively large number of individuals.

Estimates of the current prevalence of depressive disorders provide a snapshot of all those who are suffering from depression at any one time. By contrast, lifetime prevalence rates consider all those who have ever met criteria for the disorder at any point in their lives prior to interview age, and are thus necessarily higher than point prevalence estimates. Prevalence rates for 12 months yield the proportion of the population that met diagnostic criteria at any point in the past year. The most recent epidemiological study in the United States (the National Comorbidity Study-Replication [NCS-R]; Kessler et al., 2005b) assessed a representative sample of individuals 18 years and older. In the past 12 months, 6.7% of those interviewed met criteria for MDD, 1.5% for DD (Dysthymic Disorder), 1.0% for Bipolar I, and 1.1% for Bipolar II. If one considers soft bipolar diagnoses (e.g., recurrent subthreshold hypomania during an MDE [major depressive episode], or with or without subthreshold MDE), these presentations are more common, with 1.4% 12-month prevalence rates. Lifetime rates for this age group were higher—16.6% for MDD, 2.5% for DD, 1.0% for Bipolar I, 1.1% for Bipolar II, and 2.4% for subthreshold BD. Merikangas et al. (2010) reported on corresponding rates for adolescents (13 to 18 years old) who were part of a supplemental adolescent sample from the NCS-R; 11.7% of youths met criteria for a lifetime diagnosis of MDD or DD and 2.9% for Bipolar I or II.

When comparing the prevalence rates of various depressive disorders, it is important to keep in mind distinctions among lifetime and point prevalence estimates. The lifetime prevalence of chronic and recurrent forms of depression (i.e., dysthymia, chronic MDE, recurrent MDD) is lower than that of nonchronic forms (e.g., a single MDE). Thus, less serious forms of depression are less common. However, at any one time point, the bulk of depressive disorders will fall among the small proportion of individuals who experience multiple episodes of depression across their lives or chronic forms of the disorder. Therefore, point prevalence estimates are more influenced by the number of people in the population who have chronic or recurrent forms of depression than by those who have experienced only a single MDE.

There is also reason to believe that the rates of depressive disorders may be even higher than suggested by epidemiological studies that rely on retrospective reports to estimate the lifetime prevalence of these disorders. Two studies compared cross-sectional estimates of psychopathology, which are similar to those generated from epidemiological studies that complete a single assessment with participants, to prevalence estimates obtained prospectively from longitudinal studies in which the same participants are repeatedly assessed for psychopathology over multiple assessment waves. The latter have the advantage of requiring shorter recall periods, thus reducing the chances that participants forget episodes—particularly those periods of symptoms that are shorter and/or milder. Both studies (Moffit et al., 2010; Olino et al., 2012) showed that lifetime prevalence rates are much higher from prospective studies that aggregate across multiple assessments than from studies that use a single cross-sectional assessment. The differences across the two strategies were most noticeable for episodic conditions (i.e., those that wax and wane over time, rather than being chronic), such as MDD. For example, Olino and colleagues (2012) reported that rates of DD did not vary across cross-sectional and prospective assessment, but those of MDD did. Lifetime rates of MDD and bipolar spectrum disorders were twice as high when aggregated across repeated assessments as when they were generated from a single cross-sectional assessment. This suggests that even more individuals might experience depressive disorders than is indicated by epidemiological data, although the underestimates might largely be missing cases that are more easily forgotten (i.e., those that are milder or of shorter duration).

EVIDENCE FOR THE UNIVERSALITY OF DEPRESSION ACROSS CULTURES

Consistent with anecdotal reports and evidence from studies conducted globally, international epidemiological research indicates that depression is evident worldwide (Weissman et al., 1996). The prevalence of depressive disorders does appear to vary, however, across nations. At the broadest level, rates in the United States, Canada, and Europe are higher than those in East Asian countries, whereas variability within a continent is often associated with aspects of the broader sociocultural context. Thus, higher rates are evident in countries with more problematic economic and political circumstances (Chentsova-Dutton & Tsai, 2009). This mirrors cross-cultural data on subjective well-being that refers to a person's perception of an overall sense of happiness, fulfillment, and satisfaction. Data comparing a wide range of nations and cultures indicate that citizens of nations with many markers of sociopolitical upheaval, poverty, or inequality have lower mean levels of subjective well-being than those living in cultures with fewer such issues (e.g., Diener & Suh, 2000).

A recent study reported on the lifetime and 12-month prevalence of MDD across 10 countries in North America, Latin America, Europe, and Asia (Andrade et al., 2003). It found that in most nations included, the estimated lifetime prevalence of MDD was between 5% and 10%, with the lowest rate in Japan (3%) and the highest in the United States (16.9%). The typical (median) age of onset was similar across 8 of the 10 countries, and the greater risk to women than men was evident in all 10 countries.

Similarly, there is evidence that depression is *not* a purely modern phenomenon, despite the interest each new generation seems to find in chronicling the hardships and personal failings that make its own cohort unique relative to its predecessors. One can find depictions of depression in literatures across cultures and historical time. For example, the Bible's description of the first king of Israel, King Saul, includes rich depictions of a depressive state, including suicidality. In 1621, Robert Burton's *The Anatomy of Melancholy* was published. Ostensibly a compendium of medical knowledge from ancient times, the book is also a broader exposition on human emotion. Burton's definition of melancholy is quite nuanced, noting distinctions between episodic and chronic/temperamental forms of depression; the multitude of bodily, cognitive, and emotional symptoms of depression; and the universality of the experience:

> Melancholy, the subject of our present discourse, is either in disposition or in habit. In disposition, is that transitory Melancholy which goes and comes upon every small occasion of sorrow, need, sickness, trouble, fear, grief, passion, or perturbation of the mind, any manner of care, discontent, or thought, which causes anguish, dulness, heaviness and vexation of spirit, any ways opposite to pleasure, mirth, joy, delight, causing forwardness in us, or a dislike. In which equivocal and improper sense, we call him melancholy, that is dull, sad, sour, lumpish, ill-disposed, solitary, any way moved, or displeased. And from these melancholy dispositions no man living is free, no Stoick, none so wise, none so happy, none so patient, so generous, so godly, so divine, that can vindicate himself; so well-composed, but more or less, some time or other, he feels the smart of it. Melancholy in this sense is the character of Mortality.

In more recent history, Abraham Lincoln offers a fascinating example of chronic depression. As described in Shenk's (2005) biography of Lincoln, his propensity toward depression was evident relatively early in life, appeared to be chronic, and was of considerable severity that it was worrisome to those close to him. For example, after the death of a close other, Lincoln became quite depressed. A friend described his reaction in a correspondence as such:

> . . . after that Event he seemed quite changed, he seemed Retired & loved Solitude, he seemed wrapped in profound thought, indifferent, to transpiring Events, but had Little to say, but would take his gun and

> [wonder] off in the woods by himself, away from his association of even those he most esteemed, this gloom seemed to depend for some time, so as to give anxiety to his friends in regard to his mind . . .

There was a serious concern among his friends because Lincoln shared with them that he frequently contemplated suicide. Another friend recalled:

> Mr. Lincoln's friends . . . were Compelled to keep watch and ward over Mr. Lincoln, he being from the sudden shock somewhat temporarily deranged. We watched during storms—fogs—damp gloomy weather. . . . For fear of an accident . . .

There are many such compelling examples of depression and its impact that can be found outside of the scientific literature. However, we should not conclude on the basis of highly resonant anecdotes that depression is invariant across time, or particularly across culture. Given historical changes in understanding of and sensibilities regarding the experiences we now conceptualize as reflecting depression, and our tendency to view the past in light of our own knowledge and worldview, it is easy to assume (but impossible to prove) that our current conceptualization of depression is one that would provide an equally good fit for people in prior historical epochs. This concern is also relevant when we seek to understand the role that culture may play in the understanding and manifestation of depressive disorders. There are important cultural differences in norms about the expression of emotion and levels of expressed emotion (e.g., Eid & Diener, 2001), cognitions about the self, and views on agency and interpersonal connectedness (e.g., Markus & Kitayama, 1991), the perceived importance of implicit and explicit social support for buffering stress (e.g., Taylor, Welch, Kim, & Sherman, 2007), and community supports for people struggling with psychological difficulties (Barrio, 2000). Each of these factors would be expected to potentially influence the likelihood that an individual would experience depressive symptoms; that he or she would report to others that they experience these symptoms; that these would be labeled as reflecting a psychological disorder; and that the presence of such symptoms would result in significant impairment in the person's life.

Consistent with these cultural differences in aspects of emotions and their expression and norms regarding help seeking and support, considerable evidence suggests that there are differences in the rates of depressive disorders (particularly unipolar depression) across different cultures. Moreover, many scholars have argued that culture shapes the presentation of depression. Thus, the same syndrome might be expressed in the form of different symptoms across cultures, with symptom presentation adhering to culturally accepted norms for signaling distress to others. For example, in Asian cultures, depression may be expressed and experienced predominantly in terms of somatic complaints, such as insomnia, fatigue, headaches, and so on (Kleinman & Good, 1985), perhaps because Asian cultures tend to emphasize holistic representations of mind and body, rather than a conceptualization of depression in psychological terms (Kalibatseva & Leong, 2011). Ryder and Chentsova-Dutton (2012) offered several explanations for why depression may be experienced in terms of somatic symptoms, including a desire to avoid stigma associated with mental illness and to seek out treatment from medical rather than psychological providers, and a tendency to express symptoms in a way that will be more socially acceptable by not emphasizing one's own negative emotions and personal distress.

There is much work left to be done to understand the role that culture plays in the etiology, phenomenology, and course of depressive disorders. Efforts have been made to establish epidemiological research programs globally to establish basic facts about the prevalence and demographic correlates of depressive and other disorders worldwide. However, truly integrative psychopathological research that generates research hypotheses from within an understanding of these diverse cultures is in its infancy. An important goal is to increase the reach of empirical research to other cultures; however, it may be even more critical to facilitate the development of psychological research conducted by people from within those cultures. Given the importance of the social relationships and context to understanding depression, it seems likely that culturally informed and diverse research will yield important findings about those critical components of human cognition, emotion, and social relationships that underlie risk for depression, as well as those that serve to aid in recovery from these disorders.

SECULAR TRENDS IN DEPRESSION

In addition to questions about the universality of depression across cultures versus variability, there is also reason to wonder whether there have been important changes in depression over time. In the United States, there is evidence that the prevalence of depressive disorders has changed during recent history. Specifically, these secular trends take the form of an increase in the prevalence of unipolar depressive disorders across successive generations, or cohorts of individuals, born during different epochs. The presence of such effects would suggest an increase in the causal factors responsible for depressive disorders over the same period of time. This could take the form of a greater mean level of individual susceptibility factors to depression in the population and/or greater exposure to environmental risk factors for the disorder, either because a greater number of people became exposed to the critical factors or because there was a mean increase in the degree of severity of these environmental risk factors over time. The data that originally stimulated discussions about possible secular trends in depressive disorders came from epidemiological studies collected in the 1970s and 1980s that showed a linear increase in prevalence of unipolar depressive disorders among people born in more recent cohorts. This observation was not limited to the United States because increases in prevalence also appeared in data collected in other nations. Moreover, some data indicated that the age of onset of unipolar depression was decreasing (i.e., becoming younger). Epidemiological data indicated that younger cohorts had an earlier age of onset of depression than older cohorts (Burke, Burke, Rae, & Regier, 1991; Fombonne, 1994). More recent data suggest that this linear increase may be continuing among more recent birth cohorts. Specifically, using epidemiological data from the early 1990s and 2000–2001, Compton, Conway, Stinson, and Grant (2006) showed that 12-month prevalence rates of MDD increased from 3% to 7% across that 10-year period, and Andrade et al. (2003) reported evidence for secular increase in the prevalence of MDD in nine different countries. However, not all studies have replicated these findings, with some failing to find evidence of continuing secular increases over more recent birth cohorts (e.g., Murphy, Laird, Monson, Sobol, & Leighton, 2000).

The causes of these secular trends are a source of controversy. Some researchers argue that they are caused by methodological artifacts, rather than reflecting real changes in the disorder's prevalence across historical time. The magnitude of these secular changes also remains unclear. Ideally, we would have access to datasets including rigorous assessment of these conditions in representative populations that are followed and assessed repeatedly across their life spans, including many successive generations of individuals. Unfortunately, such data are not available; we must make do with largely cross-sectional epidemiological data, interpretations of which are necessarily more difficult. Moreover, there is also evidence that these secular trends are not specific to depression because rates of other psychiatric problems (such as externalizing problems) also increased over the same interval (Achenbach & Howell, 1993; Lewinsohn, Rohde, Seeley, & Fischer, 1993; Simon & VonKorff, 1992). Finally, a meta-analysis of studies exploring cohort effects on rates of depressive disorders in children and adolescents found no evidence for an increase in prevalence in cohorts born between 1965 and 1990 (Costello, Erklani, & Angold, 2006). This evidence is inconsistent with that from epidemiological studies of lifetime prevalence of these disorders as reported by adults indicating an earlier age of onset of depression among more recently born cohorts.

A number of hypotheses have been offered to explain these secular trends. First, it is possible that rates appear lower in older birth cohorts because people who are older at the time of assessment may have forgotten prior episodes of depression, especially those that are less severe or persistent. However, recent findings indicate that the lower rates of depressive disorders among older adults are not artifactually reduced (i.e., due to forgetting), but rather reflect vertically lower prevalence of depression in this age group (e.g., Kessler et al., 2010). Second, it is possible that younger cohorts have been socialized toward greater psychological mindedness and awareness of their emotional states, less stigma regarding mental illness in general, and greater openness to treatment seeking. These factors may contribute to different processing of and willingness to report on depressive symptoms among younger, as compared to older, individuals. There is some evidence that changes in vernacular use of language referring to depression and its associated symptoms can influence rates in response to particular interview items; if different interviews use terms that have fallen in or out of favor in the population, they may produce different rates of endorsement of particular items and influence the prevalence estimates of disorders involving these items (e.g., Murphy et al., 2000).

Finally, these secular trends could emerge from different time-related effects that are difficult to tease apart with available data. As noted by Fombonne (1994), increases in depression could be attributable to changes in the age structure of the population, historical changes that increase risk for the entire population exposed to those changes, or heightened vulnerability evident in a particular group of people who share experiences (because they are from the same birth cohort). For example, rates of depression could increase because of changes in the population structure. Because young people have elevated rates of current depression, any shift in the birth rate that increases the proportion of the population falling in younger age groups relative to older age groups will produce higher rates of current depression in the population as a whole. Broader societal changes that could create greater risk for depressive disorders, such as increased exposure to traumatic events, might account for these secular changes. However, the effects of an increase in exposure to environmental risk factors would depend on the potency of these risk factors in the population; unless the effects were very large, it is difficult to imagine this independently increasing the rates of depressive disorders substantially. Unfortunately, existing data do not support any one of these patterns more than another. Thus, secular trends in unipolar depressive disorders, although fascinating, remain a finding still in search of an explanation.

Although less frequently discussed in the literature, there are also studies demonstrating an increase in prevalence of manic episodes/BD over the last half of the 20th century (e.g., Chengappa et al., 2003; Gershon, Hamovit, Gurhoff, & Nurnberger, 1987; Lasch, Weissman, Wickramaratne, & Burce, 1990). Some studies have also reported earlier ages of onset of BD among those with the condition from more recent birth cohorts (e.g., Chengappa et al., 2003), consistent with a process called anticipation. Anticipation refers to the observation that among a biological family with multiple members affected by a disorder of interest, severity of the disease increases and/or its age of onset decreases across successive generations (Harper, Harley, Reardon, & Shaw, 1992). Anticipation has been discovered for several medical conditions, and one study found evidence for anticipation in BD (McInnis et al., 1993). Thus, secular trends may be evident for both unipolar and bipolar depressive disorders.

Whether or not depressive disorders have been increasing in prevalence across recent decades, there has definitely been a notable change in recognition (within the mental health community as well as society at large) of depressive disorders in terms of both their prevalence and the suffering they entail. One would expect such changes might facilitate people's willingness to endorse depressive symptoms in epidemiological studies (and thus, impact the prevalence rates), as well as potentially have a positive impact on people's willingness to seek help for their own depression or to provide support and understanding to someone else suffering from one of these conditions. Public health campaigns have also been enacted to promote recognition and understanding of mental health problems. However, at the same time, evidence from survey research indicates that over the past 50 years, there has been an increase in negative attitudes (stigma) toward the mentally ill in the United States, or at the very least no decrease in stigma (e.g., Pescosolido et al., 2010; Phelan, Link, Stueve, & Pescosolido, 2000). Other evidence from a British sample suggests that stigmatizing attitudes toward people with depression are generally less negative than those toward schizophrenia or substance-use disorders, but still more negative than toward other psychiatric disorders, such as eating disorders (Crisp, Gelder, Rix, Meltzer, & Rowlands, 2000). Thus, it is striking that there has been an increase in the prevalence of depressive disorders during the same historical period in which we also observe growing negative attitudes toward mental illness. This suggests that the observed secular trends are unlikely to be a result of greater normalization and understanding of depressive disorders.

DEMOGRAPHIC PREDICTORS OF RISK

If you know nothing else about unipolar depression, it is important to know that it is most commonly experienced by young women. This issue is revisited in more detail, describing evidence regarding this gender difference and the theoretical models generated to account for such evidence. A corollary to this is that because depression is so common in an absolute sense, there are still many men and people in different ages groups who are currently suffering from these disorders, who previously have suffered from them, or who will later suffer from them. Almost all other demographic factors that might identify those at elevated risk are far less predictive than gender, but some have been replicated in multiple studies and are thus worthy of mention and interpretation. These are reviewed before a return to gender differences for a more thorough discussion of the scientific evidence regarding the existence of and sources of these effects.

€ducation and Socioeconomic Status (SES)

Greater risk for developing a depressive disorder is disproportionately evident among those with fewer economic resources. In a cross-national study, Andrade et al. (2003) found that lower education was significantly related to MDD in two countries (the United States and the Netherlands), and lower SES (as measured by family income) was a significant predictor in three of the five countries in which it was assessed in the study (the United States, Canada, and the Netherlands). Thus, findings were relatively consistent across different countries, and indicated that having fewer resources (in terms of finances or educational background) was associated with greater risk for MDD across nations varying in their economic and sociocultural circumstances. Several studies conducted in the United States have demonstrated the importance of lower educational level for unipolar depression. For example, Maes et al. (1998) found that lower educational level was associated with MDD in two large cohorts, and the same effect also emerged from the large epidemiological sample of the NCS (Blazer, Kessler, McGonagle, & Swartz, 1994) and the NCS-R sample. BD has also been linked to lower SES and lower education (Kessler et al., 1997; Merikangas et al., 2007), as well as to being unemployed or disabled (Merikangas et al., 2007). The mechanisms underlying these associations are unknown, although both directions of effect are plausible. Lower SES and education may increase risk for disorder, perhaps because those circumstances increase stressful life circumstances that might be associated with development of the disorder. Alternatively, the presence of manic and/or depressive symptoms may deleteriously affect educational outcomes and employment, thus leading to lower levels of SES.

Rural Versus Urban Residence

Andrade et al. (2003) found evidence that residence in a rural area was associated with lower risk of MDD in five of six countries included in their study, although the size of this effect was modest. In the NCS, urban residence was associated with higher rates of BD, but was not associated with unipolar depressive disorders (Kessler et al., 1997).

Marital Status

Divorced and separated women are at higher risk for both MDD and DD than are married or single (i.e., never married) women. In Andrade and colleagues' (2003) cross-national study, unmarried individuals were at greater risk for MDD in all ten countries. In the NESARC (National Epidemiologic Survey on Alcohol and Related Conditions) study (Grant et al., 2005), BD was more common in those who were widowed, separated, or divorced than in those who were single or married. Longitudinal data found that people who married subsequently reported fewer depressive symptoms than those who did not marry over the same period of time, whereas those who were married but separated or divorced over the course of the study reported more depressive symptoms than those whose marital status did not change (Marks & Lambert, 1998). These data are consistent with other evidence showing that being married is positively associated with happiness, and that this association might be mediated by the positive financial and health benefits of marriage (Stack & Eshelman, 1998). Some studies indicate that the protective effect of marriage against depressive disorders is greater for men than for women (e.g., Kessler & McRae, 1984). Moreover, Stack and Eshelman (1998) found that the beneficial effect of marriage on happiness was not moderated by gender (i.e., its effects were not different in men and women). Thus, it is clear that marital status is a reliable correlate of both unipolar and bipolar depressive disorders, but the mechanisms underlying this association are not definitely known. The role of close interpersonal relationships in depressive disorders is discussed in Chapter 4.

Race and Ethnicity

Representative epidemiological studies in the United States have found that the lowest rate of MDD is evident among Black Americans, and the highest rate is among Hispanics (Kessler et al., 1994). One study found that the rates of depressive disorders were elevated in Native Americans relative to participants from other racial/ethnic backgrounds (Huang et al., 2006). In the NCS-R sample, Black and Hispanic Americans had lower overall rates of depressive disorders (Kessler et al., 2005b). Thus, there is no overwhelming pattern suggesting that particular racial or ethnic groups in the United States are routinely at elevated risk for depressive disorders.

Gender

Gender differences are not as striking a feature of BD in comparison to MDD and DD. Evidence from epidemiological samples suggests that the prevalence of Bipolar I does not differ across men and women (e.g., Grant et al., 2005; Lewinsohn et al., 1995; Merikangas et al., 2007; Regier et al., 1988; Weissman et al., 1993). However, there is some evidence that women are at greater risk for Bipolar II Disorder (e.g., Baldassano et al., 2005; Hendrick, Altshuler, Gitlin, Delrahim, & Hammen, 2000). Findings regarding gender differences in the number of manic or depressive episodes experienced over the course of the disorder are mixed, with some studies finding no differences (e.g., Baldassano et al., 2005), and others reporting that women have more and longer depressive episodes (Angst, 1986; Roy-Bryne, Post, Uhde, Porcu, &

Davis, 1985). This suggests that gender differences may be more strongly related to depressive episodes rather than the unipolar–bipolar distinction, leading to gender differences in Bipolar II and depressive episodes within Bipolar I, as well as MDD and DD, but less clear differences of manic episodes. However, there is evidence for a later average age of onset of mania (and thus, BD) among women rather than men by approximately 3 years to 5 years (Grant et al., 2005; Kennedy et al., 2005; Robb, Young, Cooke, & Joffe, 1998; Viguera, Baldessarini, Tondo, 2001).

Why Are There Gender Differences in Depression?

As noted earlier, one of the most reliable correlates of unipolar depressive disorders is being a woman. Across many different samples from the United States and other nations, it has been shown that women have approximately twice the risk of developing depressive symptoms and disorders (Andrade et al., 2003; Nolen-Hoeksema, 1990; Weissman & Klerman, 1977). Consistent with the notion of a spectrum of depressive disorders described in Chapter 2, there is also evidence that subthreshold levels of depressed mood/dysphoria are higher in adolescent girls than in boys (Allgood-Merten, Lewinsohn, & Hops, 1990), suggesting that greater risk is evident across the entire spectrum of severity for females. Importantly, there is also evidence that these gender differences do not appear until at least mid-adolescence (Costello et al., 2006; Hankin & Abramson, 2001), after which they are relatively persistent in magnitude across the remainder of the life span. Prior to mid-adolescence, boys actually have higher rates of unipolar depressive disorders, although these differences are statistically significant in some studies (e.g., Angold, Costello, & Worthman, 1998) and nonsignificant in others (e.g., Anderson, Williams, McGee, & Silva, 1987).

Epidemiological data show that the greater risk to women for first onset is evident across adolescence through adulthood.

This suggests that gender differences in depressive disorder can best be described as reflecting processes that cause women to be at higher risk for ever developing depressive symptoms or disorders, rather than processes that increase the severity of these symptoms or disorders in women with depression relative to men with depression. Most of the available evidence has shown that among all those who ever experience a depressive disorder, the course is similar in women and men. For example, in the NCS, women had higher lifetime and past-year prevalence of MDD, but did not differ from men in their likelihood of having a chronic depression or a recurrence in the previous year (Eaton et al., 2008; Hankin et al., 1998; Kessler, McGonagle, Swartz, Blazer, & Nelson, 1993). In the Oregon Adolescent Depression Project, the greater prevalence of MDD in women was evident for first incidences (Rohde, Lewinsohn, Klein, Seeley, & Gau, 2013); follow-up data into the participants' 30s found that women had higher overall rates of MDD and more episodes of MDD, as well as marginally longer episodes (Essau, Lewinsohn, Seeley, & Sasagawa, 2010). Thus, longitudinal assessment may detect more episodes of depression in women than in men. However, the bulk of the evidence suggests that we must first understand those processes in women that give rise to the greater likelihood of ever being depressed, and, even more specifically, why the effect of these processes first become evident in early adolescence. Importantly, these theories must do more than invoke age as the critical causal mechanism. Age is only a proxy for more specific maturational processes and changing developmental contexts that are correlated with, but not isomorphic with, chronological age.

Pubertal Transition and Hormonal Mechanisms. The phenomenon of escalation of rates in girls relative to boys that is evident in adolescence has been the source of considerable research and theorizing because it is clear that any theory proposed to explain gender differences in depression must take into account this developmental moderation. One of the most obvious potential sources of this developmental effect, given its timing in the early adolescent period, is processes related to the pubertal transition. A few studies directing measurement of participants' pubertal status have shown that the increased risk to women appears after, not before, the pubertal transition (Angold, Costello, Erkanli, & Worthman, 1999; Angold et al., 1998); however, these findings await replication and further identification of which of the many changes associated with puberty result in higher levels of depression in girls. An obvious biological candidate is the role of hormones because the pubertal transition is associated with differential changes in the levels of several hormones across boys and girls. There are very few published studies showing associations between depressive symptoms or disorders and measured hormones (pubertal status is an indirect proxy for the hormonal changes, but not a direct assessment of hormonal levels). Two studies have shown that higher levels of testosterone are linked to greater depression in girls but lower anxiety and depression in boys (Angold et al., 1999; Granger et al., 2003).

Another source of evidence for the causal importance of hormonal levels to depression is the case of the postpartum period, which involves a rapid decline (over a period of days) in the hormones estrogen and progesterone from their heightened levels during pregnancy, and a slower decline in prolactin that occurs over a period of weeks (Hendrick, Altshuler, & Suri, 1998). However, both longitudinal studies tracking covariance in depressive symptoms and broader measures of mood along with direct measures of these hormones and studies comparing mean differences of these hormones across groups with and without postpartum depression have generally found no significant associations (e.g., Heidrich et al., 1994; O'Hara, Schlechte, Lewis, & Varner, 1991). Furthermore, known risk factors for the development of an MDE in the postpartum period include a family history of depressive disorders, prior history of MDD, stressful life events, and elevated depressive symptoms during pregnancy (Gotlib, Whiffen, Wallace, & Mount, 1991; O'Hara, 2009; O'Hara, Neunaber, & Zekoski, 1984). Thus, the pattern of risk factors is not specific to the postpartum period; in fact, it is the most reliable predictor of MDD in the population in general. Moreover, there is now evidence that rates of MDE are elevated in fathers in the post-partum period, with one meta-analysis suggesting a rate of 10% and the highest risk in the period 3 months to 6 months after the birth of the child (Paulson & Bazemore, 2010). Thus, despite considerable interest in the potential role of gender differences in hormones in creating gender differences in depression, there is lack of empirical evidence.

Most researchers believe it is unlikely there is a direct effect of hormones on depression, but rather that they indirectly increase risk via any one of several mechanisms, including: (a) the effects of hormones on brain development, (b) the development of secondary gender characteristics that are generated by these hormones (and which in turn set into motion psychosocial changes that differentially affect boys and girls), or (c) the hormonal changes that occur during the pubertal transition may interact with life events and the social context. Consistent with the second possibility, some evidence indicates that it is the timing of puberty, rather than its occurrence per se, that may be most predictive of depression. For example, in girls, early puberty (relative to one's peers) has been linked to internalizing (depression and anxiety) symptoms (Ge, Conger, & Elder, 1996; Graber, Lewinsohn, Seeley, & Brooks-Gunn, 1997; Kaltiala-Heino, Kosunen, & Rimpela, 2003; Stice, Presnell, & Bearman, 2001). By comparison, pubertal onset later than one's peers may be associated with depression for boys (e.g., Kaltiala-Heino et al., 2003). These findings are typically interpreted as reflecting mismatches among the challenges brought on by puberty in girls and the psychological resources available to those who enter puberty earlier than their peers. For example, younger girls may be less prepared for the changes to their body shape and appearance that accompany puberty; they may feel more self-conscious because they are experiencing these changes before their friends or may be more naïve about or threatened by the increased masculine attention to their bodies that these changes may bring about.

Later-developing boys may find early adolescence more stressful if they are slow to experience the increase in height and muscle mass that accompanies their puberty, potentially putting them at risk for bullying or reduced status in the dominance hierarchies that are common to masculine friendship groups.

Finally, consistent with the third possibility, Cyranowski and colleagues (2000) proposed that pubertal increases in the hormone oxytocin in girls interact with socialization processes to increase risk for depression in girls. Animal studies demonstrated that oxytocin is important for a number of affiliative processes, including parenting and pair bonding, and human studies have shown oxytocin is associated with constructs such as empathy and trust (Insel, 2010). It has been proposed that increases in oxytocin in girls heighten their awareness of and motivation for affiliation with close others; when affiliation goals are blocked by threats to close relationships, such as interpersonal conflict or relationship loss, individuals with higher motivation for affiliation (girls, in these models) will be more likely to suffer depression as a result. These suggestions regarding indirect mechanisms by which the hormonal changes of puberty may shape risk to increase depression in girls relative to boys are a rich source of theorizing regarding potential biological bases of the gender difference, as well as possible transactions between biological and psychosocial processes.

A Framework for Organizing Research on Gender Differences in Depression

One system of organizing the voluminous research literature addressing this topic is to articulate the kinds of causal models that could account for the basic observation of gender differences first appearing in early adolescence; consider the patterns of evidence that would be consistent with each model; and then compare the existing evidence for particular constructs to these idealized patterns. As described by Nolen-Hoeksema and Girgus (1994), the pattern of gender differences in unipolar depression is consistent with three different causal patterns. Model 1 proposes that the etiology of depression is the same in both genders (i.e., whatever factors cause depression in men are the same factors that cause depression in women), but these causal factors increase for girls in early adolescence to a greater degree than they increase for boys. This model implies that there is an interaction between gender and age on the critical etiological factors, but no interaction between gender and the etiological factors on depression (i.e., these factors are equally important for both men and women in terms of predicting depression; however, there are mean level differences across the genders that emerge in early adolescence, causing more girls to cross the threshold for expressing depression). Of note, this model cannot account for findings that men are more likely than women to be depressed in the childhood period, unless one proposes that the etiological agents are elevated in men in childhood, or that depression in childhood is etiologically distinct from that occurring in adolescence or adulthood. Nolen-Hoeksema and Girgus's second model, by contrast, proposes that the etiology of depression is different in men and women (i.e., although they may share some causes, at least some important causal agents are only relevant to one gender but not the other), and that those etiological factors that are unique to girls become more common than those that are unique to boys in early adolescence. This model suggests that depression has different etiological correlates in both genders, and that there is an interaction between age and type of risk factor—only those risk factors unique to women increase in early adolescence, whereas those unique to men do not increase. This model is consistent with findings that men either do not differ from women in levels of depression earlier in childhood or that they have higher levels, as reviewed earlier. For this model to be validated, we would need to understand what etiological factors are shared across both genders and which are unique; furthermore, the unique predictors should vary in a specific way in their occurrence (for categorical risk factors) or in their mean levels (for dimensional risk factors) across developmental time, whereas the shared factors should not (i.e., their effects should be consistent across development).

Finally, Nolen-Hoeksema and Girgus's third model argues that the relevant etiological factors for depression are the same in men and women, but that women have greater levels of these etiological factors very early in development (well prior to adolescence). However, these etiological factors are latent until early adolescence, when they are activated by the transitions in biological and psychosocial contexts that occur during this developmental period. As a result, gender differences in depression do not emerge until this time, even though women have been at higher risk for much longer. Thus, in this model, there is a main effect of gender and no interaction between gender and age on the etiological factors. However, there is an interaction between age and the etiological factors on measures of depression, with their effects only emerging in early adolescence. As with Model 1, Model 3 cannot account for observations that men have higher risk for depression than women in childhood.

In research exemplifying Model 2 and Model 3, there has been a tendency for investigators to focus on factors characteristic of the early adolescent period believed to potentiate preexisting risk factors in girls, such as concerns about meeting societal ideals for thinness that are relatively unique to (or at least, most exaggerated in) Western cultures. For example, Hyde, Mezulis, and Abramson (2008) hypothesized that the greater risk for girls might be attributable to their greater body shame/dissatisfaction because they experience more pressure to conform to gendered expectations for appearance, particularly after the pubertal transition. However, as noted earlier, Andrade et al. (2003) found that gender was a reliable predictor of risk for MDE across 10 different countries, with odds ratios ranging from a low of 1.2 in the Czech Republic to a high of 2.5 in Japan, with most falling between 1.9 to 2.5. The relative robustness of these gender differences across cultures is telling with respect to their interpretation because it suggests their causes cannot be solely attributable to factors that are highly culture specific.

Numerous other factors have been proffered as potential explanations for the increasing gender difference in depression in adolescence including: rumination or other forms of cognitive vulnerability; stressors such as negative life events or more traumatic experiences such as rape or sexual abuse; and dependence on interpersonal relationships or greater affiliative needs (Hyde et al., 2008). It is fair to say that none of these have been shown to fully account for the gender differences in depression. However, some of these appear promising because they have received some empirical support, and these are subsequently discussed.

First, some have proposed that girls are more prone to depression beginning in adolescence because they have a greater affiliative orientation than boys. Their desire for closeness with others and tendency to be affected by turmoil in those relationships and to feel empathic distress in response to negative emotions experienced by close others is viewed as a risk factor for depression in early adolescence. The adolescent period is characterized by an increase in affective intensity of parent–child conflict (Laursen, Coy, & Collins, 1998), as well as growing intimacy in peer relationships and an increase in the centrality of these peer relationships to adolescents' well-being and identity (Furman, 2002). Achieving harmonious, fulfilling relationships is challenging, particularly as factors outside of one's control can influence the quality of one's relationships. Thus, individuals who value relationships highly and suffer greatly when they perceive threats to their relationships may be at risk for depression. To the extent that girls are more likely to engage in these processes, they would be expected to be at higher risk for developing depression during the adolescent period. This pathway would fit Nolen-Hoeksema and Gurgus's second model, wherein the causes of depression differ for boys and girls across development. Early causes (prior to adolescence) are similar in level across the two genders; however, causes more characteristic of girls' psychology become more common in adolescence (such as a need for affiliation and interpersonal closeness and success), although those causes that are more important for boys do not increase during this developmental period.

Other theories focus on the disproportionate occurrence of particular stressors among girls compared to boys. There is some evidence that girls may experience more negative life events than boys, although the magnitude of the gender difference is rather small (Davis, Matthews, & Twamley, 1999). Most of these theories have focused on one particular stressor, sexual abuse/assault. Adult women are twice as likely as men to be the victim of sexual assault, and the occurrence of sexual assault is itself linked to risk for depression (Weiss, Longhurst, & Mazure, 1999). Similarly, rates of retrospectively recalled childhood sexual abuse are approximately twice as high in women as in men (Costello, Erklani, Fairbank, & Angold, 2002; Tolin & Foa, 2006), with rates of 17% in women and 8% in men (Putnam, 2002). Cutler and Nolen-Hoeksema (1991) estimated that gender differences in sexual abuse may account for as much as 35% of the gender difference in depression in adults. Spataro, Mullen, Burgess, Wells, & Moss (2004) explored associations between childhood sexual abuse and treatment seeking for psychiatric disorders in a prospective design in which children were initially ascertained following suspicion they were the victims of sexual abuse. The found that both genders who had been sexually abused were at elevated risk for the development of depressive disorders compared to population rates; however, men and women who experienced abuse did not differ from one another on their rates of depressive disorders (consistent with Nolen-Hoeksema and Girgus's Model 1 or Model 3). Thus, it is possible that differential risk for sexual abuse/assault may account for some of the gender differences in depressive disorders. It is not clear whether sexual abuse can explain the timing of the emergence of these gender differences (in early adolescence) because it does not appear that the occurrence of sexual abuse is highest in early adolescence. Most research indicates that the peak age of vulnerability is between ages 7 and 13 (Finkelhor & Baron, 1986), but rates of abuse of children under the age of 6 are probably underestimated because the youngest victims are least likely to report experiencing such abuse.

Finally, there is one well-studied causal pathway to depression that appears to fit with at least part of Nolen-Hoeksema and Girgus's third model (i.e., that etiological factors for depression are the same in both genders, but women have greater levels of these etiological factors very early in development that are not activated until early adolescence). Early anxiety disorders appear to be important predictors of the later development of depression (Silberg, Rutter, & Eaves, 2001; Warner, Wickramaratne, & Weissman, 2008); girls have higher levels of anxiety disorders than do boys (Lewinsohn, Gotlib, Lewinsohn, Seeley, & Allen, 1998). Moreover, this anxiety pathway to depression appears to be associated with a particular temperament trait, negative emotionality (NE). Children with anxiety disorders are characterized by high levels of NE, and childhood NE has been prospectively linked to the development of anxiety and unipolar depressive disorders (Klein, Durbin, & Shankman, 2009). Moreover, the specific aspects of NE that are most closely linked to early anxiety disorders— high levels of behavioral inhibition (reticence to engage with novel social and nonsocial stimuli) and fear proneness—differ across boys and girls at a very early age, with girls exhibiting higher levels of fear proneness at least by the preschool period (Else-Quest, Hyde, Goldsmith, & VanHulle, 2006; Olino, Durbin, Klein, Hayden, & Dyson, 2013). What is unknown is what factors interact with NE to increase the risk associated with this trait during the early adolescent period. Moreover, there is evidence that individual differences in NE are correlated with depression in children prior to early adolescence (e.g., Lonigan, Phillips, & Hooe, 2003), inconsistent with Nolen-Hoeksema and Girgus's third model. Further, NE itself changes over developmental time such that increases in mean levels of this trait are evident from late childhood to early adolescence (e.g., Durbin et al., under review). This points to the need for more richly dynamic models of the etiology of depression that consider the ways in which risk factors may change in their mean levels over developmental time, as well as in their associations with depression.

Because of the ubiquity of gender differences in depression, it is important for any theoretical model of the causes of depression to be able to explain these differences. Thus, this issue is revisited in each of the following chapters that deal with etiological theories of depression (Chapters 4–9). It is important to note that it is unlikely that any of the many pathways that are probably involved in the development of depressive disorders will only be found among men or women, and thus one factor (or even a small number of factors) cannot be expected to account for the observed gender differences in prevalence. Finally, the greater risk for depression among boys in the childhood period has received less empirical attention. Understanding this finding may be important for discovering whether there are meaningful etiological differences between childhood-onset and later-appearing depressive disorders.

DEVELOPMENT AND AGE AS PREDICTORS OF DEPRESSIVE DISORDERS

Depressive disorders exhibit a characteristic developmental trajectory. Rates are low in childhood, but approach the same rate as those observed in adults by late adolescence. Although the base rates of unipolar depressive disorders are low in the preschool and childhood periods—around 2% (Egger & Angold, 2006) or 5% (Rohde et al., 2013)—it does not appear to be the case, contrary to earlier theoretical views (Glaser, 1967), that young children are incapable of experiencing depression or will necessarily mask their depression with behavioral disturbances rather than primary mood disturbances. The point prevalence of MDD increases from the childhood to adolescent period to 8% by adolescence (Birmaher et al., 1996; Costello et al., 2006; Lewinsohn, Clarke, Seeley, & Rohde, 1994). The increase in rates from childhood to adolescence and similarity between adolescent and adult rates has also been found in samples outside of the United

States (e.g., Andrade et al., 2003), suggesting it is not unique to the American culture. For bipolar spectrum disorders, rates are very low until late adolescence.

Several important aspects of the developmental trajectory of these conditions should be noted. First, the bulk of these conditions evident at any one time point are experienced by relatively younger individuals. Second, the typical age at which they are first experienced tends to be earlier in the life span, with a very long "tail"; new onsets of depression can occur at any point throughout the life span (through the older-adult period), although risk of ever developing a first episode of depression decreases with age. See Figure 3.1 for a depiction of the prevalence of first onsets of depression across the life span. Many of the episodes of depression that occur later in life are clustered among those who have a history of the disorder (thus, not new cases), reflecting the chronic nature of depression. Therefore, most people who will ever experience an MDE will have their first episode by early adulthood (Kessler et al., 2005a; Rohde et al., 2013). In the NCS-R sample, the median age of onset (assessed retrospectively) for MDD was 32 years, with one half of all cases having their onset between ages 19 and 44. The median age of onset for BD was younger (18 years), as

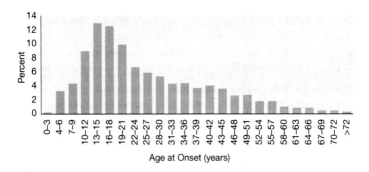

FIGURE 3.1 Age of onset of MDD as a function of age.
Source: From Zisook et al. (2007). Reprinted with permission from the *American Journal of Psychiatry* (Copyright © 2007). American Psychiatric Association.

was that for Bipolar II (20 years) and subthreshold BD (22 years). In comparison to other common psychiatric disorders, the age of onset of depressive disorders (especially the unipolar disorders) tends to be spread across a wider range of the life span; for example, median onset age for anxiety disorders and externalizing disorders is 11 years, and both of these categories have narrower age of onset distributions.

Are Depressive Disorders Occurring in Childhood or the Older-Adult Period Different From Those Occurring in Other Developmental Periods?

The modal unipolar depressive disorder onsets in adolescence or early- to mid-adulthood; far fewer cases first appear in childhood or in later life. Given this typical developmental trajectory, it is reasonable to ask whether cases that deviate from this onset are etiologically unique. Regarding late-onset cases, rates of depressive disorders (including both new onsets and recurrences) are consistently lower among the older adult than those earlier in the life span (Blazer & Hybels, 2005; Jorm, 2000; Kessler et al., 2010). Kessler and colleagues (2010) found in the NCS-R that the severity of MDEs were lower in the older participants than MDEs occurring among those in younger age groups. Moreover, rates of severe role impairment (i.e., considerable impact of depressive symptoms on the ability to perform adequately in one or more domains of functioning) associated with an MDE were lowest in the older group. Some have proposed that lower rates in older adults are driven by recall bias in this group (Simon & VonKorff, 1992). More recent studies using sophisticated means of assessing age of onset continue to find lower rates in the older population, suggesting other explanations are required for this phenomenon. It is not clear if there are protective factors that emerge later in life or factors that are overrepresented among individuals who survive into the older period (as opposed to dying younger) that buffer against the development of depression or limit its severity or impact. However, these findings are consistent with evidence from life span developmental research demonstrating that— contrary to lay perceptions of later life as a period characterized by a steady decline in life satisfaction and emotional hardiness— the older period is actually associated with significant emotional strengths that may reduce risk for depression. In comparison to younger individuals, older adults have been shown to have greater memory for positive emotional material and are more likely to set goals that are focused on emotionally meaningful aspects of their lives (Carstensen & Mikels, 2005).

Depressive disorders in the very young were relatively neglected in terms of empirical research until the 1980s, largely owing to clinical lore suggesting that young children were incapable of experiencing classic depressive syndromes. The field changed considerably after psychopathologists began to provide compelling evidence (e.g., Carlson & Cantwell, 1980) that these conditions could in fact manifest in children in ways that are strikingly similar to the presentations evident in adults. Recent research on very-early-onset depressive disorders has focused on identifying similarities and differences between childhood-onset and later-appearing (i.e., adolescent and adult onset) depressive disorders. Data on the longitudinal course of depressive disorders suggest that during the childhood period, MDD is less likely to be recurrent than in later developmental stages (Rohde et al., 2013). It may also have greater comorbidity with externalizing/disruptive behavior disorders than depression occurring later in life. Rates of co-occurring internalizing (depressive and anxiety) disorders and externalizing (conduct) disorders are as high as 45% to 80% early in development (Angold & Costello, 1993; Capaldi & Stoolmiller, 1999; Loeber & Keenan, 1994). This overlap may be driven by temperamental risk factors that increase risk for both forms of psychopathology early in development (e.g., Gilliom & Shaw, 2004), shared genetic contributions between depressive and externalizing conditions (e.g., O'Conner,

McGuire, Reiss, Hetherington, & Plomin, 1998), or environmental factors that increase the likelihood of developing both forms of disorder (e.g, Gjone & Stevenson, 1997; Tully, Iacono, & McGue, 2008).

Jaffee and colleagues (2002) compared individuals with a childhood-onset depressive disorder to those with an adulthood- onset depressive disorder and those without a history of depression on a host of potentially important etiological factors. They found that the group with childhood onset was more troubled on average in terms of their early childhood experiences than the adult-onset group. Specifically, a number of the correlates unique to this group are ones that have previously been associated with externalizing problems, including antisocial and hyperactive behavior problems, and a history of criminality in their parents. A separate study of adult women relying on retrospective recall of childhood experiences and age of onset of depression also found that childhood-onset depression, in comparison to adulthood-onset depression, was associated with greater comorbidity in childhood (Hill, Pickles, Rollinson, Davies, & Byatt, 2004). Finally, Gilman, Kawachi, Fitzmaurice, & Buka (2003) found that residential instability and family disruption were more strongly related to depression with onset prior to age 14 years than cases emerging thereafter. Taken together, the findings of these studies suggest that early-onset depression may be somewhat distinct from that with more typical onset in adolescence or adulthood—cases beginning in childhood tend to emerge in the context of greater overall psychiatric symptoms (including disruptive behavior problems) and the presence of risk factors commonly associated with externalizing psychopathology. Thus, it is possible that the long-term outcome for childhood-onset unipolar depression is quite different from that of adolescent-onset depression. Consistent with this, in a longitudinal epidemiological study, Copeland, Shanahan, Costello, and Angold (2009) found that depressive disorders in childhood did not exhibit continuity (i.e., predict later depressive disorders) in young adulthood, whereas adolescent cases of depressive disorders did predict the presence of depression in young adulthood.

There is also evidence that early-onset cases of depressive disorders may be more severe than those with later onset, although it is important to note that many studies have defined early onset by ages that are not particularly young, relative to the median age of onset (e.g., defining cases with onset before 21 years old as early onset). In BD, early onset is associated with worse outcome of the disorder over time (Carlson, Bromet, & Sievers, 2000; Ernst & Goldberg, 2004). For patients with recurrent MDD, earlier onset predicts a greater likelihood of experiencing manic and hypomanic symptoms (Cassano et al., 2004) that are in turn associated with overall psychiatric severity. Earlier onset predicted longer duration of depressive episodes in a sample of adolescents (Lewinsohn et al., 1994). Early-onset cases tend to have more extreme levels of personality traits associated with risk for depression, greater family history of depression, and worse psychiatric course (Alpert et al., 1999; Klein et al., 1999). Data from a large treatment study indicated that those with onset of an MDE prior to adulthood were more likely to be women; have a family history of depression or substance abuse; less likely to be married; have a more chronic and/or recurrent course of the disorder; exhibit overall poorer functioning; and have more suicidal ideation (Zisook et al., 2007). Thus, it is possible that an earlier age of onset is a marker of a more severe form of depression, is caused by particular risk factors that are also associated with general psychiatric functioning, or that an early onset leads to poorer course by disrupting normal developmental achievements. It is important to remember that age is itself a proxy for other developmental mechanisms, such as maturation of biological and psychological systems, and that these processes can unfold in a linear or nonlinear way. Age may also be a proxy for the tempo of changing life transitions and contexts that may be the critical factor explaining the life course trajectory of depressive disorders. These issues are reviewed in more detail in Chapter 4.

THE FULL CLINICAL PRESENTATION AMONG THOSE WITH DEPRESSION: COMORBIDITY

Epidemiological data demonstrate that most individuals (around three fourths) who experience a depressive disorder also have one or more additional psychiatric conditions, either concurrent with their depression or at another point in their life spans (Kessler et al., 2007). The typical comorbid conditions run the gamut of all other common psychiatric disorders, including other internalizing problems (anxiety), as well as externalizing conditions (e.g., substance abuse). Comorbidity is most prevalent among those with more persistent (chronic or recurrent) forms of depression.

Rates of Comorbidity in Unipolar Depression

Lifetime rates of a comorbid anxiety disorder among those with MDD are 59%, compared to 24% to 32% for comorbid substance abuse and other externalizing disorders (Kessler et al., 2007). This high level of comorbidity is not limited to a particular developmental period. Rohde et al. (2013) found in a longitudinal study of adolescents followed up into early adulthood that the rates of comorbidity between MDD and both anxiety disorders and substance abuse disorders were comparable in magnitude across childhood, adolescence, emerging adulthood, and adulthood.

Rates of Comorbidity in Bipolar Disorders

The rates of lifetime comorbidity are persistently higher for those with Bipolar I or II or subthreshold BD, approaching 88% to 98% (Kessler et al., 2007). In the NCS-R dataset, the rate of comorbid anxiety disorders among those with Bipolar I or II was 63% to 87%, compared to 35% to 71% for externalizing or substance abuse disorders.

Comorbidity With Anxiety Disorders

Comorbidity between depressive and anxiety disorders has received particular attention because it is the most common (although notably, in the NCS-R sample, higher comorbidity between depressive and anxiety disorders was driven by a few disorders, specifically Generalized Anxiety Disorder [GAD] and Panic Disorder for MDD and Obsessive-Compulsive Disorder [OCD] for Bipolar). Not only are depressive and anxiety disorders commonly co-occurring at the same time point, it also seems that anxiety disorders may precede the development of depression and strongly predict it—earlier anxiety disorders serve as a potent risk factor for the subsequent development of depression (e.g., Cole, Peeke, Martin, Truglio, & Seroczynski, 1998; Hagnell & Grasbeck, 1990; Pine, Cohen, Gurley, Brook, & Ma, 1998; Wittchen, Kessler, Pfister, Hofler, & Lieb, 2000). Moreover, one large longitudinal cohort study showed that cases of comorbid depressive and anxiety disorders were more likely to persist over time than those that were not comorbid with anxiety (Merikangas et al., 2003). The nature of this predictive association is unclear. Perhaps depressive and anxiety disorders share common risk factors, but anxiety disorders tend to onset earlier. If that is the case, then it may point to shared risk factors for both conditions; however, treating anxiety disorders may not reduce the incidence of depression. By contrast, if anxiety disorders are causally implicated in the risk for depression, successful treatment of these may prevent the development of depression.

The comorbidity between depression and anxiety has often been ascribed to overlap between the two syndromes, captured by Clark and Watson's (1991) tripartite model, which proposes that some symptoms of these two forms of psychopathology are markers of a broader general distress/dysphoria factor that is common to both anxiety and depression, whereas others are unique to anxiety (e.g., dizziness) or to depression (e.g., anhedonia). Symptoms may vary in the degree to which they measure the general distress/dysphoria factor and these specific facets (Watson, 2009). For some researchers, an important agenda is the development of purified depression and anxiety constructs that more strongly tap these unique components, with the goal being to increase discriminant validity (i.e., discover variables that correlate with one construct but not the other) and to identify unique etiological factors that are specific to one condition or the other. However, it is possible that the general distress/dysphoria factor, despite having lower discriminant validity, is a meaningful and important construct.

Structural analyses of *Diagnostic and Statistical Manual of Mental Disorders* unipolar depressive and anxiety disorder diagnoses from several epidemiological samples reveal that the overlap between these two sets of disorders are not uniform across different diagnoses (Watson, 2009). First, among the anxiety disorders, GAD, which is defined chiefly by pervasive and chronic worry, has the greatest overlap (i.e., largest associations) with MDD and DD, followed by Panic, Posttraumatic Stress Disorder (PTSD), OCD, and social phobia with moderate associations. Agoraphobia and specific phobia have the weakest overlap with unipolar depressive disorders. GAD is more comorbid with the depressive disorders than it is with other anxiety disorders; this is unsurprising because its symptom set is the most saturated with items tapping general distress/dysphoria. Watson (2009) has proposed that the internalizing disorders can be modeled as emerging from (a) a higher-order internalizing dimension including all depressive and anxiety disorders (with the possible exception of OCD), and (b) two lower-order dimensions, reflecting dimensions labeled distress/anxious-misery and fear. Distress/anxious-misery disorders include MDD, DD, GAD, and PTSD. Fear disorders include panic, agoraphobia social phobia, and specific phobia. The placement of OCD and bipolar disorder within these dimensions remains controversial, largely because their prevalence is very low in the population and they are therefore often excluded from structural analyses.

Comorbidity With Externalizing Disorders

Rates of substance abuse disorders are also elevated in those with depressive disorders. For example, in the NCS-R sample (Kessler et al., 2005b), there were significant associations between both lifetime MDD and lifetime dysthymia and lifetime Oppositional Defiant Disorder (ODD), Attention Deficit Hyperactivity Disorder (ADHD), Intermittent Explosive Disorder (IED), and alcohol and drug abuse and dependence; associations of similar magnitude were evident for bipolar spectrum disorders. Moreover, there is evidence from at least one prospective study (Fergusson, Boden, & Horwood, 2009) that there are significant longitudinal associations in adulthood from alcohol dependence to MDD, but not from MDD to alcohol dependence. By contrast, data from younger (i.e., adolescent) samples have shown the reverse pattern, with problematic alcohol use and substance abuse disorders being predicted by earlier depressive disorders (e.g., King, Iacono, & McGue, 2004). However, the effects of earlier depression on later substance abuse problems are weaker than those of earlier externalizing problems, suggesting this is a less common pathway to the development of substance problems. As noted earlier, much has been made of the temporally ordered comorbidity between anxiety and mood disorders, particularly in the early childhood to adolescent period. Interestingly, evidence from even younger samples (of preschoolers) indicates that early externalizing disorders are also predictive of the development of MDD (Luby et al., 2009). Finally, comorbidity with externalizing problems is generally associated with greater psychiatric severity among depressed individuals over time. For example, those with BD who have a comorbid substance abuse disorder tend to have poorer outcome over time, including greater treatment noncompliance and higher rates of relapse (Krishnan, 2005; Strakowski, DelBello, Fleck, & Arndt, 2000).

Comorbidity With Personality Disorders

Depressive disorders are also commonly comorbid with personality disorders (Shea et al., 1992) that are defined by persistent, maladaptive patterns of interpersonal behavior, self-perception, and cognitions. Rates of these conditions are particularly high among those with dysthymia and BD, relative to MDD (e.g., Lenzenweger, Lane, Loranger, & Kessler, 2007). Moreover, among those with depressive disorders, those who also have a personality disorder tend to have poorer outcome over time (Newton-Howes, Tyrer, & Johnson, 2006).

CONCLUSIONS

In summary, depressive disorders are relatively common and they can occur to anyone regardless of culture or age. They vary greatly in their severity, with the prevalence of these conditions decreasing as a function of this severity, such that bipolar spectrum and chronic or recurrent forms of unipolar depression are less common in the population. These more severe forms are associated with greater comorbidity with other psychiatric conditions. Although unipolar depression can onset at any point in the life span, it disproportionately affects young people, particularly young women. Any complete model of the etiology of unipolar depression must account for gender differences in its prevalence and development over time.

How Does Depression Affect Functioning?

The reach of depression disorders extends far beyond the symptoms used to identify and characterize them. In fact, one could say that it is the impact of those symptoms on other aspects of a person's life that makes them so unbearable, rather than the fact of the symptoms themselves. In many cases, it is these experiences—the difficulty of continuing on with one's typical routine, desires, and goals—that differentiate more normal experiences of sadness and malaise from syndromes of depression, and which drive people to seek treatment for these conditions. Often, people suffering from depression may manage to continue functioning in important domains despite considerable pain; when they can no longer do so, they may feel demoralized, self-critical, and dejected. For this reason, problems with functioning are likely even more serious among those who seek treatment for their depression, compared to those who do not.

89

Therefore, evidence from treatment-seeking samples will necessarily inflate estimates of the impact of depression on functioning, so it is important to consider evidence derived from community samples of those with depressive disorders.

In addition to documenting the prevalence of depressive disorders in the population, epidemiological studies have also been used to quantify the harm they cause to society at large. To do so, they focus on indicators that can be numerically rated and objectively interpreted—costs in health care dollars associated with treatment of depression itself and the additional use of health care for medical conditions among those with depressive disorders (compared to those without such disorders)—as well as lost productivity in work or school settings attributable to depressive disorders. The results of these analyses are rather grim, and suggest that far from being limited to personal suffering, the effects of depression ripple out to aspects of one's life that are critical to achieving and thriving, as well as to domains that impact the lives of others. For example, in the National Comorbidity Study-Replication (NCS-R) sample, the estimate of lost work days per year associated with depressive disorders was 27.2 for those with Major Depressive Disorder (MDD) and 65.5 for those with Bipolar Disorder (BD). Of note, much of the greater impact of BD on work functioning was attributable to major depressive episodes (MDEs) being more impairing among those with BD. Moreover, these Disorders were also associated with lower productivity on days at work. Interestingly, subthreshold Borderline Personality Disorder (BPD) was associated with equivalent role impairment as in MDD (Kessler, Merikangas, & Wang., 2007), suggesting that even symptomatically "milder" conditions may in fact be associated with considerable objective difficulty in functioning.

These data suggest that depressive disorders are harmful to those with the conditions in terms of potentially lost wages and opportunities for advancement due to absenteeism and lower productivity, as well as possibly fewer competency-related gains that can be accrued by experiencing positive work functioning. They are also economically harmful to the institutions and companies that employ these individuals, as well as to the greater society as a whole. In fact, analysis of data from multiple countries suggests that the effects of depression on functioning indices such as these are comparable to and sometimes exceed those of chronic medical conditions. Owing to data such as these, depressive disorders have received attention outside of the mental health field, including the areas of public health and policy as well as economics. Improving treatments for these conditions and access to such treatments may represent an opportunity to produce broader economic and societal benefits, such as increased productivity (perhaps by virtue of improving workers' well-being as well as reducing absenteeism and diminished productivity). The so-called "business case" for improving depression treatment and treatment access rests on such data, and the assumption of these models is that such improvements will result in lowered health care costs (most of which are borne by employers) and increased profits by virtue of heightened productivity (Donohue & Pincus, 2007). For example, the World Health Organization (WHO) estimates that depression is the fourth leading cause of disease burden in the world, accounting for 4.4% of total disability adjusted life-years (Ustun, Ayuso-Mateos, Chatterji, Mathers, & Murray, 2004), with some projections indicating that depression will rank second in this metric by the year 2020 (Murray & Lopez, 1996).

What makes depressive disorders so critical from a public health perspective is their relative chronicity and frequent early age of onset, which are even more marked for more serious forms of depressive disorders. Data from epidemiological studies suggest that depressive disorders are both intermittent and chronic in nature. Data from international (e.g., Murray & Lopez, 1996) and U.S. samples (Eaton et al., 1997; Spijker et al., 2002) suggest that the mean length of duration of an MDE is approximately 5 months to 7 months, with a median of 3 months. In the NCS-R (Kessler et al, 2007), respondents were asked to retrospectively report on the number of years they had spent in episode. The mean was 11.6 years for Bipolar II; 6.8 years for subthreshold

BPD; and 5.8 years for MDD. The effect of early onset and chronicity is to make disorders active to impair functioning for longer periods of time and across a diverse array of outcomes that characterize different developmental periods. It is not clear whether this is attributable to the duration of time the person is actively depressed, or due to the fact that depression early in life might impede success at earlier developmental milestones (such as in the domains of education and social network development), the long-term effects of which ripple further out across the life span. For example, in a 10- to 15-year follow-up of a sample of individuals with adolescent-onset MDD and nonpsychiatric controls, Weissman and colleagues (1999) found that the formerly depressed group had lower educational achievement and social class and longer durations of unemployment. One fourth of the depressed group made a suicide attempt over the follow-up interval, compared to 5.4% in the originally healthy group. Nearly two thirds had another MDE over the follow-up, whereas only 30% of the initially healthy group had an MDE over the same period.

COURSE OF DEPRESSIVE DISORDERS

The first fact that is important to understand with respect to the impact of depression on functioning is that, although the minimum duration of the most common depressive disorder identified in the *Diagnostic and Statistical Manual of Mental Disorders (DSM)* is relatively brief (i.e., 2 weeks for an MDE), most individuals with a depressive disorder are symptomatic for longer periods of time. Moreover, among those who have a chronic or recurrent course, even periods that do not meet full diagnostic criteria are often characterized by subthreshold symptoms and subpar functioning. A number of terms have been employed to describe important elements of course in the depressive disorders. Each of these is described here.

For unipolar mood disorders, the term *chronic* refers to an episode that lasts 2 years in duration (by definition, all cases of Dysthymic Disorder [DD] meet this definition; the *DSM-5* category of Persistent Depressive Disorder captures all chronic unipolar cases).

Remission refers to a period of time characterized by a cessation or significant reduction in symptoms of the disorder. It is typically defined as lasting less than 8 weeks. Well periods longer than 8 weeks are termed *recovery*. *Incomplete interepisode recovery* describes a situation in which a person has more than one MDE, and in the intervals between MDEs the person does not fully remit.

Relapse refers to circumstances in which a person initially improves in terms of symptoms, but then regresses to meeting full diagnostic criteria for the disorder. About one in five individuals who are in remission from an MDE will relapse back into the episode. Relapses seem to characterize those individuals who are likely to exhibit a chronic, recurrent course to their depressive disorder.

Recurrence is defined as a new MDE among those with a prior history of MDE and full recovery from the previous episode. Rates of recurrence (new MDEs in someone with a prior history of MDD) increase as a function of time after the initial episode, with 25% to 40% of individuals having a new MDE within 2 years; 60% after 5 years; 75% after 10 years; and 85% after 15 years (Keller & Boland, 1998). Recurrence is more common among those with MDEs of longer duration, those with DD, and those with a prior MDE (e.g., Keller, Lavori, Rice, Coryell, & Hirschfeld, 1986). Data from childhood samples indicate that rates of recurrence of MDD are 40% after 2 years and 70% after 5 years (Kovacs et al., 1984). Thus, there is an imbalance in the course data—the likelihood of recovery slows after several years (fewer additional people are achieving recovery), whereas the rate of recurrence grows with time. There is also some evidence that time to recurrence is shorter among those with more prior episodes (Solomon et al., 2000).

Typical Course of MDD

Few people who ever meet criteria for MDD exhibit a chronic course; most achieve remission or recovery at some point. There have been only a small number of studies that followed individuals with depressive disorders over very long periods of time in order to document the natural course of these conditions. However, the data from these studies are generally consistent with one another and with evidence from cross-sectional, epidemiological studies. Most individuals with MDE (about 90%) recover from their index episode within 5 years, and the bulk of these recoveries occurs within a year (Keller et al., 1982). The longer an MDE lasts, the lower the probability a person will recover from that episode within a year's time or even longer (e.g., Coryell, Endicott, & Keller, 1990). However, even though a small subset of people will experience an episode for many years, some of these people will still achieve recovery later.

Data from the Epidemiological Catchment Areas Study suggest that although about half of people with a lifetime MDD report only a single episode, about 15% experience a chronic, unremitting course, and the remainder (35%) will experience recurrent episodes (Eaton et al., 2008). For people who experience dysthymia with superimposed MDEs, often recovery from the MDE means a return to dysthymia, rather than full recovery or remission from depression altogether. Evidence from younger samples indicates that depressive disorders can be recurrent or chronic even early in development, including in early to middle childhood (e.g., McCauley et al., 1993; Rao et al., 1995), and even as early as the preschool years (Luby, Si, Belden, Tandon, & Spitznagel, 2009). Data from a longitudinal study of adolescents followed into early adulthood (Rohde et al., 2013) revealed that the length of depressive episodes occurring early in the life span is quite variable. Considering all those who met criteria for MDD up to the age of 30, the mean duration was approximately 28 weeks. However, the range was large (from a low of 2 weeks—that required for diagnosis of an MDE in the *DSM-IV*—to a high of 829 weeks). Moreover, those who met the criteria for an MDE in childhood had the longest mean duration (69 weeks), suggesting that very-early-onset episodes are particularly problematic.

Typical Course of Dysthymia (Persistent Depressive Disorder)

People with dysthymia are less likely to recover from their disorder than are those with MDD, and the course of dysthymia is frequently punctuated by MDEs that represent exacerbations of the underlying depressive state. Klein and colleagues (2006) followed a sample of patients with either dysthymia or nonchronic MDD over a 10-year period. At the 5-year follow-up, approximately 53% of those with dysthymia had recovered, but nearly half relapsed in the following 23 months; at 10-year follow-up, nearly 75% recovered, with half of these cases recovering by 52 months, but 71% of these cases relapsed. Consistent with the idea that dysthymia is a more severe disorder, dysthymics had more suicide attempts and hospitalizations, poorer functioning, and had higher overall depressive severity and persistence of depressive symptoms across the follow-up, in comparison to those who entered the study with nonchronic MDD.

Course of Bipolar Disorder

BD tends to be a highly recurrent condition. A large study of more than 1,000 individuals with Bipolar I or Bipolar II Disorder found that approximately half had a recurrence in the ensuing year, with most of the recurrences being of depressive episodes, compared to manic episodes (Perlis et al., 2006). Many manic episodes in BD cycle into depressive episodes (around 20% to 30%; Angst, 1987; Keller et al., 1986). Even among those who only have a history of manic episodes, recurrence into another manic episode is common; Keller and colleagues (1993) reported that pure mania has a high rate of recurrence (48% by 1 year; 81% by 5 years). BD tends to be less chronic (in terms of persistent symptoms without significant well periods) than some unipolar depressive disorders (i.e., dysthymia, chronic MDD); most manic episodes last about 3 months to 4 months, and Angst and Sellaro (2000) estimated that individuals with BPD spend about 2 months per year in episode. Even though episodes may remit, there is evidence that many people with BD are still symptomatic and continue to exhibit difficulty in functional domains, despite no longer meeting full threshold criteria (e.g., Keck et al., 2003)

The Collaborative Study of Depression followed participants over a 20-year period. Among those with BD in this sample, across their many recurrent mood episodes observed over the 20 year period, the median duration of MDEs was 15 weeks, with 75% of these episodes terminating (i.e., recovery achieved) by 35 weeks. The median duration of manic episodes was 7 weeks, with 75% ending after 15 weeks. Among those experiencing successive manic and major depressive episodes, the median duration was much longer (61 weeks). Likelihood of recovery from an index episode (of mania or MDE) was negatively associated with the cumulative number of years the person spent in episode over the follow-up period, and with the severity of the index episode. Moreover, rapid cycling episodes had lower probability of recovery than pure manic or MDEs. In that study, those who recovered from their index MDE or manic episode but still had residual, subsyndromal symptoms experienced faster recurrence to their next episode, when compared to those who had a symptom-free recovery (Judd et al., 2000; Judd, Paulus, & Zeller, 1999; Judd et al., 2008). Thus, the typical course of BD is recurrent and relapsing, and those with mixed episodes or rapid cycling or incomplete interepisode recovery exhibit the most severe course. Angst and Sellaro (2000) showed that there is a progressive shortening of the intervening well periods for the first few manic episodes, after which the pattern of recurrence is not consistent; the median cycling interval they observed between episodes was 18 months.

IMPACT ON FUNCTIONING OVER THE COURSE OF DEPRESSIVE DISORDERS

The following sections address the diverse and rather pervasive ways in which the depressive disorders can impact domains of functioning, including those that may be obvious only to the persons suffering from the disorder, as well as those that may be readily apparent to or even directly impact others in their social environment. Importantly, functional impairment is a critical component of our understanding of depressive disorders as psychiatric conditions. The *DSM* (and *International Classification of Diseases*) systems require as a part of the diagnostic criteria for each depressive disorder that a person exhibit significant functional impairment or distress associated with mood symptoms, in addition to meeting symptom severity and duration thresholds. Thus, it is important to understand the specific ways in which these conditions impact functioning.

Impact on Cognitive Functioning

There is overwhelming evidence that the depressive disorders are associated with characteristic patterns of cognitions, many of which appear in the diagnostic criteria themselves (e.g., trouble thinking/concentration in MDD, hopelessness in DD, flight of ideas in BD). The cognitive components are often featured in clinical descriptions of the disorders. The ways in which depression can impact cognition can be thought of as falling into one of two domains: (a) the qualitative content of one's cognitions (*what* one is thinking), and (b) quantitative dimensions of information-processing systems (*how* one's cognitive mechanisms are functioning relative to some norm). With regard to the first domain—as is immediately evident to most people who have experienced depression or mania in themselves or someone they know well—persons actively experiencing the symptoms of a depressive disorder think in ways that are highly congruent with their mood state. In this way, these conditions illustrate a more general principle of psychological science, the tight interconnection between emotion and cognition. Moreover, these thoughts can come to predominate in the person's consciousness in ways that are highly impairing. For example, in a manic episode, a person may become fixated on a grandiose plan, with grand and exciting thoughts related to how to achieve this plan and excitement about the prospects of glory upon achieving it crowding out more mundane, but necessary, thoughts about self-care. The thoughts may be so pressing that individuals cannot help but express them to everyone they meet, including strangers. In an MDE, people may become preoccupied with perceived failures, ruminating extensively about lost opportunities, gaffes, or their own inadequacy, or have intrusive, guilty thoughts about things they feel they should or should not have done. These thoughts may be so painful that the person withdraws from others or engages in unhealthy attempts to distract themselves from the cognitions, such as substance use or self-injurious behaviors.

By contrast, the second type of cognitive impairment, alterations in information processing, deals with ways in which depressive disorders change the efficiency or mechanisms of cognitive systems including those for attention, memory, and language. In some cases, empirical findings from this domain of research are interpreted as providing evidence that depression can *bias* information processing in predictable ways. Of course, some of what we know about the cognitive impact of depressive disorders deals with both types of changes—in the cognitive mechanisms underlying information processing, as well as in the output of these mechanisms (i.e., the content of the cognitions themselves). Detailed here—more about what is known from each of these literatures.

Specific Forms of Depressive Cognition. *Depressive realism.* A somewhat surprising but reasonably well-replicated fact from the cognitive literature on depression is that depression can actually make some types of information processing more accurate.

The depressive realism hypothesis (Alloy & Abramson, 1979) describes ways in which depressed people make more accurate, realistic inferences than do nondepressed people. The nature of this difference appears to be due to the failure of depressed people to exhibit a positive bias with regard to their performance, which is normative among those who are not depressed. For example, the nondepressed tend to overestimate the degree to which they have control over outcomes, whereas depressed people more accurately detect their degree of control (e.g., Alloy, Abramson, & Rosoff, 1981). Importantly, however, most studies of this phenomenon have used analogue (dimensional) measures of dysphoria, rather than samples defined by more serious levels of depression, and a recent meta-analysis demonstrated that the magnitude of these effects is rather small (Moore & Fresco, 2012). Thus, although this phenomenon is notable, it may be less important than other forms of depressive cognition.

Negative self-verification. Swann's self-verification theory (Swann, 1983) explains some surprising findings about our desire for receiving particular kinds of feedback about ourselves. In brief, we generally prefer to receive feedback that is consistent with our own views of ourselves, even if those views are negative, presumably because when one's views are corroborated by others, it results in the reassuring feeling of confidence in one's self-perception. People who are depressed have been shown to prefer to receive negative feedback (e.g., Giesler, Josephs, Swann, 1996), to actively solicit negative feedback from close others (Swann, Wenzlaff, Krull, & Pelha, 1992), and to prefer friends and romantic partners who view them negatively (Swann et al., 1992). In fact, when people who are experiencing depressed mood are given favorable information about the self, they then tend to seek negative feedback, presumably to reaffirm that their negative self-views are accurate (i.e., shared by others; Swann et al., 1992).

Rumination. Rumination refers to a tendency to respond to negative emotions by engaging in cognitive elaboration of these feelings, repetitively running over and over negative feelings in the mind, with an emphasis on distressing qualities and the negative consequences that may ensue from these feelings. Response styles theory (Nolen-Hoeksema, 1991) proposed that the tendency to passively engage in repeated rumination about one's negative emotions, rather than to engage in active problem solving to alleviate the source of the negative emotions, represents a trait risk factor for the development of depression. Rumination hijacks our human capacity to engage in meta-cognition (to reflect on our feelings and thoughts) and turns this capability into a harmful process that can prolong and exacerbate feelings of depression. As reviewed by Nolen-Hoeksema, Wisco, and Lyubomirsky (2008), rather than using processing of negative emotions to evaluate their causes and generate potential solutions, rumination tends to lead to less effective problem solving and reduced motivation to enact potential solutions. Individual differences in rumination correlate with depressive symptoms (they increase as depressive symptoms increase), and experimental induction to ruminate increases feelings of dysphoria; individual differences in rumination have also been linked to risk for developing a depressive disorder (Nolen-Hoeksema et al., 2008). Thus, when depressed, many people will engage in thinking that appears "stuck" in the fact of their depressive experience; and people who respond to feelings of negative mood with a passive style of this type are at risk for developing more serious forms of depression. Rumination has traditionally been conceptualized as being a factor unique to unipolar depression. However, there is now evidence it is associated with anxiety disorders and binge drinking/alcohol abuse (Nolen-Hoeksema et al., 2008). Moreover, one recent study found that remitted BD patients were higher on trait levels of rumination about both negative and positive emotions, and those with greater trait rumination about positive emotion had more lifetime manic episodes (Gruber, Eidelman, Johnson, Smith, & Harvey, 2011).

Cognitive triad. Beck's (1987) now classic theory of depression focuses on the tight link between depressed mood and particular patterns of cognition. He identified a number of kinds of "automatic thoughts" common among those experiencing depressed mood. These negative thoughts are characterized by self-reprisal, all-or-nothing thinking, and hopelessness; and they are readily accessible and rapidly generated (hence, automatic). In Beck's model, these automatic thoughts (instances of depressive cognition) are viewed as being generated by schemas, which are higher-order, organized belief structures that integrate our memories of the past, interpretations of the present, and predictions for the future. Among depressed individuals, these schemas are dysfunctional in that they represent excessively negative views of the self, the future, and how the world works. According to Beck, not only are the schemas of depressed persons defined by negative content that bias momentary thoughts and direct attention toward negative content, these negative schemas also exert a greater impact on momentary thoughts than do the schemas of nondepressed persons. Thus, the top-down interpretive processes guide momentary information processing so as to bias depressed individuals' attention to and interpretation of stimuli, such that neutral (or sometimes, even positive) stimuli are distorted by the influence of these negative schemas. In turn, these schemas bias behavior in ways consistent with the negative, hopeless, and passive content of these cognitions.

Effects of Depressive Disorders on Information-Processing Mechanisms. *Effects on attentional and perceptual processes.* Attentional processes are responsible for controlling the selection of environmental stimuli for more elaborate processing; thus, biases in attention towards or away from particular kinds of stimuli can constrain the information we use to understand our environment, predict the future, and engage in decision making. Because attention is a limited resource, it can be shaped by top-down processes that allocate our attention to or from certain kinds of stimuli or aspects of our environment. Negative attentional biases are a well-replicated correlate of anxiety disorders (Mineka & Sutton, 1992; Williams, Watts,

MacLeod, & Mathews, 1997). Anxious individuals engage in faster identification of negatively valenced stimuli, particularly those that are consistent with a threat to self. Given the high degree of comorbidity between anxiety and depressive disorders (see Chapter 3), one might expect to see similar effects for depression. However, although there is some evidence that depression is associated with attentional biases toward negative affective information (i.e., depressed persons allocate their attention more to negatively valenced stimuli), these findings have been rather inconsistent, with some studies finding such effects and other failing to do so. Thus, to the extent that biased attention at early stages of stimulus processing occurs in those with depression, it may be due to comorbid anxiety or may be limited to some kinds of negative stimuli. However, there is some evidence that depression may instead be associated with a failure to disengage from negative stimuli once they capture the attention (Gotlib & Joorman, 2010).

Effects on memory processes. Depressed individuals show enhanced memory for negatively valenced material (Mathews & MacLeod, 2005; Williams et al., 1997). The strongest effects are evident for tasks that require explict (rather than implicit) memory (Gotlib & Joorman, 2010). Comparing the performance of depressed and nondepressed persons across memory tasks varying in the stimuli used and the kind of processing of stimuli required, it seems that the most notable deficits among depressed people emerge when processing involves attending to the meaning of stimuli, rather than their pure perceptual features (Gotlib & Joorman, 2010).

In addition to deficits that are evident in recall of nonpersonal stimuli, depression is also associated with a particular pattern of abnormality in autobiographical memory. When asked to generate memories of events from their past that exemplify positive and negative emotions, people with depression tend to recall events at a level that is overly general, rather than specific (Williams et al, 2007). For example, they refer to a category of events that tend to elicit that emotion, not to a particular recalled event that occurred in a specific time and/or place. This phenomenon of "overgeneral memory" is important because it has been linked to experiencing longer episodes of depression (Raes et al., 2006), and slower or incomplete recovery from depression (Brittlebank, Scott, Williams, & Ferrier, 1993; Dalgleish et al., 2001). Williams and colleagues (2007) argued that overgeneral memory may arise because people with depression may retrieve memories in such a way as to block access to details that would be upsetting (i.e., would result in more negative affect). Thus, it may represent a form of avoidance of negative emotional material that deleteriously impedes improvement in depressive symptoms.

Effects on executive functioning and cognitive control. Cognitive control processes facilitate flexible shifting of attention, inhibiting previously rewarded responses, and generating new responses in ways that are flexible to environmental demands and the contingencies in the environment relevant to our goals. Ellis and Ashbrook (1988) proposed that depression is associated with deficits in effortful cognitive processing (including memory) because depression reduces cognitive capacity (i.e., resources available for processing). An alternative hypothesis focuses on the specificity of depression-related deficits to particular kinds of tasks. Siegle and colleagues (2002) articulated the affective interference hypothesis, which proposes that depressed people's cognitive resources are readily allocated to stimuli that are emotionally salient. As a result, they will perform adequately when the task requires an explicit focus on affective elements of the stimuli. By contrast, if the task demands that they focus on other aspects of the stimuli and ignore the affective components, their performance will suffer as a result. There is evidence that depressed persons exhibit more deficits in memory performance when the cognitive load of the task is increased (Hartlage, Alloy, Vázquez, & Dykman, 1993) or when task-irrelevant or personally salient thoughts interfere with attention to other aspects of the task (Ellis & Ashbrook, 1988). Gotlib and Joorman (2010) reviewed evidence from a number of different kinds of tasks, and concluded that depression is characterized by problems in inhibiting ongoing processing of negative stimuli, which interferes with the processing of other, more task-relevant stimuli, and increases the likelihood that negative mood will persist by causing the person to continue processing this material. Specifically, negative stimuli remain in working memory for too long because they are not expunged to make room for more relevant stimuli. This is consistent with evidence that those who tend to forget negative events and remember more positive events from the past have greater well-being over the life span (Charles, Mather, & Carstensen, 2003). These experimental findings also jibe with clinical observations that many people with depression can become so fixated on hurtful memories from the past that much of their available cognitive effort is consumed by these thoughts, which in turn makes it more difficult for them to focus on problem solving in the here and now.

Information-processing abnormalities in BD. There is also evidence that those with BD differ from those without BD on aspects of information processing, although this has been a less active area of research in the field of BD than in unipolar depression. These deficits may represent risk factors or trait markers for the illness; a meta-analysis showed that people with BD exhibit poorer executive functioning, verbal memory, response inhibition, and speed of processing compared to controls, even when in a euthymic (i.e., not currently meeting diagnostic thresholds for an episode) state (Robinson et al., 2006). These differences may distinguish among depressive conditions; one study found that mania is associated with greater dysfunction in executive functioning, compared to unipolar depression and bipolar depression (Gruber et al., 2011). Finally, greater memory deficits have also been linked to greater severity (i.e., history of more manic episodes, hospitalization, suicide attempts) and overall poorer performance on executive functioning and memory to worse outcomes (Martinez-Arán et al., 2004), and these deficits seem to be more marked in those who are further along in progression of the disorder (i.e., older patients and those with more prior episodes; Robinson & Ferrier, 2006). Taken together, this evidence suggests that in addition to depression, mania and mania proneness are also linked to cognitive abnormalities, although more evidence is necessary to demonstrate whether any of the observed cognitive correlates of depressive or manic episodes are specific to either state (versus generally associated with both), and whether they are outcomes of the psychopathological processes that define these conditions or causes of these conditions.

Associations between information-processing abnormalities and their biological mechanisms. Technologies for measuring brain processes, including cerebral blood flow (e.g., functional magnetic resonance imaging or fMRI), electrocortical activity (i.e., EEG), and visual attention to stimuli (eye tracking), have become increasingly sophisticated during the past 20 years. Ideally, we would be able to tie observed deficits and abnormalities in information processing defined by responses to cognitive probes and tasks to indices of the brain mechanisms that may underlie these responses. Such work is beginning to emerge, and holds considerable promise for advancing our understanding of how and why depressive disorders are associated with particular patterns of processing for different kinds of stimuli. Combining these different levels of analysis (cognitive performance at the behavioral level and brain functioning at the neural circuit level) will be critical for providing a richer depiction of the phenomena, and will hopefully generate new, testable hypotheses about the origin and development of the information-processing abnormalities and deficits that characterize depressive disorders.

IMPACT ON SOCIAL AND INTERPERSONAL FUNCTIONING

Among all the domains of functioning that may be impacted by depression, social and interpersonal functioning have received the most attention, and for good reason. Depressive disorders are associated with relatively broad difficulties in social functioning across different kinds of relationships and levels (e.g., social support, peer relationships, romantic relationships, and so on; Hirschfeld et al., 2000). Intimate relationships, in particular, are critical to understanding the pervasiveness of depression's effects and the contexts in which it is most likely to be felt.

In her blog, *Hyperbole and a Half*, Allie Brosh described the impact of her depression on her interpersonal experience:

> Months oozed by, and I gradually came to accept that maybe enjoyment was not a thing I got to feel anymore. I didn't want anyone to know, though. I was still sort of uncomfortable about how bored and detached I felt around other people, and I was still holding out hope that the whole thing would spontaneously work itself out. As long as I could manage to not alienate anyone, everything might be okay! However, I could no longer rely on genuine emotion to generate facial expressions, and when you have to spend every social interaction consciously manipulating your face into shapes that are only approximately the right ones, alienating people is inevitable. It's weird for people who still have feelings to be around depressed people. They try to help you have feelings again so things can go back to normal, and it's frustrating for them when that doesn't happen. From their perspective, it seems like there has *got* to be some untapped source of happiness within you that you've simply lost track of, and if you could just see how beautiful things are . . . At first, I'd try to explain that it's not really negativity or sadness anymore, it's more just this detached, meaningless fog where you can't feel anything about anything—even the things you love, even fun things—and you're horribly bored and lonely, but since you've lost your ability to connect with any of the things that would normally make you feel less bored and lonely, you're stuck in the boring, lonely, meaningless void without anything to distract you from how boring, lonely, and meaningless it is. But people want to help. So they try harder to make you feel hopeful and positive about the situation. You explain it again, hoping they'll try a less hope-centric approach, but re-explaining your total inability to experience joy inevitably sounds kind of negative; like maybe you WANT to be depressed. The positivity starts coming out in a spray—a giant, desperate happiness sprinkler pointed directly at your face.

And it keeps going like that until you're having this weird argument where you're trying to convince the person that you are far too hopeless for hope just so they'll give up on their optimism crusade and let you go back to feeling bored and lonely by yourself. (May 2013)

Marital/Couple Relationships

There are well-replicated and relatively large concurrent associations between depression and distress in close relationships (e.g., Whisman, 2001). Although more studies have been conducted exploring associations between marital distress and MDD, data from the NCS-R sample showed that there was a stronger association between BD and marital distress than between MDD and marital distress (Whisman, 2007). Moreover, this study also found that the link between MDD and marital distress was larger among older participants, suggesting that relationship functioning may be more adversely affected by depressive disorders among older individuals. There is also evidence from a large epidemiological sample that marital dissatisfaction predicts the onset of a new MDE over a 1-year follow-up interval for both men and women (Whisman & Bruce, 1999). Other studies have shown that measures of general interpersonal functioning are reliable predictors of the course of depression and the length of episodes (e.g., Brown & Moran, 1994; Lara, Leader, & Klein, 1997). These findings indicate that the quality of partner relationships may play an etiological role in the development and course of unipolar depression. Other evidence suggests that depression leads to subsequent problems in close relationships (e.g., Fincham, Beach, Harold, & Osborne, 1997), including an elevated risk for divorce among married couples (e.g., Merikangas, 1984). Thus, the relationship between unipolar depression and interpersonal functioning seems to be a bidirectional one (Davila, Karney, Hall, & Bradbury, 2003; Davila, Stroud, & Starr, 2009; Karney, 2001).

There is also some evidence that those with depressive disorders are more likely to marry others with the same conditions.

Mathews and Reus (2001) found data for assortative mating for both bipolar and unipolar depressive disorders, with higher rates among those with BD. There is also evidence for mating across depressive and other disorders, including alcoholism and anxiety disorders (Maes et al., 1998). Therefore, one reason why depression may be associated with relationship discord may be because of an additive effect of the deleterious influence of psychiatric problems evident in both partners.

Why is depression associated with intimate relationship problems? Some theorists have focused on the impact of depressive symptoms that may sever some important relationship-maintaining behaviors (e.g., loss of interest in sex in the depressed partner may decrease intimacy between the partners; anhedonia may reduce the depressed partner's willingness to engage in shared hobbies), or serve as irritants to the partner (e.g., sleep problems may be disruptive for the partner; lack of energy in the depressed partners may lead them to contribute less to household tasks, burdening the other partner). One study of individuals with unipolar depression, bipolar depression, or schizophrenia found that across these groups, impulse control symptoms were particularly associated with lower marital satisfaction (Hooley, Richters, Weintraub, & Neale, 1987). This suggests that some of the problems associated with BD may be particularly destructive with respect to relationship functioning.

Others have explored specific behaviors common among depressed people that may contribute to relationship dysfunction. For example, one interpersonal pattern common to those with unipolar depression is excessive reassurance seeking, which refers to a tendency to repeatedly seek reassurance from others about one's value and worth to the others, even when the others have already provided a reasonable amount of such assurance (Coyne, 1976; Joiner, Metalsky, Katz, & Beach, 1999). Coyne (1976) argued that some depressed people respond to depressive symptoms of guilt and worthlessness by developing a concern about whether others concur with these perceptions and will therefore reject them. In order to obtain information about whether their relationships are in fact in danger, they seek reassurance from close others about self-worth and value. The typical pattern is that others will initially provide such reassurance; however, some depressed people continue to question, seemingly not assuaged by others' statements. Eventually, close others feel frustrated by this behavior and may begin to express rejection of the depressed person. This may bring about the very thing that the depressed person feared in the first place—the loss of an important source of social support. Consistent with this, people with MDD report that they are most likely to engage in excessive reassurance seeking when they feel threats in their close relationships or when they have doubts about their performance or competence (Parrish & Radomsky, 2010). Depressed persons may also generate other kinds of stressors that contribute to conflict with their partners, which in turn worsens their depression (e.g., Davila, 2001; Davila, Bradbury, Cohen, & Tochluk, 1997). The role of stress generation in depressive disorders is discussed more fully in Chapter 8.

Parent–Child Relationships

There is a large literature examining the impact of depressive symptoms and disorders on aspects of the parent–child relationship, including parenting behaviors and the overall quality of the parent–child relationship. The importance of the parenting role as a potential source of functional impairment in the depressive disorders is heightened by the fact that these conditions tend to have very high prevalence rates during the early and middle adult years (see Chapter 3)—the time in the life span when the burden of parenting is heaviest. Most of the empirical research examining the effects of depression on the parent–child relationship has focused on women and their roles as mothers, with fathers and the paternal–child relationship relatively neglected. There is considerable evidence that women with depressive disorders and elevated depressive symptoms report themselves as experiencing more problems in parenting and with the quality of their relationships with their children in comparison to nondepressed mothers (Downey & Coyne, 1990; Rutter, 1990). Moreover, the smaller literature using direct observations of parenting by women has also shown that depression in mothers is linked to objective measures of parent–child interaction. Specifically, higher levels of depression in women are associated with more observed irritability, coercion, and hostility directed toward their children, and these effects appear to be greatest when the parent is actively depressed, as opposed to not in episode, and for younger, as opposed to older, children (Lovejoy, Graczyk, O'Hare, & Neuman, 2000). Fewer studies have been conducted with fathers, but the available evidence suggests that the effects are comparable to those observed in mothers (Wilson & Durbin, 2010).

IMPACT ON WORK AND EDUCATIONAL PERFORMANCE

Depressive disorders are associated with significant impairment in competency domains (i.e., work and educational performance). The societal burden of this form of functional impairment has been quantified in numerous studies showing that the overall costs of depressive disorders are enormous. The economic burden of depression can be driven by the costs associated with treatment of depression, lost lifetime earnings owing to suicide, and lower productivity (missed days and lower performance). Greenberg et al. (2003) estimated the total economic costs of MDD, DD, and BD to be $83.1 billion dollars in 2000. The costs appear to be even higher for women with depressive disorders, as well as those who have other comorbid psychiatric conditions in addition to a depressive disorder (Birnbaum, Leong, & Greenberg, 2003; Kessler & Frank, 1997). When interpreting these data, it is important to keep in mind the age distribution of depressive disorders. Because they tend to be most prevalent among those in the early to middle adulthood periods, depressive disorders impact functioning during those developmental periods in which people are most commonly pursuing educational and career advancement that affects their earning potential and career advancement across the long term in their lives.

One means by which depression affects work performance is by virtue of missed days at work. Those with depression tend to take more sick days than those with chronic medical conditions (nearly 10 days per year versus 7 days per year for conditions such as diabetes, high blood pressure, back pain; Druss, Schlesinger, & Allen, 2001). Other studies have more directly assessed work productivity on the job. One longitudinal study (Wang et al., 2004) measured work performance using ecological momentary assessment; participants were electronically alerted at five random times over a 7-day period, asking them to report on their level of concentration, task, focus, efficiency, and productivity. This study found that MDD was associated with poorer task focus and work performance, whereas other chronic conditions (such as arthritis, back pain, hypertension) were not. Data from the NCS-R sample show that both MDD and BD are linked to poor work functioning, with the overall costs due to lost workplace functioning attributable to BD of $14.1 billion in the United States (Kessler et al., 2006); overall costs of MDD were higher ($36.6 billion) because of its greater prevalence. However, BD was associated with more lost work days than MDD, with this greater impairment driven by the fact that the MDEs occurring among those with BD were more impairing than those occurring to people with MDD.

Depressive disorders are also linked to poorer academic functioning and educational outcomes in adolescence and emerging adulthood (Birmaher et al., 1996; DeRoma, Leach, & Leverett, 2009). Thus, one means by which early depressive disorders may exert a long-term effect on functioning is via their negative impact on academic performance and advancement.

IMPACT ON PHYSICAL HEALTH, HEALTH CARE USAGE, AND MORTALITY

Epidemiological data indicate that depressive disorders are associated with greater health care costs, with much of the costs attributable to untreated depression or treatment-resistant depression (Greenberg, Corey-Lisle, Marynchenko, & Claxton, 2004; Simon, VonKorff, & Barlow, 1995). Annual health care costs for depressed individuals rival those of people who have one of several serious chronic medical conditions (e.g., diabetes, heart disease, hypertension), with estimates of $4,373 per depressed person-year (in 1995 dollars), compared to $949 (in 1995 dollars) per year among those without a depressive disorder. Among those with depressive disorders, those with a chronic course utilize the greatest amount of general medical services (Howland, 1993).

Depression is also associated with poorer overall health, and with numerous chronic medical conditions, particularly chronic pain (Blair, Robinson, Katon, Kroenke, 2003). For example, Kessler and colleagues (2010) found in the NCS-R study that 11 of 14 physical disorders assessed were significantly elevated in those with MDD compared to those without MDD, including back or neck problems, seasonal allergies, asthma, frequent/severe headaches, and chronic pain conditions. The rate of comorbid physical disorders was much higher in older adults (65 years of age or older) than in the younger age groups; however, the strength of association between MDD and these conditions generally decreased with age, perhaps because the rates of MDD decrease with age whereas the rates of medical problems increase, lessening their association in the oldest group. Alternatively, the older population may adopt a different attitude toward physical illness (perhaps a more accepting one) that reduces the depressogenic effect of these conditions (Ernst & Angst, 1995).

Specifically, there is also evidence that depression is prospectively associated with the occurrence of cardiac events, with the greatest risk evident among those who have anhedonia

(Davidson et al., 2010), or recurrent or severe MDD (Kendler, Gardner, Fiske, & Gatz, 2009). The effects of anhedonia may be mediated by hypercortisolemia, inflammation, or autonomic arousal (Kendler et al., 2009); or catecholaminergic dysfunction (see Chapter 9 for a more complete description of these models); failure to engage in healthy behaviors that are protective for cardiac health, such as exercise and a healthy diet; or a tendency for those with anhedonia to underreport their symptoms to their physicians (Davidson et al., 2010). There is also prospective evidence for a link between coronary artery disease and the subsequent development of MDD (Kendler et al., 2009). Some of these associations between depression and serious medical conditions may be driven by the effects depression has on self-care routines and health behaviors. For example, meta-analytic evidence suggests that there is a reciprocal relationship between depression and being obese or overweight (Luppino et al., 2010). Finally, depression may be correlated with medical problems because they share etiological processes. For example, chronic psychosocial stress is associated with both depressive disorders and chronic medical problems; growing evidence suggests that chronic psychosocial adversity exerts a toll on major biological systems responsible for health (the allostatic load hypothesis). These data are discussed in more detail in Chapter 9.

SUICIDALITY AND SELF-HARM

Finally, one very important outcome often associated with depressive disorders is suicidality, ranging from passive suicidal ideation to nonlethal self-injury to actual suicide attempts and completed suicides. Suicide attempts are rare in the population, with only 1.6% of all deaths in the U.S. in 2010 attributable to suicide (McIntosh & Drapeau 2012). This rarity makes prediction of suicide and precision in identification of risk factors for suicide very difficult. Nonetheless, there is convincing evidence that nearly all cases of suicide—upwards of 95%—occur among those with mental illness (Cavanagh, Carson, Sharpe, & Lowrie, 2003). Rates are especially high among those with MDD (Bostwick & Pankratz, 2000) and BD (Harris & Barraclough, 1997).

Suicidality is common among those with depressive disorders. For example, Verona and colleagues (2004) found that nearly 25% of those with depression will make a nonfatal suicide attempt at some point in their lives. Rates of suicidality vary across the life span, with the highest risk evident among older adults. However, youngsters are not immune to suicidality. Nock and colleagues (2013) reported on the prevalence of nonlethal suicidal behaviors among adolescents in the nationally representative sample of the National Comorbidity Study-Adolescent (NCS-A) supplement. The rates of suicidality were relatively high; 12.1% reported experiencing suicidal ideation at some point in their lifetimes. The rates for suicidal plans and attempts were 4.0% and 4.1%, respectively. Only one third of those who experienced ideation ultimately developed a plan for suicide and another one third made an attempt. Risk for suicidal ideation was low in childhood and increased across adolescence (ages 12 years to 17 years). Girls had higher rates of ideation and attempt (odds ratio [OR] = 1.7 and 2.9, respectively). Most of those adolescents who reported a history of ideation (89.3%) or attempts (96.1%) met lifetime criteria for at least one mental illness. Consistent with evidence from smaller samples (Lewinsohn, Rohde, & Seeley, 1994), the most common mental illness among those with a suicide attempt was a unipolar depressive disorder (MDD, dysthymia), although elevated risk was also associated with BD, externalizing disorders, and anxiety disorders. In clinical samples, the rates are even higher. Weissman and colleagues (1999) reported that in their follow-up of depressed adolescents, 5% to 10% attempted suicide within 15 years of their first MDE. In the Oregon Adolescent Depression Project (OADP) sample, rates of suicide attempts were highest in the adolescent period (ages 13 years to 17 years), compared to the emerging adulthood and adulthood periods (Rohde et al., 2013). Among those who met criteria for MDD at any point up to age 30, 19% had at least one suicide attempt between adolescence and age 30, much higher than the rate among those without a history of MDD across the follow-up—3%. This suggests that for those with depressive disorders, the adolescent and early adulthood periods may be associated with particularly high levels of risk for suicide.

Predictors of Suicidality

The most important predictors of suicide attempts and completions are a prior history of suicidal behaviors, being physically ill, and being isolated from sources of social support (reviewed by Van Orden et al., 2010). In addition to one's own mental illness and family history of mental illness, it also appears that a family history of suicide contributes additional predictive validity. For example, Brent and colleagues (2002) found that children of parents who made a suicide attempt had six times the risk of making an attempt themselves. Joiner's interpersonal theory of the causes of suicide (Van Orden et al., 2010) emphasizes a number of factors that are particularly relevant to those with depressive disorders. The theory proposes that those who ultimately commit suicide have feelings of thwarted belongingness (i.e., they are isolated from the affective bonds and responsibilities to others that act as barriers to ending one's life); high perceived burdensomeness (i.e., they feel that their circumstances, such as being ill or unemployed, create more difficulties than advantages for their families and close others); and they have lost the fear of death and pain that enacting suicide necessitates.

CONCLUSIONS

Depressive disorders are associated with profound and pervasive effects on all of those domains of functioning that are critical contributors to our self-concept as thriving individuals. Not all of those who have a depressive disorder experience dysfunction in all of these domains, but most have considerable difficulty in one or more. Because the symptoms may be more bearable than the impairment, difficulty in functioning is often the problem that drives those suffering from depression to seek out treatment.

Why Does Depression Exist?

ny theoretical model of depressive disorders must be consistent with our broader understanding of human psychology, including the origins and functions of our psychological processes. The existence of depressive disorders must make sense in light of the evolutionary context of our species, and theories of the mechanisms that produce depression must be biologically plausible (i.e., they must honor our understanding of the processes by which the brain accomplishes the tasks it evolved to manage). The field of evolutionary psychology deals with these very issues; it attempts to explain psychological phenomena by reference to their functions in evolutionary context, or how psychological processes might represent adaptations that emerged from natural or gender selection to solve life challenges that faced our species in our ancient environments. As applied to depression (and psychiatric conditions in general), evolutionary psychology paradigms attempt to answer *why* human beings should even have the capacity to experience the features we identify as central to depressive syndromes. Given the evidence discussed in Chapter 4—showing that depressive disorders are associated with serious and often chronic deficits in the ability to function well in domains that are essential to survival and success (both personally and in terms of promoting the survival and success of those with whom one shares one's genes)—it may seem paradoxical to view depressive processes as reflecting adaptive mechanisms. However, that is precisely what evolutionary models of depression propose. Thus, the challenge of these theoretical models is to simultaneously account for the possible advantages to the organism that emerge from the capacity to experience depression, while also explaining how these same advantages can produce such negative outcomes.

The logic underlying evolutionary models of psychological disorders is that these conditions are not diseases in the traditional sense, but rather are manifestations of broader neurobiological mechanisms that are themselves normative. The dysfunction that characterizes psychological disorders is a result of a misfit between evolutionary older phenotypes that evolved because they were adaptive at the time and the new environments in which human beings are now situated (Wilson, 1998). Psychological mechanisms that were previously associated with fitness in the environment of evolutionary adaptation have survived, although they may no longer be associated with advantageous functioning in the same way in our current environments. One important goal of theorizing in this domain is to explain how psychological processes that characterize psychopathology may have operated in the environment of evolutionary adaptation because there is good reason to believe that this environment was quite different from the ones in which human beings are currently developing. Phenotypes that have survived must have been selected for in our evolutionary past, and thus must have conferred a selective advantage. A second goal is to explain how these systems potentially produce both beneficial (adaptive) and harmful outcomes in humans' current environmental context. Different evolutionary models of depression may focus on distinct elements of these conditions and diverse ideas about the functional significance of these elements; however, they all have in common the notion that human beings can (and do) experience depressive disorders—in our evolutionary past, the psychological mechanisms that produced these syndromes yielded advantages that allowed individuals with the capacity to engage in these mechanisms to survive themselves, as well as to promote the survival of those who shared their genes.

A number of theorists have offered models of depressive disorders that emphasize the possible adaptive significance to our species of these conditions and related emotions. The purpose of such models is twofold: (a) to provide a conceptualization of depression that is consistent with evolutionary theory, and (b) to describe how the etiology of depression may be understood as involving normal processes of adaptation. It is important to note that such models focus less on individual differences in depression risk, and more on understanding universal psychological mechanisms that explain the existence of such a negative state in humans in general. The presumption of these models is that there must be some adaptive value to depression (or related states that are produced by the same psychological mechanisms that produce depression), at least in the sense of promoting adaptation to situations that our ancestors routinely faced in their environment.

IS DEPRESSION AN ADAPTATION?

An adaptation is a characteristic that is heritable and originally arose in our species as a function of natural selection processes; because those with the characteristic had greater fitness than those without the characteristic, adaptations become more common in the gene pool (Buss et al., 1998). Adaptations that do not become universal in the gene pool must have a more complex association with fitness (otherwise, everyone would have the adaptation). In the case of depression, the capacity to be depressed may be adaptive in some environments and not in others, or appear only in some developmental periods or in response to certain environmental triggers (Nettle, 2004).

Many psychological processes are easy to imagine as adaptations that evolved to solve important challenges that faced human beings in our ancestral past; psychiatric conditions pose more of a challenge. Nesse (2000) noted that we can think of depression in one of two ways: (a) it is a disease or defect, a conceptualization consistent with the inclusion of depression in psychiatric classifications that emphasize "harmful dysfunction" as the hallmark of psychiatric illness, or (b) depression is a defense mechanism that arises from (but is not itself) a disease. Diseases are produced by defects (maladaptations) and have no usefulness to the person with the disease; thus, they do not have adaptive significance to the organism. By contrast, defenses have been shaped by natural selection; they are compensatory in nature and may serve to remediate some manifestations of the disease (e.g., pain is a defense that serves many adaptive functions in the context of physical illness). In many instances, defenses may not be harmful to the person, and in others, attempts to block these defenses may actually prove harmful (e.g., people who cannot perceive pain will incur harmful tissue damage). Thus, we can view depression as an ultimately harmful state resulting from one or more defects that can exist in important psychological mechanisms, or as the adaptive output of defense systems that were shaped by natural selection, perhaps to favor those with better abilities to regulate their mood states or to manage their engagement with particular kinds of environmental contexts.

As described in Chapter 1, our use of the word "depression" to describe narrower or broader manifestations can belie our underlying conceptualization of what depression is. Using the term *depression* to refer to more severe and uncommon states is consistent with a model of depression as a disease.

By contrast, when we see similarities across more and less severe states of depression or across depressive symptoms and normal range variations in mood, this reflects the notion that depression is a normal state that likely has adaptive value in some of its manifestations. If depressive disorders and normal experiences of grief, sadness, and guilt emerge from shared mechanisms, then perhaps depression shares with these normal experiences their adaptive functions as well. For example, the gradation of negative emotional experience may have evolved to provide a means of acknowledging and responding effectively to unfortunate circumstances. Some theorists have argued that depression may be adaptive precisely because it is painful, in that its function originates in the ability of this pain to motivate and support adaptive behavior to change the circumstances that originally caused the pain (e.g., Watson & Andrews, 2002). This may be most true for milder states of depression that are subjectively painful, but not so impairing that they prevent the person from engaging in active efforts to resolve the troubling circumstances.

We could view these states (normal negative moods, depressive conditions) as lying on a continuum, although also acknowledging that at some point along this continuum, these normal mechanisms become too protracted, excessive, or inappropriate relative to the person's context to be helpful to the person, and are instead dysfunctional. This requires us to (a) understand how the effects of depression and the functions it may serve may be quite different depending on its level of severity, and (b) identify the processes that cause a "normal," adaptive reaction to become excessive or inappropriate, and explain why such processes exist. Regarding the latter, it is possible that such processes are defects, rather than adaptations, and are therefore only evident in a subset of the population (unlike "normal" depressive mechanisms presumed to be observable in all human beings, given the appropriate eliciting circumstances).

One commonly invoked line of evidence against the view of depression as a disease (rather than an adaptation) is the fact that depressive disorders are relatively common in the population.

Moreover, they are most common in developmental periods that coincide with one's peak reproductive value (adolescence and early adulthood); most conditions we view as fitting the model of a disease have neither this age distribution nor this high a prevalence. Another factor that differentiates defenses from diseases/defects is that defenses are regulated by situational cues that signal the defense will be adaptive, whereas defects are not. As noted by Nesse (2000), the reliable association between loss experiences and depression suggests that depression may be an adaptation that evolved to provide effective strategies for dealing with loss. However, as described more fully in Chapter 8, the relationship between losses and depression is not uniform, and some evidence suggests that in serious cases of depressive disorders, the occurrence of depressive episodes may be loosed from environmental contexts. Such cases seem unlikely candidates for the expression of an adaptive defense process.

MODELS OF THE EVOLUTIONARY ADAPTIVENESS OF DEPRESSION

Depression Is A Signal for Help

Many of the evolutionarily based models generated to explain the existence of depression focus on the interpersonal and social contexts of depression. Many early evolutionary theorists, such as Lewis (1934), proposed that depression may function as a signal to close others that the person is in need of help; thus, depression may be adaptive to the extent that it elicits resources important for survival. For this process to be adaptive, the signal (i.e., depressive symptoms) should in fact elicit resources and assistance from others. However, as noted by Nesse (2000), more serious depressive disorders are frequently associated with negative reactions from others (see Chapter 4 for a detailed discussion of the negative interpersonal repercussions of depressive disorders).

Depression As A Resource Conservation Strategy

Depression may be part of a set of mechanisms that allows us to respond adaptively to stressors, given finite resources. This may be accomplished by one of two strategies: (a) limiting nonproductive allocation of resources and energy, or (b) putting a pause on ongoing resource expenditures, thus granting time for internal resources to return to their prestressor level. For example, Cannon (1929, 1932) described the body as having a "natural wisdom" that allows for rest and renewal following a stressor. Some evolutionary theorists have interpreted depressive symptoms of withdrawal and malaise as reflecting these "renewal" processes. The withdrawal that accompanies depression is proposed to serve the function of removing depressed persons from direct contact with stressors, thus providing them the opportunity to recover from the negative feelings elicited by the stressor (Akiskal & McKinney, 1973). This response may be adaptive when the stressor will resolve on its own or when it is fundamentally unsolvable. Theories such as these do not explain how adaptive processes of withdrawal that are meant to be part of transient periods of renewal can sometimes result in more protracted depressive episodes or disorders. In addition, they do not account for situations in which depressive withdrawal actually creates additional stressors for the person (e.g., lack of interest and motivation can lead to problems with work functioning and potentially cause new stressors such as job loss, or they can create interpersonal strife, another source of additional stress).

Depression As A Means Of Modulating Goal-Related Activity In Response To Changing Environmental Circumstances

Other evolutionary models are built around explanations of the possible functional role of depressive symptoms of anhedonia and amotivation in regulating goal-setting and goal-driven behaviors. These models propose that anhedonia specifically produces disengagement from goal-related behaviors; this pause on goal-setting and -seeking allows individuals time to reassess their goals, or to set aside goals that may be unrealistic or unattainable (Nesse, 2000). Consistent with these models, theory and evidence from empirical studies on normal variations in mood suggest that emotions are in fact intimately tied to goals. Normal variations in positive and negative mood states seem to be related to our perceptions of our proximity to and speed of approaching valued goal states—positive moods decrease and negative moods increase when we sense we are moving away from, or advancing more slowly than desired toward, our goals (e.g., Carver & Scheier, 1990; Higgins, 1997). Emotions also shape goal-directed behaviors. Positive moods facilitate cognitive and behavioral strategies that are novel and riskier (Fredrickson, 2001), whereas negative moods reduce risk-taking (e.g., Allen & Badcock, 2003). Depressive symptoms reduce the perception of potential rewards in the environment (anhedonia), increase estimation of the energy involved in pursuing them (fatigue), and the pessimistic cognitive style that characterizes depression will reduce the perception that efforts will ultimately pay off (Nettle, 2008). The end result of these mood changes is a shift toward a cognitive style that is more reflective and systematic, which might engender a tendency to reevaluate goals and/or one's strategy for attaining those goals.

Nesse (2000) argued that depression may represent an extreme variation of normal processes that evolved as part of systems responsible for maximizing return on investments. When one's environmental circumstances are generally auspicious, opportunities are ripe for gaining more resources by engaging in additional efforts, including those that are riskier but have a likelihood of a high payoff. By contrast, when cues in the environment suggest that opportunities are low and the risk of loss is high, it is wise to disinvest effort, particularly efforts that have a lower probability of paying off. Mood states (both positive and negative) may be the intermediary between perceptions of environmental affordances and investment in effort, such that advantageous environments spur positive affect, which in turn motivates riskier, more expansive endeavors. By contrast, less certain environments generate negative mood that serves to facilitate a more cautious approach, or even to halt action if circumstances are so disadvantageous that action might be dangerous or futile. These negative moods dampen risk until environmental circumstances improve. Nesse (2000) noted that there are many circumstances in which inaction may be preferable to effort, particularly when caution is warranted. For example, some psychosocial goals require a considerable amount of time, effort, and social resources to build, and shifting one's goals drastically in these domains could have far-reaching consequences. Another example: commitments to significant others, friends, careers, and social groups should seldom be overthrown rashly, as errors of judgment in this regard could be devastating. Thus, it might be wise to have a period of anergia, reflection, or failure to act so as to prevent oneself from making decisions that might worsen one's social resources. However, this logic does not account for the fact that those with depressive disorders seem to be at higher risk for engaging in social structures that are less than optimal, including problematic marriages and social networks (see Chapter 4). Moreover, it is important to note that much of the empirical evidence that is used to support these models relates to normal variations in positive and negative moods, not the more extreme levels characteristic of depressive disorders. However, it is possible that evolution may have provided these mechanisms related to normal variations in mood that somehow become misapplied, excessive, or elicited in inappropriate contexts in clinical conditions such as depressive disorders.

The Social Competition Hypothesis

Price and colleagues (1994) argued that the function of depression may be to cut one's losses when locked in a conflict that is unwinnable and ultimately too costly to continue. Depressive symptoms encourage the person who is bound to lose to accept this loss, to behave in a submissive manner that is likely to elicit a cessation of hostility by the victor, and to accept the loss of rank that ensues. In this way, resources, rather than wasted on a losing battle, can be preserved for future efforts that are more likely to result in gaining resources. In this model, depression that persists reflects dysfunction in this system, in that it emerges when someone refuses to accept a loss.

The Social Navigation Hypothesis

Watson and Andrews (2002) expanded upon earlier models of the evolutionary value of depression by arguing that depression evolved to provide an adaptive strategy for responding to disadvantageous social circumstances. The crux of their argument is that depression creates rumination about one's social circumstances and serves as a signal to close others that one needs to receive more resources. The former serves to direct the person's limited cognitive resources away from pursuing other goals and toward figuring out how to solve complicated interpersonal/social problems. The latter is thought to elicit such resources from those who have an interest in the depressed person's fitness (i.e., kin). For example, significant others may be motivated by the person's pain and signals of floundering to step up their assistance of emotional, logistical, and tangible support to the depressed person because they perceive that the costs of providing this support are less than the costs of continuing to endure the consequences of the person's depressive symptoms.

This model proposes that depression will emerge in the context of stressful social situations so as to facilitate better problem solving about the social stressors and cultivation of more resources to solve these problems. However, as described more fully in Chapter 8, depression can emerge in the absence of significant social stressors, and there is little empirical evidence that depressed persons engage in more effective social problem solving.

The Social Risk Hypothesis

This model proposes that depression evolved because one recurrent challenge that faced our species concerned the ability to navigate social hierarchies; individuals who were capable of successfully monitoring their social resources and preventing themselves from being excluded socially were at a fitness advantage (Allen & Badcock, 2003). Depression emerges when individuals perceive that they are at risk of losing important social resources because their contribution to their larger social group is low or their costs to the group are too high. Depressive symptoms cause the person to be risk averse in such a way as to create a preference for small gains and the stemming of losses of resources, and away from risky strategies that might prompt social exclusion. The net outcome of these consequences is to preserve existing resources. Depressive behaviors preserve social resources because they (a) reduce social conflict with others higher in the hierarchy by communicating to others that one is not a threat to existing dominance hierarchies, and (b) elicit additional resources by signaling to others that one needs resources.

Individual Differences in Mood Systems Hypothesis

Nettle (2004) proposed that depression is not an adaptation, but is a by-product of individual differences in systems for emotion that are adaptations. Emotion systems that facilitate the allocation of attention and energy toward goals that are salient for humans, such as managing social hierarchies and relationships and pursuing opportunities, serve a number of important adaptive functions. Nettle argued that depression is a by-product of individual differences in the sensitivities of systems for positive and negative mood. People with sensitive systems for negative moods can experience benefits in terms of avoidance of punishing contexts and caution in uncertain situations; optimal functioning of these systems promotes fitness, whereas extremely high or low levels may result in problems in some environmental contexts, including depression. Because the range of situations in which different levels of sensitivity of basic emotional systems are adaptive is quite broad, there remains a high degree of individual differences in these systems in the population (none is selected out by uniformly reducing fitness). Thus, emotion systems capable of producing weak to strong experiences of positive and negative moods are themselves adaptations. Individual differences in these systems were preserved across evolution because individuals varying in the strength or sensitivity of these systems could achieve high fitness, depending upon their particular environmental contexts. A side effect of these individual differences is that some people with extreme levels of functioning of these systems will experience maladaptive expressions of positive and negative emotions (e.g., depression) in some environmental circumstances.

CONCLUSIONS

Evolutionary models endeavor to address a critical issue—how conditions associated with as much pain and dysfunction as depressive disorders emerged and persisted in our species. The challenge for all such models is how to marshal evidence in favor of or against any particular evolutionary hypothesis. The critical causal mechanisms that need to be explained occurred in our evolutionary past and cannot be replicated in the laboratory. Thus, we are left to piece together consistent and inconsistent evidence from other kinds of research. As a result, evolutionary models are judged more by their internal consistency, the elegance of their formulation, and their ability to account for disparate lines of evidence. Such models are also interesting in that they force us to think about more basic underlying biological processes that may underlie depression, and prompt us to consider whether other species with who we share an evolutionary past might also be capable of depressive-like experiences. However, such models are limited in that they generate fewer novel predictions to be tested in empirical study, they have poor specificity for predicting who is at risk for depression and why, and they account less readily for some important aspects of depressive disorders (such as mania and chronic depression).

6

What Models Help Us to Understand the Causes of Depression?

From a scientific perspective, the most critical task in understanding depressive disorders is to discover their causes, both at the level of the population and for the individual person. At the population level, our task is to identify which factors and processes (within persons and their environments) exert the largest effects on individual differences in the development of depressive disorders. Locating causes means that we seek to identify: (a) all of the factors that differentiate between individuals who develop depression and those who do not; (b) processes or events that emerge or change in close temporal proximity to the timing of onset of the disorder; and (c) factors that explain variation in the severity of depression (e.g., course, comorbidity, or outcomes) in the population. Factors that play a role in causing depression for more individuals (i.e., are more prevalent causes) and whose effects are larger (i.e., are more potent causes) will emerge in this research as the most important.

We have long since abandoned the idea that there is a single, unifying cause for all cases of depression and the idea that factors that initially cause depression are necessarily the same as those that explain variation in its course or outcome. Depressive disorders are characterized by *etiological heterogeneity*, which means that many diverse causal factors or causal pathways (chains or constellations of factors) can lead to the same clinical outcomes. This is an important point—it suggests that what we observe at the level of signs and symptoms is not lawfully related to a single process or set of processes, and that there are also individual differences in the routes by which people become depressed. Several implications follow from this logic. The first is that clinical descriptions of depressive disorders that focus on signs and symptoms may not be the most useful scientific starting point for etiological research; perhaps alternative conceptualizations of (presumably more basic) underlying pathological processes that give rise to observable signs and symptoms will be a more tractable target for understanding etiology. The second is that one important agenda for etiological research is to identify more homogeneous pathways to depression or groups of individuals who share a common pathway to depressive disorders. Etiologically homogeneous subgroups can then be the target population for research aimed at detailing more precise mechanisms by which a particular etiological factor leads to depression. If etiologically homogeneous groups are distinguishable on the basis of their clinical presentation, then this suggests that depression is a "family" of interrelated disorders with similar but discriminable causal pathways. If groups of people with different causal paths to depression cannot be reliably identified on the basis of their clinical presentation, then this suggests that many different etiological pathways, originating from different sources, converge upon some more proximal processes that produce the signs we see and the symptoms that individuals with depression experience. This is referred to as a *final common pathway*. There has been much interest in testing whether there is in fact a final common pathway to depressive or manic symptoms and understanding its nature. For example, some have proposed (e.g., Siever & Davis, 1985; Stone, Lin, & Quartermain, 2008) that different pathways to depression, such as adverse environments, negativistic cognitions, or genetic differences in the sensitivity to negative events, all ultimately lead to neurochemical changes in the brain that produce altered patterns of feeling, thinking, and behaving consistent with the symptoms of depression. To date, such models are useful for informing research on etiology, but have not been conclusively shown to meet the criteria for a final common pathway.

Etiological heterogeneity poses a number of challenges to research. First, there is the conceptual problem of how to think about different sources leading to the same outcome. Second, if our clinical syndromes do not distinguish among people who have different etiological pathways, designs that contrast groups defined by the presence versus absence of depression will lump together in the depressed group individuals for whom different etiological factors are relevant. This will necessarily "water down" the number of individuals in the depressed group for whom any one particular etiological factor of interest is relevant, making it more difficult to detect the signal of the potential etiological factor's effect amid the noise of multiple etiological pathways. This makes clear why so much research has been devoted to identifying subtypes of depression defined either by particular constellations of symptoms, different course patterns, or other correlates; the aim of this research is to potentially discover groups that more cleanly relate to particular etiological pathways.

At the level of individual cases, we want to understand what factors within people and their environments, and all the transactions between these domains, ultimately lead to development of their disorders. Treatment can be meaningfully informed by such a model, particularly when it focuses on identifying changeable targets for intervention, either within the person's environment or psychology (i.e., patterns of thinking or behaving). Etiological research can help us to identify the most common pathways to depressive disorders (those present in the largest proportion of depressed individuals), but it does not tell us the relative importance of these factors within any one case.

WHAT DOES IT MEAN TO UNDERSTAND ETIOLOGY?

The primary goal of research on etiology is to discover and then to describe the processes that cause the disorder. For psychopathology, this means identifying factors that tell us *which* individuals will develop the condition of interest, as well as the *processes* or *mechanisms* by which that occurred. Much of our research is necessarily limited to identifying factors that correlate with depression (either concurrently, or over time/predictively). Incrementally identifying new correlates that allow us to explain more of the variance in risk for depressive disorders is important in that all such correlates are candidates for processes that might actually be involved in causing these conditions. The more correlates we identify, the better able we are to correctly identify more people who will ultimately develop depression, which serves important applied goals. However, not all correlates are in fact causally related to the development of depression; they may be *markers* that indicate who is at risk without telling us how or why (Kraemer et al., 1997). Given the etiological heterogeneity of depressive disorders, some risk processes that cause depression may actually account for only a small proportion of the variance in risk in the population as a whole; nonetheless, they may be critically important (and perhaps even necessary) in some cases. For this reason, it is implausible that any single theoretical model of the etiology of depression will satisfy all of our wishes—the need to account for a large proportion of people who develop these conditions; to play a powerful role relative to those that play a smaller role; or to accurately point to the actual mechanisms that produce the clinical phenomenon. Accordingly, there are many theoretical accounts offered to explain the etiology of depression, varying in their scope (the range of disorders and presentations they are meant to explain), breadth versus simplicity (the degree to which they focus on the pathways to depressive disorders attributable to a narrow set of mechanisms or they integrate the action of many disparate forces), and the extent to which they attempt to explain both normal variations in mood and depressive disorders using the same causal factors. Similarly, empirical studies conducted to test these models can vary in their ability to provide more or less dispositive evidence for the claims in any one model. Particular research designs and methods of composing populations to study are more useful for testing certain kinds of claims. A relatively limited number of designs and strategies can actually provide evidence that is causally informative, that is, able to distinguish between factors that are correlated with risk versus those that may be actually involved in causing the disorder. In this chapter, the primary paradigms that these etiological models fall into are highlighted first. Then there is a description of what the author believes to be the most important observations about depressive disorders that must be explained by any etiological model of these conditions. Finally, the author comments on the types of research designs that may prove most useful for distinguishing among different theoretical accounts and between risk markers (as opposed to risk processes or mechanisms).

THE DIATHESIS-STRESS FRAMEWORK

Many etiological models of unipolar and bipolar depressive disorders draw upon the conceptual model first offered by Meehl (1962) and Rosenthal (1963), the diathesis-stress model.

This conceptual framework was a philosophical attempt to identify the sources of different kinds of influence on psychopathology and to clarify their relative causal importance and the nature of their causal role in the development of psychiatric disorders. It also offered a practical way forward for researchers in terms of how to model and test hypotheses regarding pathological processes. The paradigm identifies two sources of influence on psychopathology—the diathesis and stress. In Meehl's and Rosenthal's original formulation, the diathesis refers to some aspect inherent to the person (traditionally viewed as genetic in nature) that reflects a propensity toward a particular disorder (such as Major Depressive Disorder [MDD] or Bipolar Disorder [BD]). Diatheses persist over time; people "carry" diatheses with them in whatever environment they encounter. Diatheses are typically seen as being specific to a particular disorder; thus, the diathesis for MDD is proposed to be distinct from the diathesis for BD.

There are two general versions of the diathesis–stress model. In the *interactive* version (see Figure 6.1), the diathesis interacts statistically with stress; stress refers to the environmental conditions under which the *diathesis produces the disorder*.

Therefore, stress provides the circumstances under which the diathesis creates the pathology. In this formulation, the diathesis has causal priority in that it identifies the most important causal mechanisms that lead to the disorder. Stress merely releases the diathesis to exert its causal influence; thus, the level of stress one experiences is irrelevant to understanding the risk for the disorder unless a person has the diathesis. In original articulations of the diathesis–stress model, stress was seen as more general than the diathesis; it is the distinction among different diatheses that tells us which disorder a person will develop, whereas stress does not differentiate among different clinical phenomena. This is another way in which this model privileges the role of the diathesis in the etiology of disorders. Thus, both the diathesis and the stress are necessary for individuals to develop a disorder; people must possess the diathesis

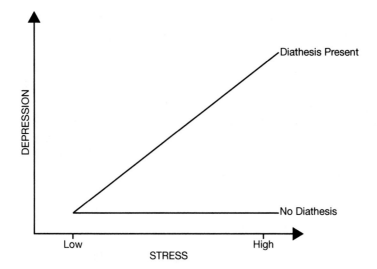

FIGURE 6.1 Interactive diathesis–stress model.

for the disorder (either categorically, or beyond some threshold if the diathesis can vary dimensionally across people) and they must experience sufficient stress to activate the diathesis. The interactive version of the diathesis–stress model asserts that only those who have sufficient stress and a sufficient amount of the diathesis will develop the disorder; all others will remain well. A number of implications follow from this model. First, many people who have the diathesis for depressive disorders will never develop the condition because they do not experience sufficient stress. This suggests certain realities that impact our ability to identify diatheses through research. All those who have a depressive disorder, such as MDD, should have both the diathesis and the stress. One might think this would make it easy to identify the diathesis. However, many people without MDD (who would form one's contrast group in a study testing differences between those with MDD and without MDD) would also have the diathesis (if they had not experienced sufficient stress to develop MDD). Thus, the difference between the group with MDD and the group without MDD on the diathesis would be smaller than the actual importance of the diathesis for understanding the disorder.

An alternative formulation of the diathesis-stress model is the *additive* version, depicted in Figure 6.2. In the additive model, neither the diathesis nor the stress is thought of as categorical. Rather, each is viewed as varying broadly across the population, such that a person can have anywhere from a very low to a very high level of each. Individual differences in each (the diathesis and the stress) are smoothly related to the likelihood of developing the disorder. There is no threshold beyond which the diathesis or stress is sufficient for producing the disorder. Rather, the two sources sum together smoothly to define a person's level of risk. In this model, people with low levels of the diathesis may still develop MDD if they experience a high level of stress; similarly, only low levels of stress will prove sufficient to provoke the

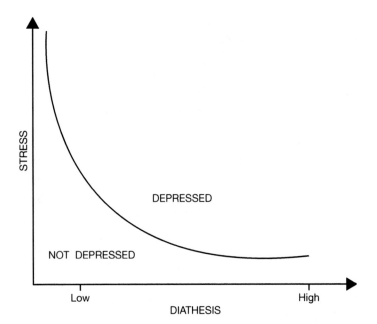

FIGURE 6.2 Additive diathesis–stress model.

disorder among those with a high level of the diathesis. This model implies that those with higher levels of the specific diathesis are more stress reactive (lower levels of stress provoke the disorder than among those with lower levels of the diathesis). Accordingly, it predicts that those with the disorder whose environmental circumstances are relatively favorable (i.e., lower in stress) must have higher levels of the diathesis. The following chapters review the extent to which specific etiological models that follow the diathesis–stress framework fit the implications of these models.

Potential Diatheses for Depressive Disorders

Meehl's and Rosenthal's model inspired (and continues to inspire) a broad range of research seeking to identify characteristics of the person that may reflect a heightened propensity toward depressive disorders. As typically conceptualized, diatheses are trait-like, meaning they are thought of as stable over time (i.e., those with high levels of the diathesis at one time point will still have a high relative standing on the diathesis at a later time point). This captures the initial depiction of the diathesis as something that individuals carry with them from situation to situation. However, it is also important to note that a diathesis need not be unchanging over time; some trait risk factors for depressive disorders may exhibit developmental change in their mean levels or only be apparent during particular developmental stages. Because the diathesis is proposed to interact with stress, these models must also characterize how stress activates the diathesis or how the diathesis increases one's sensitivity to stress (interactive model), or the process by which the diathesis and stress sum together to produce the disorder (additive model).

The most commonly proposed diathesis for depressive disorders is genetic loading for these conditions. Individual differences across persons that originate in genes are proposed to increase risk for depressive disorders because these genetic differences result in psychological processes that predispose individuals to become depressed. As described more fully in Chapter 9, familial/genetic loading for depressive disorders is the best-replicated risk factor for these conditions. One common means of quantifying familial or genetic loading for a disorder is the number of biological family members who have ever had the disorder; most researchers typically focus on measuring history of the disorder among those with the highest degree of genetic similarity, or first-degree relatives (parents, siblings, offspring). Consistent with the additive diathesis–stress model (and with the notion of etiological heterogeneity), not all people who develop one of these conditions actually have a high familial loading for depressive disorders. For example, most people with MDD, DD (Dysthymic Disorder), or BD do not have first-degree relatives with the condition. Thus, one wonders whether those without significant familial loading represent an etiologically distinct subgroup from those who do have elevated genetic risk. It is also unknown precisely how familial loading operates to increase the likelihood that one will develop these disorders. For example, there is evidence that those with a high familial loading for depressive disorders may in fact be more sensitive to stress than those with a lower familial loading (e.g., Kendler et al., 1995; Wichers et al., 2007). Familial loading is an excellent example of a proxy variable. It stands in for genetic and environmental factors that are transmitted in families; however, familial loading is not a direct assessment of these factors or the more proximal psychological or biological mechanisms coded for by these genes or influenced by the family environment that produces the disorders themselves. Some people without a family history of depression may themselves develop a depressive disorder that is genetic in origin; some with a high familial loading may develop depression as a result of other processes that are separate from their familial risk; and some people with very high familial risk may never become depressed (as implied by the interactive diathesis-stress model). Thus, it is not surprising that although familial loading is a significant predictor of risk, its association with these disorders is not large. As described further in Chapter 9, the specific genes that confer risk for depressive disorders have yet to be conclusively identified. Without knowing what those genes are, we cannot know how the genes operate to increase risk. We do not know the function of these genes or how variations in poly-morphisms in these genes may be related to different biological and psychological processes that are relevant to the etiology of depressive disorders.

Other researchers have focused on identifying trait differences that define more precisely the mechanisms that increase risk dif-ferentially across people. Many, but not all of these traits are ones that are substantially heritable, and thus consistent with the idea that diatheses are genetic in nature. For example, personality traits concerning individual differences in emotional reactivity (clarified more in Chapter 7) may describe the processes that cause some individuals to develop depression. Others have identified diathe-ses in the domains of biological differences or cognitive styles.

Stress

In the original conceptualization of the diathesis–stress model, stress was viewed in general terms as a releasing factor that poten-tiated the effects of the diathesis. The specific disorder that resulted under circumstances of stress was determined by the nature of the diathesis, not the nature of the stress. Since its original formula-tion, however, considerable empirical and theoretical advances have been made to our understanding of stress and how it might operate to influence the development of depression. In fact, it now seems clear that the *kind* of stress one experiences is impor-tant for understanding whether or not one will develop depres-sion. More on this evidence is elaborated upon in Chapter 8.

Criticism of the Diathesis–Stress Model

The diathesis–stress framework has been enormously influen-tial in terms of the research it stimulated. However, a number of conceptual and practical issues with the model have also been identified. First, the model does not tell us how to understand disorders for which there is more than one possible diathesis (depressive disorders, as noted earlier, are characterized by etiological heterogeneity). The early promise of genetic research into psychopathology—the hope that we might identify a specific gene (or even a small set of genes) necessary for the development of a depressive disorder—has not proven to meet with empirical reality. Thus, any single depressive disorder includes individuals who have different diatheses, or perhaps different combinations of diatheses, for the disorder. Moreover, some diatheses appear to be shared across disorders defined as distinct in our classification systems. For example, MDD and Generalized Anxiety Disorder (GAD) appear to be influenced by overlapping (rather than separate) genes (Kendler, Neale, Kessler, Heath, & Eaves, 1992), some of which likely include genes for high levels of the trait neuroticism/ negative emotionality (NE) (Fanous, Gardner, Prescott, Cancro, & Kendler, 2002; Hettema, Prescott, & Kendler, 2004). Moreover, the statistical interaction model underlying both the additive and interactive versions of the diathesis–stress model implies that these two domains (the diathesis and the stress) are independent of one another (and thus, can interact). However, it is now clear that the best-replicated diatheses for depressive disorders (i.e., familial loading for depressive disorders, personality traits) are not separate from measures of stress—many are significantly correlated with the likelihood of experiencing different kinds of stressors and emotional reactivity to stressors. The implications of these findings are more fully described in Chapters 7 and 8.

ALTERNATIVES TO THE DIATHESIS–STRESS MODEL

As an alternative to the diathesis–stress model, Joseph Zubin proposed an even more general *vulnerability model* (Zubin & Spring, 1977). In this framework, people's propensity for the disorder in question (e.g., DD) is understood as the additive sum of their standing on all the factors that contribute to risk for the disorder. Factors within (e.g., diatheses) and outside of (e.g., stress) the person are considered equivalently important contributors to risk. The advantage of this framework is that it provides a neat fit to common methods of analyzing the predictive validity of a range of risk factors for a disorder. Researchers commonly employ multivariate models to determine the degree to which a set of variables (e.g., multiple risk factors) explains variance in an outcome of interest (e.g., BD) in a sample. The vulnerability model does not require exploration of interaction terms as in the diathesis–stress model. All predictors thought relevant can be tested for their additive impact on risk for the disorder, with the goal being to maximize the predictive validity of the overall set of potential risk factors rather than testing a specific hypothesis about one diathesis and a measure of stress. From a research perspective, the vulnerability model encourages measurement of many different domains of potential risk and it capitalizes on etiological heterogeneity (variables tapping many distinct causal pathways can be entered into the same predictive model to maximize the likelihood of accounting for as many cases of the disorder as possible). However, in order to provide a thorough causal explanation of the disorder, the vulnerability model requires that we generate some notion of the ultimate or final process by which different sources of risk combine to produce the disorder.

Another alternative to the diathesis–stress model is to set aside diatheses and instead consider only stressors or broader environmental measures that may predispose to risk or which may have a tight temporal association with the onset of symptoms. For example, several studies have shown that stressors involving interpersonal losses, such as bereavement or the loss or threat of loss of a significant relationship, have particularly strong associations with the onset of depression (e.g., Paykel, 2003).

OBSERVATIONS ABOUT DEPRESSIVE DISORDERS THAT MUST BE ACCOUNTED FOR BY ANY ETIOLOGICAL THEORY

There are a number of well-replicated findings regarding depressive disorders that any plausible model of their etiology must account for; their success is partially judged by their ability to explain these phenomena:

1. Women are at higher risk for depressive episodes beginning at early adolescence and then throughout the life span.
2. Unipolar depressive disorders can onset at any point in the life span, but are most prevalent in late adolescence through early to mid-adulthood. BDs generally onset before mid-adulthood (typically in late adolescence or early adulthood); new cases are rare thereafter.
3. More severe cases of unipolar and bipolar disorders are characterized by a chronic/recurrent course (i.e., episodes of longer duration or more frequent episodes).
4. Both unipolar and bipolar disorders are commonly comorbid with other forms of psychopathology; overall severity and poorer outcome over time is associated with comorbidity.
5. Both unipolar and bipolar disorders tend to run in families.

RESEARCH DESIGNS THAT ARE THE MOST USEFUL FOR TESTING HYPOTHESES ABOUT CAUSES

By definition, etiological factors are present prior to the onset of disorders; they may be evident years before a disorder or shortly before, and they may exert their effects over a variable time interval. They may be variables that one can measure at a single time point (because they do not change over time) or they may themselves be dynamic (change over time). They may be from domains that are relatively easily measurable (such as self-perceptions) or those that are more challenging (such as those requiring biological assays or repeated measurements over time). Given what we know about the onset and development of depressive disorders, it is obvious that the most informative research designs have one or more of the following features:

1. Etiological factors are measured in participants before any of the participants have yet developed a depressive disorder.
2. Etiological factors are measured using approaches that minimize bias.
3. Etiological factors are assessed in ways that are developmentally sensitive (i.e., the measurement is informed by knowledge about how that factor manifests at a phenomenological and causal level during the particular developmental period under study).
4. If gender differences are of interest, the effects of potential etiological factors are measured in persons of both genders and their associations with depressive disorders are statistically compared across genders.
5. Etiological factors are indexed as directly as possible (i.e., not using proxy variables).
6. Attempts are made to consider and rule out potential confounds (i.e., other variables that may be driving the association between a depressive disorder and a potential etiological factor).
7. Research studies testing the predictive validity of an etiological factor follow participants through the typical age of risk for developing the depressive disorder to maximize the test of the importance of these factors.
8. Tests of hypothesized environmental causal agents are conducted using designs that can distinguish between mechanisms that occur via the environment and those that are attributable to genetic influences.

9. Designs that assess variables at multiple levels of analysis (e.g., self-report, observation, laboratory, neuroscience, and biological measures) allow for greater certainty that effects are attributable to constructs themselves, rather than to something unique about the measurement approach.
10. Designs that allow for an aggregation of effects across samples (such as meta-analyses) are more convincing.

There is no single research design that can conclusively rule out or prove the validity of any hypothesized etiological model. Moreover, practical considerations of time and monetary resources, burden to participants, and constraints on how many things can be validly measured at any one time point, mean that no single study—no matter how large or how convincing the findings—can persuade us to accept a particular hypothesis. Most etiological models will either disappear or gain ascendancy based on a record of failure or success across many different tests performed across different samples and research groups, and ideally using different methods and measures. The chapters that follow focus on describing the current evidence for different models and hypotheses regarding the etiology of depressive disorders. The elements detailed earlier are considered as providing more evidence for an etiological model and therefore literatures with these elements receive greater focus in subsequent chapters.

What Is the Role of Personality in Depressive Disorders?

Long before the development of our modern systems for classifying and studying psychiatric disorders, scholars pointed out that troubling signs and symptoms of mental illness were not visited randomly upon people. Rather, they seemed to develop among those whose functioning prior to the onset of symptoms presaged troubles ahead. For example, Hippocrates's and Galen's theory of the four humors—a model both of the causes of health and illness and of their proper treatment—viewed the four natural elements of the body as shaping a person's characteristic personality. This model informed medicine (including the treatment of mental illness) for centuries; the four humors of the body were seen as emitting vapors that reached the brain, thus influencing one's behavior and temperament. Those with an excess of yellow bile, the choleric type, were seen as aggressive and driven; the melancholic type (excess black bile) was viewed as apathetic, reticent, and sentimental; the phlegmatic type was seen as lazy and cowardly; and the sanguine temperament was characterized by positive affect and agreeableness. Thus, chronic imbalances among the four humors were seen as the etiology of emotional problems such as depression.

The early originators of descriptive psychopathology also noted that people who experienced depressive disorders were characterized by patterns of maladaptive personality functioning (even before the emergence of frank depression) that were similar to, if less extreme than, some of the features of depression. For example, Kraepelin asserted that serious mood disorders emerged among those whose inherited temperamental style was one of anxiety, reticence, low self-confidence and vitality, stress reactivity, and a tendency toward despair and self-reproach. This temperamental style was the underlying context in which depressive episodes developed, or in Kraepelin's words, these episodes "rise like mountain peaks from a structurally similar pain" (Slater & Roth, 1969). Similarly, Kraepelin also recognized temperamental versions of Bipolar Disorder (BD), using the term *excitement* to describe manic mood states. He defined *constitutional* manic depression as consisting of pronounced mood lability, even over the course of a day, including emotional reactions that seem excessive given their environmental precipitants: "a mood of gloom and pessimism in the morning gives place to a state of liveliness and exhilaration in the evening . . . the man who at one time is recognized as 'the life of the party,' at another is especially liable to exhibit himself as the proverbial 'wet blanket'" (Kraepelin, 1921).

Modern personality science has made considerable advances in terms of understanding the nature and distribution of core individual differences across people that offer a more nuanced understanding of personality than prescientific models such as the humoral theory. Nonetheless, current models of personality risk for depression share much in common with these ancient notions—including the proposition that personality and temperamental dispositions toward depressive disorders emerge from biological systems, the properties of which can vary across people, creating differences in their basic reactivity to important classes of stimuli. Moreover, the ancient models and theories guiding current research are aimed both at explaining some basic observations that often occur to people experiencing depressive disorders or those who know them well. For example, some people who suffer from more chronic forms of depression can find it difficult to make distinctions between the symptoms of depression and their own personality makeup; their symptoms seem to be so integral to their experience of the world that they begin to feel as though they are a part of the self, rather than a temporary experience being imposed on the self. In other cases, some people may feel that long before they ever became depressed, they acted or felt in ways that were similar to the symptoms of depression—they may describe themselves as being characteristically hopeless, dejected, or negativistic, even as very young people. In such cases, the time at which the depressive symptoms began may prove very difficult (or even impossible) to pinpoint because the distinction between these symptoms and the person's normal level of functioning is not at all clear. These examples highlight that, for many people, depressive disorders are intertwined with their characteristic tendencies or personalities.

MODELS OF PERSONALITY AND TEMPERAMENT

Personality refers to individuals' unique variation on basic evolutionary design for human nature, expressed dynamically over the course of their development, in the form of basic dispositions or traits (i.e., styles of feeling, thinking, and behaving), characteristic adaptations (i.e., goals and developmental tasks), and structures for understanding their identity and creating a coherent life narrative that provide meaning to their lives (McAdams & Pals, 2006). Thus, personality includes a broad range of individual differences in psychological systems operating at both more basic and higher order levels. The term *temperament* is sometimes used synonymously with personality; however, a more precise use of this term applies to those aspects or dimensions of individual differences that are among the earliest-appearing traits and that relate centrally to the experience, expression, and regulation of emotion. These traits govern our responses to stimuli and situations that represent the most basic incentive contexts encountered by our species, such as opportunities for rewards and punishments. There is often a presumption that temperament traits may be more directly linked to biological systems than aspects of personality, tapping other individual differences, and that their origins may be more heritable than learned. In this way, temperament is distinguishable from those dimensions of personality that deal less centrally with emotional reactivity and instead concern interpersonal or agentic goals (e.g., willingness to comply with others' wishes, as in the personality trait of agreeableness) or that may be shaped more by environmental processes (such as the political liberalism components that form a part of the personality trait of openness to experience).

The extent to which this distinction between personality and temperament holds empirically is questionable, but practically speaking the distinction may be a useful one in terms of theoretical models. Conceptually, temperament traits are distinct from depressive disorders in several ways. First, the traits are related to the operation of systems present in every person that evolved to deal with important scenarios, including the pursuit of reward and avoidance of punishment, as well as the necessity of navigating complex social systems that characterize human culture. Systems that instantiate behaviors reflective of these traits are necessary for human survival, but survival is possible for those with very different levels of the behaviors that emerge from these systems. Thus, individual differences in these traits were enhanced and preserved across evolution. By contrast, the behaviors that characterize depressive disorders (syndromes) are not necessary to human survival (see Chapter 5 for models that differ from this conclusion). Second, temperament traits are normally distributed in the population, meaning the variance in expression of these traits is very wide, with individuals falling at all levels from very low to very high and most being somewhat moderate. By contrast, the symptoms of depression and mania are not normally distributed in the population, although one can see gradations along a continuum of severity; most people have very low levels, and a small number of people have many symptoms. Third, traits refer to a person's characteristic pattern of thinking, feeling, and behaving, and cannot refer to behaviors that are only evident for a short period of time. Even though chronicity is relatively common among people who are prone to depressive disorders, even those with chronic depression may not exhibit the same degree of consistency in their expression of symptomatic behaviors that they do for more basic temperament or personality traits.

The relationship between personality traits and depressive disorders has been tested in a variety of ways, and it is fair to say that these two domains may not have one consistent pattern of relationship with each other. First, the pattern may vary across different personality traits and different depressive disorders. Second, multiple kinds of relationships may hold true; for example, a trait may be causally related to the development of a disorder and it may also shape how the disorder is manifested. Following are highlighted how personality traits are currently defined and measured to place their relationship with depressive disorders in context; then various models of how the two may be related are described; and, finally, the empirical evidence relating these two domains of variables and how it may be interpreted with relation to these models are delineated.

Structural Models of Personality

In contrast to the ancient Greeks, modern personality science proposes (and has convincing evidence) that the most meaningful differences across people in their basic dispositions are a matter of quantity, not kind. People are not best distinguished as belonging to different humors or "types" that sort them into coherent, relatively homogeneous groups. Rather, each person falls somewhere in a multidimensional space defined by the level of several different characteristics (traits), each of which maps a unique area of personality "space" that cannot be accounted for by the other traits. Much of the recent focus in personality science has been on identifying the optimal number of these traits, although "optimal" may depend upon the aim one is trying to accomplish by considering the role of personality in any one outcome of interest. The current consensus in the field is that most of the variance that exists among individuals in their basic dispositions can be captured by a small number of traits (between three and five). The Five Factor Model (FFM; McCrae & Costa, 1999) includes five traits: neuroticism, extraversion, conscientiousness, agreeableness, and openness to new experience. The Big Three Model (Tellegen, 1985) includes neuroticism (often called negative emotionality, or NE), extraversion (often called positive emotionality, or PE), and constraint ([CON], which includes elements of both agreeableness and conscientiousness). As such, much of the modern research targeted on the role of traits in the development of depressive disorders has focused on the smaller number of dimensions that fall under the rubric of temperament, specifically NE, PE, and effortful control or constraint (EC). PE and NE are defined by individual differences in frequency and intensity of experiencing different basic emotions (joy, happiness, contentment for PE, and sadness, fear, anger, and anxiety for NE); related cognitive tendencies (e.g., optimism for PE and ruminative worry for NE); and interpersonal behaviors (e.g., aspects of sociability for PE and features of hostility, interpersonal sensitivity, and alienation for NE). EC refers to processes (both conscious and unconscious) that modulate behavioral reactivity, including mechanisms for inhibiting certain behaviors and initiating others in the service of reaching one's goals, as well as engaging in planning and modulation of behaviors. The Big Three Model has the added advantage of identifying traits with considerable developmental continuity; each of these traits has also been identified in children (e.g., Rothbart, Ahadi, Hershey, & Fisher, 2001).

The Big Three traits are indeed identifiable across developmental time because aspects of each of these traits can be measured as early as infancy (e.g., Gartstein & Rothbart, 2003). Thus, they are reasonable targets for identifying early-appearing risk factors for depressive disorders. Several characteristics of the broad-band personality traits identified by the Five Factor and Big Three models are important for understanding how they might relate to these conditions. First, these traits exhibit moderate rank-order stability across lengthy developmental periods (Roberts & DelVecchio, 2000). This means that individuals, as they age, generally maintain their relative level of each trait in comparison to their peers. However, whereas these traits demonstrate consistency over time, they are not rigidly fixed in an absolute sense as was often implied by early models of personality. People can and do change in their level and manifestation of basic traits over time. These mean-level changes appear to be influenced by developmental context because there is a normative pattern to such changes (Roberts, Walton, & Viechtbauer, 2006); however, importantly, there is also individual variation in these developmental changes, suggesting that not everyone follows the same trajectory of mean-level changes in traits over time (Roberts & Mroczek, 2008). Second, we know that developmental processes act to change the mean levels of these traits over time within the population (Caspi, Roberts, & Shiner, 2005; Srivastava, John, Gosling, & Potter, 2003), such that higher or lower expressions of these traits are more or less normative at different ages. Specifically, mean levels of NE decrease from late adolescence to young adulthood, although levels of EC increase during the same developmental period. If these traits are causally related to depressive disorders, then periods in which the mean levels are changing might also represent those in which risk for the disorders is changing in parallel fashion. Such mean-level changes can occur alongside relative rank-order stability—even as mean levels of a trait rise, those lowest on the trait continue to exhibit lower levels than their peers, despite exhibiting higher levels than they did at any earlier age. Third, genetic effects on traits are generally more substantial at later than at earlier ages and longitudinal studies have shown that stable components of traits are largely attributable to genetic influences (e.g., Blonigen, Carlson, Hicks, Krueger, & Iacono, 2008). This is consistent with the idea that genes contribute to stable dispositional characteristics, perhaps partially via the effects these traits have on one's selection of or responses to environmental contexts. Each of these points is returned to in the following, discussing models of how these basic traits are related to depressive disorders.

THEORETICAL MODELS OF THE RELATIONSHIP BETWEEN PERSONALITY TRAITS AND DEPRESSIVE DISORDERS

Personality traits and depressive disorders may be related to one another in a number of ways; the nature of this relationship has implications for understanding etiology as well as potentially for informing treatments. Some models propose that traits and depressive disorders are fundamentally the same things; other models suggest that they are distinct entities that nonetheless share the same causes; and, finally, some models propose that one causes or impacts the other. It is important to note that these different models are conceptual frameworks for interpreting evidence, rather than separate visions of how the world actually works. For any one trait, more than one model could be the best explanation for the pattern of empirical data linking it to a depressive disorder. Different traits may be best fit by different models, rather than a single model explaining the relationship between all traits and a disorder. Finally, not all of these models actually make different predictions about what findings would be obtained for a particular study; as a result, distinguishing among these models is less a matter of conducting a single critical test comparing the models than it is of evaluating a much larger body of evidence with respect to the models' various predictions.

The *spectrum* model argues that some traits and depressive disorders are fundamentally describing the same phenomena (i.e., dimension or trait), but in a quantitatively ordered sense. Depressive syndromes reflect the extreme end of the trait distribution, such that high levels of the trait shade continuously into the phenomena described in diagnostic criteria wherein they are given a different label (depression) despite reflecting only a more intense variant of the same process evident at lower levels. The implication of this model is that because the trait and the diagnosis/disorder are measuring the same underlying dimension, they should have all of the same external correlates. Similarly, whatever factors cause the trait must be the same factors that cause the syndrome because they are fundamentally the same thing. This model is an important component of some structural models of psychopathology (e.g., Krueger & Markon, 2006) that conceptualize psychological disorders as being represented by a small number of dimensions (rather than discrete categories) that are themselves related to broader personality traits. Following the logic of this model to its end, if the spectrum model were accurate, then we would no longer study disorders per se, but rather the traits or dimensions of which they are a part. Finally, if this model were true, we would expect the trait and the disorder in question to have a fairly specific association; that is, one trait and one or a small number of highly similar disorders should be related to one another, rather than a single trait being related to many different disorders (Klein, Kotov, & Bufferd, 2011).

The *precursor* model proposes that a trait may represent an early point along the trajectory toward the disorder; the phenomenology of the trait is therefore a manifestation of a weaker or incipient version of the disorder's symptoms. Thus, it is similar to the spectrum model in that both imply the disorder represents a more severe variant of the underlying phenomenon than the trait itself. However, the precursor model is inherently a developmental one; it proposes that people must "pass through" a period in which they are exhibiting high (or low, depending on the trait) levels of the trait prior to expressing symptoms of the disorder. Also, similar to the spectrum model, the precursor model implies that the trait and disorder are caused by the same factors or processes. However, in contrast to the spectrum model, the precursor model suggests that some additional processes must occur in order for the person to progress on to expression of the disorder itself. This infers that the trait and disorder do not occupy exactly overlapping conceptual or etiological space because some additional factors must be invoked to explain why some people with high (or low) levels of the trait go on to manifest the disorder, whereas others do not. One might also think about the precursor model as developmental in the sense that trait manifestations might represent developmentally early or developmentally specific versions of the disorder itself (e.g., depression may manifest differently in youngsters than in adults). This version of the precursor model suggests that the trait and disorder are in fact the same underlying construct, but that there are some developmental constraints that prevent a person from manifesting the symptoms of the disorder as identified in the diagnostic criterion set. Rather, extreme levels of the trait are the way in which the underlying processes that define the disorder are manifested at early developmental periods. One might expect, if the precursor model were accurate, that measures of the trait and measures of the disorder would have similar (but not exactly the same) external correlates because the additional causal processes that move someone along the trajectory from the precursor to the disorder introduce the likelihood of other outcomes being associated with the disorder that are not associated with extreme levels of the trait. One type of finding consistent with the precursor model is if high levels of a trait predicted a more rapid escalation to the disorder or a shorter time to onset of symptoms (Fanous, Neale, Aggen, & Kendler, 2007).

An example of the precursor model can be found in the writings of Kraepelin (1921), who proposed that BD is preceded by one of four precursor patterns of personality: cyclothymic, manic, irritable, or depressive. Similarly, Schneider (1958) identified patterns of personality that represent diminished versions of depressive disorders, but he viewed them as personality disorders that should be seen as distinct from depressive disorders. Schneider's observations became the basis for the description of Depressive Personality Disorder (DPD) that was included in the appendix of the *Diagnostic and Statistical Manual of Mental Disorders, fourth edition (DSM-IV)* (as a category for further study). These observations include some elements similar to normal personality traits, and others focusing on depressotypic cognitions and interpersonal styles. Those with DPD are described as being extremely introverted (passive, unassertive, and quiet); driven to high standards (highly conscientious, responsible, self-disciplined), often to the point of harshness (being self-critical or even self-denigrating, prone to preoccupation with one's own personal shortcomings, feelings of inadequacy). Excessively high standards may be applied to other people (being highly skeptical, hypercritical, and hard to please), lending an irritable air to their interpersonal interactions. They are also described by characteristically negative patterns of thinking (brooding, worrisome, preoccupation with negative events), and trait anhedonia (overly serious, gloomy, and incapable of fun). Modern data on DPD and its association with unipolar mood disorders suggest that it may be transmitted in families along with these disorders, particularly chronic forms of unipolar depression (Klein, 1999; Klein & Miller, 1993). Prospective longitudinal studies are consistent with the precursor model because the presence of depressive personality among those who have never had a depressive disorder predicts the development of dysthymia (Kwon, Kim, Chang, Park, & Kim, 2000) and elevated depressive symptoms in youngsters (Rudolph & Klein, 2009).

The *common cause* model is distinguished from the prior two models in that it views depressive disorders and traits as reflecting different underlying entities. Their relationship emerges from the fact that they share at least some (and perhaps more than some) of their causal factors. Because the same causes produce the disorder(s) and the trait(s) in question, they will be correlated with one another, but not as strongly as if they were measuring the same underlying dimension. The strongest version of this model is that the two constructs will not have any direct causal relationship with one another after accounting for their shared etiology. Presumably, any overlap in their external correlates will also be accounted for by these shared etiological factors.

Thus, all three of the models discussed above (common cause, precursor, and spectrum) propose that depressive disorders and trait(s) emerge from shared causes, although the extent of this overlap is highest in the spectrum model, then the precursor model, and finally the common cause model. The common cause model is consistent with findings from twin studies indicating overlap in the causal influences on a trait and a depressive disorder (e.g., Fanous, Gardner, Prescott, Cancro, & Kendler, 2002).

The *predisposition, pathoplasty, concomitants,* and *scar* models all suggest that there is a causal relationship between the two sets of constructs, and conceptual distinctions remain between depressive disorders and traits in each of these models. The predisposition model argues that the trait precedes and acts to create or bring about the disorder. The factors that lead to the development of the trait are not the same ones that lead to the development of the disorder (they do not share common causes); rather, individual differences in the trait (that emerge from one set of processes) increase risk for the development of the disorder (e.g., BD). In this model, the trait is but one among a number of factors that are etiologically implicated in the disorder. This model is most similar to the diathesis–stress model described in the Chapter 6. The trait and the disorder need not share any surface phenomenological features (unlike in the spectrum model). The relationship between the trait and the ultimate development of the disorder is itself a complex pathway, potentially involving many mediators (intervening causal variables) and moderators (other factors that change the relationship between the predisposition and likelihood of developing the disorder) that link the trait(s) to the disorders. Like the precursor model, the predisposition model is a developmental one in that the trait appears prior to the disorder. However, it is even more richly developmental in that the trait is the starting point of a causal pathway of processes that unfold over time to ultimately end in the disorder (as opposed to being merely an early marker that such a trajectory is underway).

In the pathoplasty model, the trait(s) do not operate to cause the disorder; however, once a person has the disorder, the trait(s) influence the presentation or course of the disorder over time. The trait may result in a different pattern of symptoms or a greater severity of symptoms, in a longer or shorter duration of symptoms, or to moderate the person's response to one or more treatments. Much as personality traits shape or color other aspects of functioning, such as social relationships or work functioning (Roberts, Kuncel, Shiner, Caspi, & Goldberg, 2007), the traits may create a characteristic style of presentation of the disorder. It is important to note that traits may also predict outcome or treatment response not because they have a pathoplastic influence, but merely because trait levels are elevated among those who have a more severe variant of the disorder (as implied by the spectrum model). In that case, the trait is an epiphenomenon of severity, rather than a causal influence on the disorder itself. One example of pathoplastic effects is that DPD predicts worse outcome and poorer treatment response in unipolar mood disorders (Laptook, Klein, & Dougherty, 2006; Ryder, Quilty, Vachon, & Bagby, 2010).

The scar model proposes a different causal order; the occurrence of a depressive disorder changes one's personality such that the traits are different after the disorder onsets and remain so even after the disorder remits. This model is interesting in that it proposes that clinical phenomena, even those that are episodic rather than chronic in nature, can fundamentally alter one's personality.

The concomitants model argues that associations between traits and depressive disorders are a confound of measurement concerns. This model proposes that the effect of depressive symptoms is to change how individuals view and report upon their traits, even in the absence of real changes in these traits. This is consistent with evidence from the literature on cognitive effects of depression, demonstrating that acute depressive symptoms are associated with more negative self-perceptions. The concomitants model is most relevant to understanding trait–disorder associations as evidenced by self-report measures of traits.

EVALUATING MODELS OF PERSONALITY–DEPRESSION ASSOCIATIONS

The models articulated thus far describe relatively idealized conceptions of the nature of links between personality traits and depressive disorders that are useful in generating testable predictions that can be compared to empirical findings. There are some important limitations to these models, however. First, several of the models advance highly similar predictions, making it difficult to conduct a critical test that could provide evidence for one model and against another. Second, they are imprecise in some ways. For example, the precursor model does not describe the nature of the causal influences that lead someone to develop the disorder out of the precursor, and the spectrum model does not clarify how symptoms that may fluctuate over time (or appear only at certain times) lie on a continuum with trait expressions that are persistent over time.

Furthermore, most of these models do not adequately integrate the reality of data indicating that personality undergoes normative (and in some cases, nonnormative) development across the life span. As noted by Klein and colleagues (2011), this suggests that more dynamic variants of these models that take into account these normative developmental patterns of change may provide a better fit to the reality of the complex relationship between personality traits and depressive disorders, as well as the complicated forces that operate to influence personality development. For example, if a trait is a precursor for depression but also increases in the population during a particular developmental interval, are all of those with elevated trait levels during that period exhibiting early signs of the disorder, or only those who also had elevated levels at an earlier developmental period? Do the common causes that contribute to both a trait and a depressive disorder overlap with developmental influences on the trait? How should our research studies be designed in order to take into account the dynamic development of traits, when exploring their association with risk for depressive disorders?

Evidence Necessary to Provide Support for or Against One or More of These Models

Several types of studies are particularly useful for testing the predictions of one or more of these models. First, studies that can identify etiological influences on traits and depressive disorders are useful for testing claims of the common cause, spectrum, and precursor models. For example, twin studies have documented that NE and Major Depressive Disorder (MDD) share considerable overlapping genetic influences, compared to weak overlap between genetic contributors to PE and MDD (Fanous et al., 2007; Kendler, Gatz, Gardner, & Pedersen, 2006; Kendler, Neale, Kessler, & Heath, 1993). The most powerful designs are those that are causally informative, such as twin and adoption studies that can provide evidence for the role of genes and environmental influences on traits and depression. Family studies that explore whether depressive disorders in one family member are associated with traits in other family members who do not have the depressive disorders are also useful in this respect; however they are less definitive than twin and adoption studies in which genetic and environmental influences can be more clearly isolated. Prospective longitudinal studies that assess traits prior to the onset of a depressive disorder and follow participants through the age of risk are useful for testing whether the claims of the precursor and predisposition models are accurate (i.e., that prior measures of the traits predict the new onset of the disorder). Longitudinal designs that assess people before the emergence of a depressive disorder, during the disorder, and after recovery from the disorder provide useful evidence for precursor and predisposition models, as well as the scar and concomitants models. Issues of specificity (the degree of association between a trait and depression in comparison to its association with other forms of psychopathology) are also important for distinguishing the spectrum model from the precursor and predisposition models, and require designs that assess multiple disorders.

In addition to design issues, the decision about how to measure each construct (traits, depression) as well as moderators and mediators (such as environmental factors) is also critical for conducting definitive tests of these models and interpreting their findings. First, any measures that artifactually confound the two domains will inflate estimates of their overlap, thus spuriously supporting some models (e.g., spectrum, common cause). For example, the vast majority of studies testing associations between depressive disorders and personality traits have been conducted using self-report (questionnaire) measures of both constructs (traits and depressive disorders). The effect of employing the same method of assessing both constructs is to inflate the associations because both variables are saturated with the same method variance (i.e., similarities in the structure of the measure and biases that come from someone with the same perspective providing information on each construct). Thus, it is likely that our conclusions regarding the strength of association between traits and depressive disorders are overly strong. Indeed, the effect sizes for these associations are largest when both are assessed using questionnaires rather than when either is assessed using some other approach. Moreover, among individuals with psychopathology, self-reports may be influenced by poor insight into one's behavior or interpretive biases emerging from current negative mood. There is considerable overlap in item content across many questionnaire measures of some traits (e.g., NE) and depressive symptoms. This will also increase the magnitude of the association between the two variables. Second, some models, such as the precursor model, require rather careful timing of assessments and a high degree of sensitivity to the presence of symptoms. Third, there is no substitute for longitudinal data when exploring the predictive validity of traits; however, the most compelling tests of these models also require a consideration of the appropriate intervals for assessment as well as the most telling ages at which to conduct these assessments.

WHICH TRAITS MIGHT BE IMPLICATED IN THE VARIOUS DEPRESSIVE DISORDERS?

Negative Emotionality

As noted earlier, NE includes individual differences in reactivity of basic emotional systems relevant to our reactions to aversive stimuli, including punishment and nonrewards. Most models of NE include emotional states of fear, anxiety, sadness, and anger, as well as cognitive styles, such as worry, rumination, self-denigration, and hostile attributions, associated with greater intensity and frequency of experiencing these states. NE has broad and consistently replicated effects on a variety of measures of operating in the domains of health, relationship, and occupational functioning, even after accounting for other important individual characteristics such as socioeconomic status and cognitive abilities (Roberts et al., 2007). Of note, many of these external correlates are among the same that are associated with depressive disorders (more fully described in Chapter 4). Unsurprisingly, therefore, NE has been linked to nearly every conception (e.g., categorical, dimensional) and measure of depressive disorders, including MDD, DD (dysthymic disorder), and BD diagnoses, as well as subthreshold depressive symptoms (e.g., Clark, 2005). All of these syndromes are associated with higher levels of NE, and this association has been documented not just in adults, but earlier in the life span as well in childhood (e.g., Muris & Ollendick, 2005). These effects are most pronounced in cross-sectional designs that assess NE's association with depression. In many of these studies, the associations are of such a significant magnitude that they have been interpreted as providing conclusive support for the spectrum model (e.g., Tackett, Waldman, Van Hulle, & Lahey, 2011). Drawing upon such data, some have proposed that NE and depression are in fact indistinguishable from one another (e.g., Griffith et al., 2010). Unfortunately, these designs are the least informative for yielding evidence that could distinguish between models in which NE and depression are causally related or between designs that distinguish among those models that propose different forms of causal relationships. It is important to also note, however, that NE is broadly correlated with a wide variety of psychopathologies (Ormel, Rosmalen, & Farmer, 2004); thus, its specificity to depressive disorders is low, which is inconsistent with one presumption of the spectrum model.

This last piece of evidence is in fact the primary reason to dismiss the spectrum model because this explanatory account proposes that the association between the trait and the disorder should be rather specific. NE might fit the spectrum model, but it has associations with so many different disorders that are not that highly overlapping with one another (e.g., both internalizing and externalizing disorders) that it is hard to imagine that they are all lying on a single continuum. We would have to break apart the constituent pieces of quite dissimilar disorders and reassign them to different dimensions in order to simplify the trait–disorder associations evident for NE.

NE is generally more strongly related to the unipolar mood disorders than to the bipolar disorders, although there is some evidence that high NE is associated with both the manic and depressive episodes of BD (Quilty, Sellbom, Tackett, & Bagby, 2009). One meta-analysis (Kotov, Gamez, Schmidt, & Watson, 2010) showed that both unipolar mood disorders (MDD and DD) are associated with very high levels of NE, with more extreme levels evident in those with DD compared to those with MDD. However, it is important to mention that this effect is smaller than the association observed between NE and anxiety disorders, arguing a level of specificity not entirely consistent with the spectrum model. There is also evidence consistent with the claim that NE may be a concomitant of depressive disorders. With respect to MDD, NE is elevated when people are depressed compared to when they are not depressed (e.g., Ormel et al., 2004). However, those with a history of depression (currently remitted) still tend to have higher levels of NE than those who were never depressed, suggesting the concomitant model alone cannot account for these associations.

NE seems to account for much of the genetic risk for depression (Fanous et al., 2007; Kendler et al., 2006; Kendler et al., 1993). Kendler and colleagues (1993) found that most of the overlap between NE and MDD is due to shared genetic factors that contribute to both. Although women score higher on measures of NE (e.g., Costa et al., 2001), the degree of genetic covariation between NE and MDD is either equivalent or stronger in men (Fanous et al., 2002). High levels of NE may be more indicative of pathology among men, perhaps because NE tends to be elevated in women relative to men in a normative sense.

NE does predict poorer course and treatment response among those with depression (e.g., Quilty et al., 2009; Tang et al., 2009). This is consistent with NE's broader effects on a range of normal and pathological outcomes, and is also suggestive of a model in which high trait NE is a marker of a more severe variant of depression.

One study did find some evidence of a scar effect, such that MDD predicted higher NE at a later time point, controlling for NE at an earlier time point (Fanous et al., 2007). Two other studies have failed to find a scar effect for NE (Duggan, Sham, Lee, & Murray, 1991; Zeiss & Lewinsohn, 1988). In the same study by Fanous and colleagues (2007), there was strong evidence for a state effect of MDD on NE; moreover, this effect was larger than the effect of NE on subsequent DD and of MDD on subsequent NE—consistent with the idea that cross-sectional associations between NE and MDD are much larger than any longitudinal associations. This pattern of findings suggests more evidence for spectrum and concomitant models than for those implying a causal relationship (e.g., predisposition, precursor).

Positive Emotionality

Low PE is an important component of many models of unipolar depressive disorders (e.g., Clark, Watson, & Mineka, 1994) that propose this trait distinguishes depressive from anxiety disorders. However, the empirical reality is that PE is less strongly related to unipolar mood disorders than is NE; the effects are generally modest and are more inconsistent across the literature. One exception to this is dysthymia, which has a stronger association with low PE than MDD. Of note, a meta-analysis found that anxiety disorders seem to have a stronger association with low PE than does MDD (Kotov et al., 2010). Inconsistent findings linking low PE to unipolar depression may be because different studies have employed varying conceptualizations of PE in the literature, emphasizing different elements of the construct that are more or less strongly linked to depression. It appears that the positive mood elements of PE are more central to depression than sociability facets (e.g., Naragon-Gainey, Watson, & Markon, 2009). Importantly, two large longitudinal studies have shown that measures of low PE constructs in young children predict later depressive disorders (Caspi, Moffitt, Newman, & Silva, 1996; Van Os, Jones, Lewis, Wadsworth, & Murray, 1997). For BD and mania, there is evidence that high levels of PE are correlates of these conditions (e.g., Quilty et al., 2009; Bagby et al., 1997) and predict manic and hypomanic episodes (e.g., Kwapil et al., 2000). These data are consistent with theoretical models emphasizing the role of reward-related brain processes in mania (e.g., Depue & Iacono, 1989). Thus, although the literature is smaller, there is some evidence that PE may represent a precursor or predisposition for both unipolar and bipolar disorders.

Constraint

Kotov and colleagues' (2010) meta-analysis revealed that low conscientiousness is associated moderately with MDD and strongly with DD. Measures of impulsivity have been shown to be elevated in those with BD both during manic episodes and during remission (Peluso et al., 2007; Swann, Dougherty, Pazzaglia, Pham, & Moeller, 2004), and to be associated with hypomanic proneness in a community sample (Schalet, Durbin, & Revelle, 2011). Because fewer studies have focused on the role of individual differences in CON in risk for depressive disorders, there is little evidence useful for distinguishing among the different models discussed for this trait.

Other Traits

Recent theoretical and empirical models of associations between personality traits and psychopathology have attempted to fit both sets of constructs in the same conceptual and empirical space (e.g., Markon, Krueger, & Watson, 2005). These analyses focus on the broadest traits and the most common disorders, and have often excluded bipolar spectrum disorders. The samples in which these models are tested are typically comprised of undergraduates or unselected community individuals, among whom the prevalence of bipolar spectrum disorders will necessarily be very low. However, a few studies have attempted to fit bipolar disorders within these structural models. Two such studies have found that BD and mania are associated with high levels of openness to experience (Meyer, 2002; Tackett et al., 2008).

Related to openness is the construct of creativity. Associations between creativity and bipolar spectrum disorders are a common assumption among the lay public, a core of many a biography of accomplished artists and intellectuals, and are occasionally the topic of empirical research. Among samples of individuals known to have high levels of creativity by virtue of documented creative achievements, it seems that milder versions of bipolar spectrum disorders (e.g., Bipolar II or cyclothymia) and family history of bipolar spectrum conditions are more prevalent than more serious forms of the disorder (Johnson, Murray, et al., 2012). Moreover, it is likely that among those creative individuals who do have Bipolar I, their periods of greatest productivity are during well periods, as opposed to during symptomatic periods. Other lines of evidence support the interpretation that milder, as opposed to more severe, versions of bipolar conditions (or elevated familial loading for bipolar spectrum disorders) are associated with creativity, including findings regarding choosing creative pursuits as a career, achieving creative accomplishments in one's lifetime, and engaging in higher levels of divergent thinking (Johnson, Murray, et al., 2012). People with bipolar spectrum disorders also appear to be elevated on measures of drive and ambition, and there is speculation that these motivational features may propel the association between the disorder and creative accomplishments (Johnson, Edge, Holmes, & Carver, 2012).

IF THE ASSOCIATION BETWEEN A PERSONALITY TRAIT AND A DEPRESSIVE DISORDER IS CAUSAL, WHAT ARE THE PROCESSES BY WHICH THIS OCCURS?

For NE, and to a lesser extent for PE, there is sufficient evidence for longitudinal associations to warrant further exploration of the idea that individual differences in these traits act to place people at higher risk for the development of a unipolar or bipolar depressive disorder. However, it is also clear that likely only a subset of people with these conditions arrived there via a personality pathway, with chronic mood disorders seemingly much more tied to personality/temperament risk than nonchronic depressions (see Klein et al., 2011). Thus, to the extent that traits are etiologically implicated in depressive disorders, they may provide a means of discerning more etiologically informative subgroups that do a better job of mapping onto pathways to depression than do current diagnostic distinctions. It is also possible that traits may play a different role in familial forms of depressive disorders than in nonfamilial forms of the disorder. Given evidence for genetic contributions to personality traits including PE, NE, and CON, and that genes for some for these traits overlap with genes for depressive disorders (e.g., Kendler et al., 2006), one plausible model is that depressive disorders run in families because they are caused by more basic individual differences in personality traits that are transmitted genetically.

Personality risk factors for depressive disorders are likely not independent of other important etiological factors. For example, individual differences in traits may increase exposure to environmental risk factors, or may moderate the impact of these environmental exposures. For example, NE is associated with experiencing stressful life events (e.g., Magnus, Diener, Fugita, & Pavot, 1993), presumably because the effect of high NE behaviors is to negatively impact functioning across multiple domains, thus generating stressors. Moreover, high NE may potentiate the effects of stressors by eliciting more subjective distress in response to stress (e.g., Bolger & Schilling, 1991). Evidence suggests that those with high NE and stressful life events are at higher risk for a first MDE than those with lower levels of NE (e.g., Kendler, Kuhn, & Prescott, 2004; Van Os & Jones, 1999). Thus, early NE may set individuals on a path toward environmental adversity that then itself leads to depressogenic processes.

Less evidence is available regarding the mechanisms by which PE or CON may lead to depressive disorders. Low PE may result in depressogenic processes because of its impact on the quality of interpersonal relationships and social support, or because of its link to engagement in effortful behaviors directed toward attaining rewards. High PE may place individuals at risk for mania because high levels of this trait are associated with aberrant and maladaptive overvaluing of rewards and allocation of effort toward rewards, and a failure to be satiated after achieving rewards (Johnson, Edge, Holmes, & Carver, 2012); these cognitive and behavioral processes may interact with environmental contingencies to produce manic patterns of behavior.

Very little is known about the possible mechanisms by which low CON may increase risk for either depressive or manic episodes. By definition, mania and hypomania are associated with disinhibited behaviors; thus, this trait may lie on a continuum with these symptoms. Depressive episodes are not characterized by disinhibition, but other elements of low CON (such as poor planning and follow-through, low diligence) may be an outcome of depressive behaviors. Alternatively, those who habitually behave in disinhibited ways are exposed to more stressful events (e.g., Compas, Connor-Smith, & Jaser, 2004), thus resulting in greater risk for depression.

CONCLUSIONS

Personality traits are important correlates of depressive disorders, and a rich tradition and large empirical literature indicate that traits relevant to basic emotional processes (PE and NE) may predict risk for these conditions. It has yet to be fully resolved whether they do so because they directly cause mania or depression, interact with aspects of the environment to do so, or because they are subject to the same causes as depression or mania. However, there is good reason to believe that, particularly for more chronic forms of depression, individual differences in NE and perhaps PE evident before onset of symptoms are markers of those at elevated risk. Given evidence that these traits can change across development (as does the prevalence of depressive disorders), longitudinal designs incorporating measures of possible causes of individual differences in traits and potential mediators of their effects will be critical for understanding the underlying nature of personality–depression associations.

How Do Stress and the Environmental Context Impact Depression?

tress is a central component of many lay conceptions of the causes of depression. When we become aware that someone we know is suffering from depression, we often look toward events in their environment that might explain their symptoms. When close others experience stressors that are culturally recognized as being severe, such as the loss of a loved one, we are often prone to observe them with concern and to offer additional supports in the hopes of preventing the emergence of depression. These phenomena reveal that our lay conceptual models of depressive disorders (particularly unipolar depression) typically involve some presumption that depression is in many ways a reaction to events and circumstances in the environment.

Various etiological models of depressive disorders have also focused on the role that stress plays in these conditions, although theories vary considerably in terms of their conceptualization of the relevant stress processes and the degree to which stress itself is the core etiological process (versus a factor that potentiates other, theoretically more central, etiological processes). Moreover, measurement issues loom large in the literature on stress and depressive disorders. The concept of stress, so ubiquitous and easily understood when used in common language to describe psychological distress and challenge, is actually a rather complex construct to measure and model for scientific study. Researchers must contend with how to determine the actual aspects of stressors that create distress; how best to measure those aspects (by reference to objective indicators of the "stressfulness" of events or contexts or by tapping individuals' perceptions of the threat or challenge engendered by an event); how to avoid biases that may occur when people are asked to recall events from the past; how to capture the time frame over which stress exerts its effect; and how (and if) to aggregate different kinds of stress.

In addition to the *how* of measuring stress, a critical piece of etiological models that emphasize the role of stress in depressive disorders is articulating the *why*. What is it about experiencing stress or the biological or psychological processes that are engendered by stress that leads to the development of depression? As self-evident as the notion of stress as a predictor of distress seems, determining its mechanisms has proven controversial. The sections that follow describe what is known about the kinds of stress that seem to be most relevant to depressive disorders; how this stress may exert its effects (both psychologically and biologically); and other factors that may help to explain individual differences in the stress–depression relationship.

MEASURING STRESS

There are a limited number of research designs that are actually adequate for exploring the role of stress in depressive disorders. Thus, although there is a large literature that has measured both stress and depression, only a small proportion of this work included measures and designs that are actually informative with respect to providing a useful test of the hypothesized role of stress. The first issue facing such research is to employ measures that accurately and validly tap the most important elements of stress. Unfortunately, the most common assessment method— questionnaires that ask participants to indicate which of a list of stressful events occurred to them over a specified interval— is neither particularly accurate nor valid (Monroe, 2008). The most sensitive measurement approach involves direct interview assessment of participants that allows the interviewer to probe the person for details of potential stressful events, including their context, timing, and meaning. The second issue concerns the importance of ensuring that the predictor (stress) is not confounded with the outcome (depression). Thus, retrospective designs are problematic because people in general may misremember the occurrence or timing of an event. Moreover, the nature of depression is such that people may misremember an event as having occurred before the onset of symptoms rather than after because this narrative—of an event triggering the depressive syndrome—provides a compelling way to understand the condition. This "effort after meaning" may cause people to perceive a connection between a stressor and their symptoms, even when one does not actually exist.

A third challenge, both conceptually and from a measurement standard, is tapping into the very meaning of stress as it bears on the development of psychopathology, ensuring that the measure is capable of assessing the extent to which or the reasons why an event or condition is experienced as distressing.

This requires a more idiographic (i.e., person-centered) approach to the measurement of stress. There are two components to this concept of stress that are best assessed using very different techniques: the objective nature of the event, and the psychological processes generated by the person in response to the event that produce distress. The gold-standard approach to this problem is interview methods wherein the event's stressfulness is determined by evaluating the meaning of the event relative to the context in which it occurs. This is in contrast to questionnaire methods of assessing stress. A common method is the life events checklist that asks people to indicate which of many putatively stressful events have occurred to them over a particular time period (e.g., the past month, the past year). The checklist approach cannot take into account the person's circumstances, and therefore an assumption is relied on that the events are indeed stressful in the same way to each person. For example, divorce is an event that may be experienced differently depending upon its context. For some individuals, it may be experienced as a loss that can also result in a cascade of other challenges, such as financial strain and the need to create new co-parenting relationships. For others, a divorce may be a resolution to an ongoing stressor, as when the divorce ends a conflictual or abusive relationship. Only measures that place events in context by collecting relevant information from the participant can tell the difference between these two scenarios.

George Brown developed a means of ascertaining the stressfulness of an event to a particular person. This approach, the contextual assessment of stressor severity, assigns ratings to events that are based on the degree to which an event would be considered threatening (i.e., stressful) by a typical person living in the same circumstances as the participant. Thus, in the case of divorce, elements of context would include understanding things such as whether or not the person initiated or wanted the divorce; the person's social, personal, and financial context in the wake of the divorce; and so on. These contextual elements allow one to consider how "objectively" threatening the event in that particular context would be. This is different from having participants rate how stressful, difficult, or upsetting they perceived the experience to be. Such measures focusing on the perceived stressfulness of an event or one's general circumstances are indeed related to depression because those who perceive their lives as more stressful report higher levels of depression. However, this approach may spuriously suggest depression–stress relationships because a person's mood state or depressive symptoms may create bias in the recollection of events or timing. Empirical evidence indicates that objective measures (such as contextual threat interviews) are more effective than questionnaire checklist approaches in collecting precise and accurate data on the occurrence and dating of events; they are less biased by mood, and they have greater predictive validity (see Monroe, 2008).

WHAT KINDS OF STRESS ARE ASSOCIATED WITH DEPRESSIVE DISORDERS?

The label "stress" can be applied to many different kinds of experiences. It can be used to refer to the subjective experience that one is overwhelmed by circumstances that are undesirable; to the occurrence of a major, life-changing event that interrupts and challenges one's current approach to the world; or to the grind of mundane, everyday hassles that wear away at one's well-being. All these conceptualizations of stress have been included in empirical research on depressive disorders—to varying degrees. If stress operated such that all challenges collectively wore away at psychological resources to produce a depressive state, then one would expect that measures of the cumulative effects of all kinds of stress would be the most powerful predictors of depression. However, the evidence indicates that it is the type of stressful event that is most important for predicting the onset of depression, not the cumulative amount of stress in general that a person is experiencing.

Threat and Loss

George Brown and Tirril Harris (1978) developed a sensitive measure of stress and demonstrated its validity for depression in several samples of high-risk women in England. Their interview, the Life Events and Difficulties Schedule (LEDS), evaluates the occurrence of stressors and assesses the meaning of these stressors. After the interview, these events are considered in the light of the person's current context and life trajectory to assign a rating of how threatening the event would be to the typical person experiencing such an event in that life context. These contextual threat ratings thus provide a more objective measure of the likelihood that the event would be perceived as stressful. Evidence from studies using the LEDS has shown that the onset of depression is often preceded in the prior weeks by the occurrence of events that have long-term threat for the person (Brown, 1993). Threatening events include those that carry with them the likelihood of loss, danger, or disappointment. Such events that also entailed entrapment or loss are the most predictive of depression. The loss category covers a broad range of events, including the obvious loss of close others, as well as loss of a role (e.g., a job), or a cherished idea (e.g., one learns that an idealized parent has been engaging in criminal activity). Danger events (those that imply the *possibility* of a future loss) seem to be more related to anxiety disorder. The most potent loss events are those that occur in a domain of high importance to, and investment by, the person (Brown, Bifulco, & Harris, 1987). For example, a woman who passes up an important career opportunity in order to relocate with her boyfriend in the hopes this relationship will result in marriage will be particularly distressed upon discovering the boyfriend has been unfaithful to her. Two other categories of events also appear to be relevant to the onset of depression (Taylor, Gooding, Wood, & Tarrier, 2011): defeat (events that involve a loss of social rank) and entrapment (events and contexts that severely limit the person's resources for escaping an aversive situation). For manic episodes, there is evidence that events that represent disruptions to social rhythms, such as sleep or eating patterns, are common precipitants of mania (e.g., Ehlers, Kupfer, Frank, & Monk, 1993; Malkoff-Schwartz et al., 2000, 1998).

Different stressors may also shape the presentation of depressive disorders. Specifically, there is evidence that diverse stressful life events are associated with different profiles of symptom presentation. Keller, Neale, and Kendler (2007) reported that deaths of loved ones and romantic losses were associated with high levels of appetite loss and the two core depression symptoms (sadness and anhedonia), whereas chronic stress and failure experiences were associated with higher levels of fatigue and hypersomnia and lower levels of sadness, anhedonia, and appetite loss. In that sample, people who reported that their episodes were not precipitated by any event noted more fatigue, appetite gain, thoughts of self-harm, lower levels of sadness, and concentration problems. The authors argued that particular symptom presentations are determined by the nature of the context in which they occur, rather than a tendency for individuals to have particular kinds of symptoms when depressed.

Hans Selye, one of the "fathers of stress research," proposed that the mechanism by which stress produces disorder is the changes in behavior that are prompted by a stressor. This suggests that even events that are typically perceived as positive developments, but still bring about changes (such as marrying or starting a new job), could also result in disorder. A few studies (e.g., Brown, Lemyre, & Bifulco, 1992; Tennant, Bebbington, & Hurry, 1981) have found that positive events may be related to recovery from depression, specifically positive events that represent an end (or hope of an end) to chronic stress or ongoing deprivation. This provides further evidence for the role of stress in depressive episodes by demonstrating that termination of a stressor or its resolution by a new event is followed by recovery from symptoms. Relevant positive events can include what Brown termed *fresh starts*—events that give hope that an ongoing problem will have a successful resolution, and involve a change in routine or behavior that exposes the person to new environments and opportunities—as well as those that connote greater security, such as gaining employment or moving into a safer neighborhood. Positive events involving goal attainment also appear to be risk factors for manic episodes. Other evidence has shown that both positive and negative events are associated with mania, including suicide by a family member, job loss, divorce, and getting married (Kessing, Agerbo, & Mortensen, 2004).

Dependent and Independent Life Events

One important distinction when considering the depressogenic role of stressful life events is between dependent and independent life events. Independent life events, sometimes referred to as fateful events, are those whose occurrence is visited upon people through no fault of their own and whose proximal cause cannot be attributed to a person's behavior (e.g., experiencing an earthquake; losing a family member in a car accident in which one was not involved). Dependent life events are those that are influenced by the individual's behavior, such as having a serious falling out with a family member or being incarcerated for criminal acts. Dependent events are more common than independent events, and are also more challenging to interpret in the context of psychopathology. Behaviors that occur during a depressive or manic episode may bring about dependent stressors—thus, the fact that these events occur in close temporal proximity to the onset of an episode cannot be interpreted as clear evidence they caused the episode, as the reverse causal pattern may be in effect. Dependent events may also be generated by personality risk factors for mania or depression. For example, a person low on constraint (CON) may experience work-related stressors by virtue of their irresponsible behavior. There is evidence that high levels of negative emotionality (NE), prior depressive episodes, and genetic risk for depressive disorders are all associated with experiencing a greater number of dependent life events (e.g., Hammen, 1991; Kendler, Gardner, & Prescott, 2003; Kendler

& Karkowski-Shuman, 1997). Thus, risk factors for dependent life events overlap with risk factors for depression, complicating efforts to determine the causal status of dependent life events. Because of the considerable evidence that depression and mania are associated with problems in functioning in important life domains (as described in Chapter 3), rigorous assessment and fine-grained longitudinal research designs are needed to provide data that dependent events are causes rather than consequences of depression or mania. Independent events do not pose the same challenge, and there is evidence that they may be more potent for predicting major depressive episodes (MDEs) than dependent events (Stroud, Davila, Hammen, & Vrshek-Schallhorn, 2010), particularly at younger ages (Harkness, Bruce, & Lumley, 2006). However, researchers continue to be interested in the role of dependent events and have developed strategies for ruling out possible confounds. In one such study, Kendler and Gardner (2010) showed that among identical twin pairs in which one twin experienced a serious dependent life event and the other did not, MDEs were more common in the exposed twin. Although the effect of dependent life events was modest, this design did demonstrate a causal effect of these types of events on depression.

Evidence From a Prototypical Loss: Bereavement

Bereavement is a term that refers to the common, and culturally sanctioned, experience of sadness and depression that follows the death of a close other. Such losses are events that are commonly perceived as highly stressful and distressing. Close analogues of this normal human experience have also been observed in other animal species such as primates (Anderson, 2011). Beginning in the *Diagnostic and Statistical Manual of Mental Disorders, third edition (DSM-III)*, special status was accorded to bereavement in that if a depressive disorder followed from the death of a loved one and its presentation was similar to that of "normal" grief, such cases were labeled uncomplicated bereavement. Thus, if the depression was relatively brief (less than 2 months in duration), was not associated with significant impairment, and did not have more serious symptoms (such as suicidality), then the person would not receive a diagnosis of Major Depressive Disorder (MDD). The idea behind this exclusion was to prevent those likely experiencing a normative (and perhaps adaptive) response from receiving a diagnosis of a mental illness. This also emerges from concerns that our psychiatric nomenclature may pathologize reactions that are typically seen in our society as expected reactions to normal human experiences. The *DSM* also recognized an intermediate definition, complicated bereavement. Complicated bereavement was used for the subset of individuals who experienced bereavement of longer duration (longer than 2 months) or which was particularly severe in its symptom profile (defined by the presence of morbid preoccupation with worthlessness, suicidal ideation, psychomotor retardation, psychotic symptoms, or marked functional impairment). The assumption underlying this subtype was that these indicators (duration, more pathological symptoms) were evidence of greater underlying psychopathology, more akin to an MDE not related to bereavement than to normal bereavement. The complicated bereavement subtype was thought of as a normal reaction that evolved into a problematic psychiatric condition. In fact, prolonged and particularly severe cases of depression can follow losses, although these are not particularly prevalent. Consistent with this notion, Gilman et al. (2012) found that bereavement cases (those who were excluded from an MDE diagnosis because of the presence of a loss) were less pathological than cases of MDE (i.e., not bereavement-related) in terms of their course. Specifically relative to those with MDE, people with bereavement had fewer depressive episodes over their lifetime, less psychosocial impairment, and less likelihood of receiving treatment. Compared to MDD, complicated bereavement cases had lower numbers of lifetime MDEs, less psychosocial impairment, and less treatment seeking. Bereavement cases and complicated bereavement cases generally did not differ from one another on family history or on long-term outcomes.

One problem with the bereavement exclusion is that it singled out a particular stressor for exclusion; moreover, it articulated an assumption regarding the etiology of the depressive symptoms, namely that the symptoms are caused by the loss. This was not consistent with the *DSM*'s purportedly agnostic stance on etiology because, historically, the *DSM* has relied on identification of syndromes by their signs and symptoms, not their etiology. The critical questions are whether the nature of the trigger should be taken into consideration when deciding whether someone has the disorder; whether we can ever determine which responses are normal following a trigger; and which responses should be viewed as indicative of disorder.

Many scholars have questioned whether special treatment is warranted for bereavement, relative to many other stressors of other types that may be implicated in depressive disorders. There is evidence that antidepressant and psychosocial treatments are effective for treating bereavement-related depression (e.g., Reynolds et al., 1999; Zisook & Schuchter, 2001), suggesting that these conditions respond to the same interventions as other MDEs.

Furthermore, several recent studies have questioned whether bereavement produces a clinical state that is meaningfully different from depressive episodes that occur following other kinds of stressors. For example, Kendler, Myers, and Zisook (2008) compared MDEs that occurred in the context of bereavement to those that occurred in the context of other stressors: relationship loss (divorce, separation, or breakup), illness (illness, accident, serious health event), and job loss. The two groups (bereavement-related and other stressor-related) were largely similar to one another. They did not differ on duration of the MDE, number of prior episodes, most symptoms of the MDE, lifetime comorbid diagnoses, or the likelihood of having a subsequent MDE.

Moreover, the groups did not differ on their likelihood of exhibiting a pattern of symptoms typically described as indicative of normal grief (i.e., brief duration, lack of substantial impairment, no suicidality, psychomotor retardation, and so on). Similarly, Wakefield, Schmitz, First, and Horwitz (2007) used data from a large epidemiological sample, and compared four groups with MDEs related to stressors: uncomplicated bereavement triggered, complicated bereavement triggered, uncomplicated other loss triggered, and complicated other loss triggered. The uncomplicated cases (triggered by bereavement versus triggered by other losses) did not differ on most clinical indicators, such as melancholic features, duration, and so on. The complicated groups (complicated bereavement and complicated other loss) differed from the uncomplicated groups (uncomplicated bereavement and other loss), such that the complicated cases were generally more severe/pathological than uncomplicated cases (i.e., they were higher on severity, proportion of cases meeting criteria for melancholia, suicide attempts, treatment seeking, and medication). The authors interpreted their findings as supporting the validity of the distinction between uncomplicated and complicated bereavement, but also indicating that the same distinction may be important to make for other kinds of losses as well. Applying the same exclusion rule to other losses in the epidemiological sample would decrease the lifetime prevalence of MDD from 15% in the sample to 11.3%. Based in part on data such as these, the *DSM-5* will remove the bereavement exclusion from a diagnosis of MDE. Those who meet the symptom criteria for an MDE will receive a diagnosis of the disorder even if the development of the symptoms occurred immediately in the wake of a loss.

Regardless of whether bereavement is fundamentally distinct in its causal relationship to depression, it is clear that the lay understanding of bereavement reflects culturally sanctioned grieving that occurs upon loss of a loved one. Expectations that one will experience a period of sadness, withdrawal, decreased functioning, and preoccupation with the loss and the loved one are normative. Thus, it is likely that others' responses to the aggrieved person will be quite different from responses to people experiencing depression in the wake of a different form of loss (e.g., of a job) for which less provisions are made. This may impact the course of depressive episodes that occur following different kinds of losses.

TIME FRAME OVER WHICH STRESS EXERTS ITS IMPACT

An important part of understanding how stress impacts depression is considering the time frame over which it exerts its effects. How long does it take for a stressor to result in depression, and does this vary depending on the nature of the stressor? How long may the effects of a stressor lie dormant before resulting in symptoms? What might this time frame tell us about the psychological and biological mechanisms by which stressors act to increase risk? Evidence suggests that for major stressful life events, their effects are relatively short-lived; if they are going to result in a depressive episode, they will likely do so within 1 month to 3 months of their occurrence (e.g., Brown & Harris, 1978; Harkness & Monroe, 2006; Kendler, Karkowski, & Prescott, 1999).

PREDICTORS OF STRESS EXPOSURE AND STRESS REACTIVITY

Any model of the role of stressors in creating depression must also take into account factors that increase exposure to stress and individual difference characteristics that are associated with greater reactivity to stressors. Stressors are not distributed randomly across the population, nor do people respond equivalently to the same stressor. Many of the factors that have been linked to stress exposure and reactivity are also related to depressive disorders. For example, higher genetic/familial risk for depression is associated with greater reactivity to stress, defined as the likelihood of developing depression, given a stressor (Kendler et al., 1995; McGuffin, Katz, & Bebbington, 1988). Consistent with their greater risk for depression, women also seem to be more reactive to certain kinds of stressors, particularly those in the interpersonal realm (e.g., Nazroo, Edwards, & Brown, 1997). Women are more sensitive to the depressogenic effects of low levels of social support (Kendler, Meyers, & Prescott, 2005). They also seem to be exposed to more interpersonal stressors; Kendler, Thornton, and Prescott (2001) found that women are also more likely to report experiencing interpersonal stressors such as loss of a close friend, conflict with close others, illness of close others, and housing problems. By contrast, men report higher rates of occupation and legal problems (e.g., job loss, work problems, robbery, and legal problems). It is not clear if these gender differences in likelihood of experiencing diverse events are attributable to behavioral disparities across the genders that may precipitate these events, differential placement in these contexts, or in differences between men and women in how stressful they perceive negative events in various domains to be (e.g., relationships versus work). In addition to gender differences in the occurrence of these stressors, men and women also differed in the depressogenic effects of some events in Kendler and colleagues' (2001) study. Specifically, the effect of difficulty with close others on depression was stronger for women, whereas the effects of divorce/separation and work problems on depression were stronger for men. Finally, there has been considerable interest in the idea that particular genes are involved in stress reactivity; some versions (polymorphisms) of these genes are associated with greater likelihood of developing depression, given a stressor (e.g., Caspi et al., 2003). These findings regarding gene–environment interactions are addressed more fully in Chapter 9.

Persons at risk for depression are also likely to be exposed to more stressors than those at lower risk because many factors correlated with risk for these disorders are also associated with overall stress exposure. In particular, those living in lower socio-economic circumstances are exposed to greater risk for acute negative events, as well as chronic stressful experiences (such as unemployment, unsafe neighborhoods, and discrimination) that are associated with poverty. Finally, there is evidence that the same personality traits that have been linked to elevated risk for depression (described in full in Chapter 7) are themselves correlated with stress exposure. Selection effects refer to processes by which individual characteristics of people shape their choice of environments. For example, those high in NE may select romantic partners who are less psychologically healthy, thus increasing the risk they will be exposed to interpersonal stressors. In adults, there is evidence that high levels of NE are correlated with greater stressful life event exposure (e.g., Kendler et al., 2003). Even stronger evidence for the power of these selection effects comes from two longitudinal studies of samples assessed initially in childhood that found early behavioral and emotional problems (Champion, Goodall, & Rutter, 1995) and high NE in childhood (Van Os & Jones, 1999) predicted greater exposure to stressors in adulthood. Obviously, data such as these call into question the clarity of the diathesis–stress paradigm (see Chapter 6). Findings demonstrate that these two domains are not independent of one another, making it much more difficult to interpret statistical interactions between a diathesis and a stress variable that are significantly intercorrelated.

Stress Generation

Exposure to stressors may be driven by a number of characteristics of those at risk for depression. Hammen (1991) argued that depression is characterized by *stress generation* processes, wherein those with depression engage in behaviors that create or exacerbate stressful experiences in their life (i.e., increase occurrence of dependent life events), particularly in the interpersonal domain. As noted, these processes seem to characterize even those who are not currently depressed but have a history of a depressive disorder, suggesting that the causes of stress generation might lie in preexisting characteristics of those at risk for depression, rather than being a function of the depressive syndrome itself. To illustrate, those with a history of depression also have higher rates of interpersonal stressors even when they are in remission (e.g., Hammen & Brennan, 2001). Stress generation may help to explain the predictive validity of dependent interpersonal events on depression (e.g., Kendler et al., 1999). Finally, one study found that high levels of NE partially accounted for the association between depression and subsequent exposure to life stressors (Uliaszek et al., 2012).

Stress Sensitization

Stress generation describes the ways in which individual differences in personality and behavior are intimately tied to the creation of stressful circumstances. Stress sensitization refers to hypothesized processes by which the power of stress to elicit a depressive response changes as exposure to stress accumulates across the life span. The concept of stress sensitization was introduced by Robert Post (1992), who claimed that the relationship between major stressors and the occurrence of depression changes over the course of the disorder; over time, episodes become decoupled from stress (a process he called "kindling"). Thus, serious stressors should be more important to first episodes of depression than they are to subsequent episodes (recurrences). The literature on kindling/sensitization theory is somewhat mixed; some studies support its predictions and others do not (Hammen, 2005). In particular, some studies have shown that lower severity life events are associated with MDEs, particularly recurrences (e.g., Hammen, Henry, & Daley, 2000; Harkness et al., 2006; Monroe et al., 2006), which is consistent with the predictions of stress sensitization. Stress sensitization may characterize only some people who ultimately develop depression. For example, Kendler and colleagues (2001) found that those at genetic risk for depression had a weaker association between stress and depressive episodes; those at low genetic risk showed the most evidence for sensitization to stress with increasing episodes. Subsequent theoretical work has focused on two variants of kindling theory that may account for these discrepant observations: stress sensitization and stress autonomy. The stress sensitization model proposes that with successive depressive episodes, events of weaker and weaker potency are capable of triggering an episode. Thus, severe events may be even less likely to be tied to episodes with time, because lesser events (which are more likely to occur than severe events) beat them to the punch (so to speak) and elicit episodes on their own. Whereas first onsets of depression may be linked to a severe life event, such as loss of a loved one, later onsets may be triggered by events of lower severity. For example, Kraepelin (1921) made the classic observation of his patient who became depressed "after the death first of her husband, next of her dog, and then of her dove" (p. 179).

Stress autonomy is consistent with Post's kindling model, and it proposes that episodes begin to occur autonomously of stress; thus, the relationship between stressors (both more and less severe stressors) and depressive episodes should weaken over time, as episodes begin to occur even in the absence of stressors. Teasing apart stress sensitization and stress autonomy variants of this model requires longitudinal data that allow us to test whether serious stressors lose their impact over time, and whether they are less likely to occur prior to an episode, as well as whether the impact or occurrence of less severe life events increases across the course of MDD. The existing evidence suggests that although neither model is a perfect fit, there is more support for stress sensitization than for the stress autonomy model. For example, Stroud et al. (2010) found that there was a decreased occurrence of severe life events over subsequent MDEs, whereas lower severity life events became increasingly impactful over the course of the disorder (particularly those involving relationship loss). Lower severity events did not become more common over the course of the disorder (i.e., with subsequent recurrences), which also suggests that stress generation processes for lower severity events may not be caused by depressive symptoms or episodes per se.

Although originally conceptualized as a model of how stress contributes to Bipolar Disorder (BD), there is only weak evidence that the role of stress diminishes or that weaker stressors are capable of eliciting episodes across the course of BD (Bender & Alloy, 2011).

CHRONIC STRESS

Most of the focus of diathesis–stress research and empirical tests of the role of stressors in depressive and manic episodes has focused on events, or acute stressors that have a relatively identifiable onset and offset. However, other kinds of stressful circumstances that are characterized by events of longer duration (e.g., many weeks or months) and those that persist without a clear onset or offset may also play a causal role in the development of depressive disorders. These are typically referred to as chronic stress, a label that has been applied to a broad set of circumstances (e.g., health problems, disabilities, poverty, and so on). There is evidence that chronic stressors are associated with depression (Brown & Harris, 1978), and some indication that they may be even more strongly related than are events/acute stressors (McGonagle & Kessler, 1990). Of course, because such conditions are chronic, they are even more likely to overlap temporally with depression and it may be more difficult to determine that they preceded the episode. Acute and chronic stressors may also interact—an acute stressor may be more powerful if it occurs in the context of an ongoing/chronic stressor in the same domain, or persistent stress may reduce the power of a new acute event to prompt depression (Hammen, 2005). Of the various chronic stressors that may be important for understanding risk for depression, those occurring early in life have received special theoretical and empirical attention.

Early Adversity and Depressive Disorders

Early adversity refers to a variety of experiences and contexts that occur early in development and are believed to increase risk for psychopathology because of their formative influence on psychological processes that then increase risk for depression later in the life span. For example, negative experiences early in life may alter children's expectations for their lives, including the kind of treatment they can expect from others. These expectations contribute to the development of maladaptive patterns of interpersonal behavior traits that increase risk. Such experiences may be particularly common among those who develop chronic forms of depression. McCullough (2003) argued that the early home environment stressors common among the chronically depressed lead to expectations that others will hurt them if given the opportunity. He described four themes common among those exposed to maltreatment: (a) an early family environment failed to address the child's physical and/or emotional needs; (b) the family environment was characterized by danger to the child and others; (c) the child experienced chronic pain (physical and emotional) that produced feelings of tension, anxiety, and fear/terror; and (d) the child often had to serve the emotional needs of the caregiver. The hypothesized outcome of such events is the development of maladaptive schemas that summarize a person's perception of self-worth and relationship to others. Young (1999) described such early maladaptive schemas as being defined by feelings of incompetence, insecurity, vulnerability, self-criticism or entitlement, insufficient self-control, enmeshment, or mistrust and alienation. Such schemas may be depressogenic through selection processes (e.g., entering into relationships with others that confirm these negative self-perceptions) or by interacting with stressors.

Empirical tests of these models have shown that aspects of early adversity are particularly common among those with chronic depression, and that greater early adversity is associated with a poorer course of depressive disorders. For example, McLaughlin and colleagues (2010) reported that adverse early home environment factors (parental mental illness, substance use disorder, criminality, family violence, physical and sexual abuse, and neglect) were associated with persistence of mood disorders over time. Early environmental adversity (such as physical or sexual abuse) has been linked to more severe (i.e., rapid cycling, longer duration of ill times, higher suicidality, higher comorbidity with other Axis I disorders) and treatment-resistant courses of BD, as well as an earlier onset of the condition (e.g., Garno, Goldberg, Hamen, & Hitzler, 2005; Leverich et al., 2002). The effects of early adversity may be mediated by changes that occur in the person's responses to subsequent stressors (sensitization). To illustrate, Dienes and colleagues (2006) found that bipolar patients with more severe early adversity had a greater likelihood of experiencing a recurrence over a 1-year follow-up when exposed to mild levels of stress, compared to patients with less early adversity.

There is also evidence that less extreme manifestations of such adversity, particularly in the interpersonal domain, may be associated with elevated risk for depression. For example, variations in parenting are related to depression in youngsters; effects are small, but consistently suggest that children who are exposed to rejection by their parents are at elevated risk (McLeod, Weisz, & Wood, 2007). Among adults, there is a great deal of evidence showing that the interpersonal climate of those with unipolar and bipolar depression plays an important role in determining course over time. Patients who are exposed to an environment characterized by high levels of "expressed emotion" by close others fare the worst over time. High expressed emotion refers to a critical attitude by close others toward the depressed person; interview measures of this construct predict relapse in a variety of conditions aside from depressive disorders, including alcoholism and schizophrenia (Butzlaff & Hooley, 1998).

BIOLOGICAL PROCESSES BY WHICH STRESS MAY CAUSE DEPRESSION

The past 20 years have seen increasing emphasis on identifying the biological pathways by which stressors get under the skin (so to speak) to influence medical and psychiatric health. Sterling and Eyer (1988) and McEwen (1998, 2003) introduced a theoretical model of these processes that describe the short- and long-term adaptations that occur in response to stressors. This model emphasizes the adaptive processes that allow humans to respond effectively to life challenges, both large and small, by allowing for changes in our internal systems that produce functional responses to new circumstances (*allostasis*). Although these processes are adaptive, they also exert a toll; if internal parameters are repeatedly forced to change, particularly if the processes that do so are extreme or inefficient, then there will be "wear and tear" on the body, referred to as *allostatic load*. Allostatic load refers to the cumulative toll resulting from adaptation processes elicited by stressors. Allostatic load is believed to play a role in both the aging process as well as the development of medical and psychological disorders.

Chronic cortisol production is one marker of allostatic processes. Although cortisol secretion is a critical and adaptive part of human stress response, excessive cortisol production (because of exposure to repeated stress or because of abnormal stress reactivity) is problematic. In fact, it is linked to a variety of medical problems, and is evident in a minority of patients with unipolar depression. It is believed that one of the mechanisms of cortisol's negative effects on psychological health may be the effect it exerts on brain processes important for depressive disorders. There is a bidirectional association between cortisol production and activity in brain circuits—including the prefrontal cortex, hippocampus, amygdala, and hypothalamus—important for emotion and its regulation. Stress appears to have toxic effects on the hippocampus, leading to changes in hippocampal structure (e.g., Woolley, Gould, & McEwen, 1990). One study showed that compared to healthy controls, those with MDD exhibited more decline over a 3-year period in their gray-matter density in the hippocampus, the anterior cingulate cortex (ACC), right dorsomedial prefrontal cortex, and left amygdala (Frodl et al., 2008). Some have proposed that one of the mechanisms by which early adversity increases subsequent risk for depression is because these negative experiences shape biological stress responsivity systems in a way that make them sensitized to later stressors (Heim & Nemeroff, 2001).

Biologically informative measures are increasingly being incorporated into empirical studies of depression and depression risk, including measures of overall (baseline) levels of cortisol (thought to potentially reflect the long-term effects of stress exposure) and reactive cortisol (tapping the body's ability to mount a cortisol response to an acute stressor). Such research is potentially promising but progress to date has been slow. This is likely because elevated cortisol does not seem to characterize all people with depression, and because there is not yet a gold standard for how best to measure reactive cortisol. Similarly, there is also great interest in other measures of allostatic load linked to aging, including shortening of telomeres (the outermost part of chromosomes, which shorten progressively as a function of genomic replication and oxidative stress), which is a marker of accelerated aging. There is emerging evidence that depressive disorders are associated with accelerated telomere shortening (Simon et al., 2006; Wikgren et al., 2012). Thus, as measures of biological processes involved in stress improve, it is possible we may have new insights into the mechanisms by which stress is involved in the development of depression and the effects depression exerts on physical health.

CONCLUSIONS

Exciting new developments in the measurement of biological markers of the body's response to stress await empirical integration with other methods from psychological science, including rich assessments of psychosocial stressors and individual differences in people's perception of and response to these stressors. In particular, full tests of these models will require in-depth longitudinal studies that take into account maturation of stress-response systems and the cumulative psychological effect of stress across the life span in order to fill in the links across these different literatures. An important note of caution when considering the state of the field is that the emergence of sophisticated biological measures cannot replace continued efforts toward the measurement and understanding of psychological processes that explain humans' understanding of and behavioral responses to stress, and how these responses interact with their ongoing environmental circumstances to increase or decrease risk for psychopathology. Connections between these psychological and biological processes are bound to be complex, necessitating continued efforts to advance stress models using a number of different paradigms.

The fairly straightforward notion that stress must play a role in causing depression or mania and complicating people's efforts to recover from these conditions has proven to be insufficiently nuanced to capture the empirical reality of how these processes are interrelated. Nonetheless, findings demonstrating complex interplay between people's behavior and their environments (as they encounter and perceive them) are rich sources of hypotheses regarding the potential mechanisms by which depression develops. The existing evidence for the role of stress is consistent with the idea that depressive disorders are etiologically heterogeneous; some cases may emerge in the absence of stress, some may be primarily attributable to stress, and people may vary in the kinds of stressors that are most potent for them. Stress can be an outcome of depression, and it can be a marker of the behavioral processes that precede and predict the development of depressive disorders.

What Genes and Biological Systems Are Implicated in Depression?

s is often the case in science, a long-standing theoretical interest awaited new technological developments before it could begin to bear fruit in terms of empirical findings. Ancient models such as the humoral theory of depression emphasized the biological underpinnings of depressive disorders. However, for centuries there was insufficient knowledge of the brain and its workings and no direct means of assessing the relevant biological processes, leading to stagnation in attempts to more precisely describe these biological underpinnings. Very little progress on this front was made until the somewhat unlikely discovery of chemical agents that had beneficial effects on depressive symptoms. The first major theory to emerge from this discovery was the catecholamine hypothesis (Schildkraut, 1965). This theory proposed that depression was caused by abnormal levels of particular neurochemicals (the catecholamines), based on observations that drugs that impacted these neurochemicals (monoamine oxidase inhibitors [MAOIs] and norepinephrine uptake inhibitors) showed significant antidepressant effects. It is important to note that even this evidence was rather indirect. It relied on the logical inference that because medicines that increased available levels of a particular neurochemical produced reductions in depressive symptoms, then the original source of those symptoms must have been reduced levels of those same chemicals. The simplest version of this logical model is now known to be inaccurate; however, it nonetheless was incredibly generative in terms of spurring novel hypotheses, approaches, and research designs for uncovering the biological processes that are implicated in depression. Current research on these processes is wildly varied in terms of the kinds of variables that are foregrounded (e.g., brain circuits, neurochemistry, autonomic nervous system processes, genes) and due to the technological demands of much of this research, progress is often slow, particularly with respect to integrating knowledge across different research domains. However, several of these literatures have produced replicated findings that have the potential to deepen our understanding of processes illuminated in psychosocial and psychiatric research on depressive disorders. In the following, findings are reviewed regarding brain processes at the level of neurochemistry, neuroanatomy, and brain functioning; the role of hormones; and the role of genes.

NEUROCHEMICAL PROCESSES

The discovery of antidepressant medicines led to a flurry of research on neurochemical processes in depression and mania that continues today. This work has obvious applied value in addition to its contribution to our basic understanding of depression; greater knowledge regarding the role of neurotransmitters in depression can potentially facilitate the development of novel medicines with effective antidepressant properties. With regard to basic science, this knowledge also furthers our understanding of molecular mechanisms that are implicated in mood and behavior. Most of this work has focused on a small number of neurotransmitters that have the following characteristics: receptors for these neurotransmitters are widely distributed across a number of brain regions; pharmacological agents that act on the levels of these neurotransmitters or affect the action of other processes at their receptor sites are lawfully related to aspects of mood and behavior; and their mechanisms can be modeled in nonhuman animals (animal models allow for the use of more invasive measurement techniques that yield more precise information about their mechanisms).

The advent of the use of antidepressants and lithium (for Bipolar Disorder [BD]) was so successful and transformative in psychiatric practice that it forever influenced the way scientists and lay people alike think about the biology of these disorders. This is reflected in the common parlance, in which depression is often described in popular culture as being caused by a "chemical imbalance" in the brain. This metaphorical phrase has proven remarkably appealing, so much so that many people do not know it is *not* an accurate representation of the role of neurotransmitters in depressive disorders. There is no single neurotransmitter (or set of them) that bears a direct linear, causal relationship with either depression or mania. It does not appear that simply increasing or decreasing the amount of a neurotransmitter available in the brain is the key causal process that produces the symptoms of depressive disorders (or reverses them). Even effective antidepressant medicines tend to have a slow onset of their effects, much slower (approximately 3 weeks) than what one would expect if their benefits were attributable to merely increasing the levels of available neurotransmitters in the brain. This suggests that their mechanisms of action are slower emerging, and thus likely take the form of changes in receptor density, postsynaptic processes, and longer term alterations in brain circuits. Thus, the biological processes by which neurotransmitters relate to depressive syndromes (and even to normal functioning) remain poorly understood, and are now acknowledged to be complex in nature. Despite the challenges, however, basic research on both animals and humans continues to clarify the nature of these processes and to confirm that they are an important part of the emotional and behavioral changes that accompany depression and mania. Following, evidence is highlighted regarding a handful of neurotransmitters that seem to play an important role in depressive disorders.

Serotonin

Considerable data from multiple streams of research indicate that systems involving the neurotransmitter serotonin are involved in depressive disorders. Experimental evidence consistent with this claim comes from studies of manipulations of serotonin systems. Specifically, treatment studies show that drugs known to increase circulating serotonin in the brain, selective serotonin reuptake inhibitors (SSRIs), are effective in treating depression. This is true for a wide range of medicines that vary in their chemical structure; effective antidepressants from all classes (e.g., SSRIs, MAOIs, norepinephrine uptake inhibitors) increase the release of serotonin in the brain (Mongeau, Blier, & DeMontigny, 1997) and increase the density of serotonin receptors, thereby providing more targets for serotonin to exert its effects on brain circuits (Haddjeri, Blier, & DeMontigny, 1998). Moreover, symptoms of depression can be precipitated by administration of agents such as tryptophan that decrease production of serotonin. Taken together, these findings suggest that a deficit in functional levels of serotonin may be causally involved in the processes that give rise to depressive symptoms. Serotonin appears to play the same role in depression occurring in those with BD as in those with unipolar depression, but its role in mania is less clear (Mahmood & Silverstone,

2001). Also consistent with this logic, serotonin has a broader role in normative mood, sleep, and sexual functioning, and has been linked to individual differences in a variety of personality traits associated with depressive disorders, including impulsivity/ low constraint (CON) and some aspects of negative emotionality (NE) (Carver, Johnson, & Joorman, 2008; Carver & Miller, 2006).

Dopamine

A number of lines of evidence also suggest that low levels or reduced transmission of dopamine are implicated in unipolar depression, particularly the anhedonic and amotivational aspects of the syndrome (Dunlop & Nemeroff, 2007). Dopamine is critical for brain functions that relate to pleasure, reward-driven behavior, motivation, and some aspects of cognitive functioning such as concentration and performance speed. For example, studies of rodents have shown that reduced concentration of dopamine in reward-related brain regions is associated with reduced efforts in these animals to obtain rewards (Salamone, Aberman, Sokolowski, & Cousins, 1999). In humans, there is evidence that severe forms of depression may be associated with greater responsivity to the rewarding effects of stimulants (e.g., Tremblay, Naranjo, Cardenas, Herrmann, & Busto, 2002), with the hypothesized mechanism being that lower release of dopamine results in compensatory processes, including upregulation of postsynaptic dopamine receptors. Early biological models of BD proposed that mania resulted from excess of dopamine but existing data suggest this is overly simplistic. Stimulant medicines can prompt manic-like behavior, presumably because they activate brain pathways involved in reward-seeking and impulsive behavior (Seamans & Yang, 2004). Evidence regarding the role of dopamine in mania includes studies showing that antimanic medicines are dopamine antagonists; and functional and structural brain imaging techniques have shown that circuits innervated by dopamine may be abnormal in those with BD (Cousins, Butts, & Young, 2009).

Brain-Derived Neurotrophic Factor

Brain-derived neurotrophic factor (BDNF) is a protein that acts on neurons in particular brain regions, including the hippocampus, cortex, and basal forebrain, acting to support the survival and differentiation of existing neurons and the growth of new neurons. It plays a critical role in neurogenesis, neural development, and long-term memory (Post, 2007). Interest in this protein dovetails with theories of depression that focus on the role of neuroplasticity, specifically that depression is associated with cell loss, reduced neurogenesis, and neuronal atrophy that is the outcome of exposure to repeated and/or chronic stress (e.g., Kuma et al., 2004). The impact of this loss is thought to negatively impact the functioning of the prefrontal cortex and hippocampus, and this may in turn result in abnormalities in emotion regulation, memory, and/or learning that are characteristic of depressive disorders. There is evidence from animal studies that some effective treatments for unipolar depression (including some antidepressants and electroconvulsive therapy) increase *BDNF* mRNA expression in brain regions implicated in depression (see the following), including the hippocampus and prefrontal cortex (Nibuya, Morinobu, & Duman, 1995; Russo-Neustadt, Beard, Huang, & Cotman, 2000). Moreover, low levels of BDNF have been linked to high levels of NE (Lange et al., 2005). Finally, as described in the following text, polymorphisms in a BDNF promoter gene have also been linked to BD, especially rapid-cycling forms of the disorder (Green et al., 2006), although other studies have failed to find such an association.

BRAIN REGIONS AND BRAIN CIRCUITS IMPLICATED IN DEPRESSIVE DISORDERS

Given the profound emotional, cognitive, and behavioral sequelae of depressive and manic episodes, it is likely that these conditions encompass multiple areas of the brain that are involved in important components of both normal and abnormal functioning. It should go without saying that depression and mania are disorders of the brain in that all of our cognitive, motivational, and emotional systems are produced by the action of brain processes. Discovering the precise mechanisms, however, is considerably more challenging because our understanding of how the brain accomplishes its tasks is still somewhat in its infancy. Moreover, it is clear that there are many variations on the evolutionary blueprint for our brains. Individual differences are evident at every level of analysis of the brain, including its structure and functioning. Linking brain structure and function to individual differences in risk for and manifestation of depressive disorders will necessarily involve considerable effort to discover universal principles of brain–behavior associations, as well as the ways in which variations in these are responsible for differences across people in their risk for depression.

Researchers have focused on a variety of brain markers, including differences in the structure (e.g., size and shape) of various brain regions, functioning of brain regions and circuits (i.e., their pattern of activation/involvement during tasks designed to engage people in the processes that might be aberrant in depressive disorders), and more molecular components, such as neurochemistry. Much of this work has focused on group differences across those with and without the disorder in question (e.g., Major Depressive Disorder [MDD]). Far less research has used designs capable of sorting out the nature of the relationship between these neurophysiological measures and depressive disorders. Thus, for many measures, we do not know if they are an epiphenomenon of depressive or manic symptoms; if they are the outcome of the disease processes; or if they are risk markers that may differentiate people who will ultimately develop a depressive disorder from those who will not. Nonetheless, these research avenues hold promise for understanding more precisely the biological mechanisms that define these conditions. As we learn more about the way risk and disease processes are manifested in the brain, we have the potential to learn about the normal functions of the implicated processes, as well as how they may generate the signs and symptoms we observe at a behavioral and psychological level. This knowledge may help us to understand the etiology of these conditions, as well as potentially suggest novel avenues for treating and preventing them.

Differences in Brain Structure

A meta-analysis of structural differences in brain regions across those with BD and control participants revealed that only a few structural differences appear to be replicated in the existing literature, perhaps because the differences between those with and without BD are small in magnitude, thus necessitating relatively large samples (uncommon in structural imaging studies) to detect such effects. Those with BD have larger ventricles and higher rates of deep white matter hyperintensities (small areas in which the signal intensity is high relative to surrounding tissue, unusual signs that are very rare in young, psychiatrically healthy people, but more common in aging populations and those with cerebrovascular disorder; Kempton, Geddes, Ettinger, Williams, & Grasby, 2008), as well as abnormalities in cerebellar structures (Stoll, Renshaw, Yurgelun-Todd, & Cohen, 2000). It is not clear from the existing evidence whether these differences are evident before the onset of the disorder, only during the illness, or if they are also evident when patients are in remission. Both MDD and BD have also been linked to structural abnormalities in the anterior cingulate cortex (ACC; Coryell et al., 2005).

Meta-analytic evidence shows that MDD is associated with larger ventricles, greater cerebrospinal fluid volume, and smaller volumes of the hippocampus, frontal lobe, orbitofrontal cortex, thalamus, and basal ganglia (Kempton et al., 2011). Hippocampal reductions were greater in currently depressed than in remitted MDD patients. There is also evidence of some structural differences between those with MDD and those with BD, including fewer deep white matter hyperintensities in those with MDD, and smaller hippocampal and basal ganglia volume in those with MDD. The two disorders were similar to one another (but differed from controls) in terms of having increased lateral ventricle volume and greater subcortical gray matter hyperintensities. Thus, some abnormalities in brain structure are similar across unipolar and bipolar disorder, whereas others are unique; the latter hold the potential to explain the origins of mania.

Differences in Brain Activation and Functioning

Functional imaging of brain regions, using electroencephalogram (EEG) and functional magnetic resonance imaging (fMRI), involves mapping patterns of brain activity (assessed by electrocortical activity, glucose metabolism, or cerebral blood flow) to performance on tasks designed to elicit the processes of interest (such as attention to different kinds of stimuli, interpretation of higher order information, responsivity to emotional cues, and so on). Depressive disorders and markers of risk for these conditions have been linked to functional differences in several different brain regions.

Amygdala. The amygdala has been linked to a broad variety of emotion-related processes. This brain region, located in the limbic cortex, appears to primarily play a role in determining the emotional salience of stimuli, both at a conscious and nonconscious level. People with MDD have increased blood flow in the amygdala that persists after recovery, and amygdala activation correlates with depression severity (Drevets & Raichle, 1992). Among those with unipolar depressive disorders, there is evidence of exaggerated amygdala activity to negative stimuli, such as sad or fearful faces (e.g., Surguladze et al., 2005; Victor, Furey, Fromm, Ohman, & Drevets, 2010). Nondepressed persons appear to have a positivity bias; for example, relative to depressed people, they show stronger amygdala responses to happy faces in comparison to sad faces (Killgore & Yurgelun-Todd, 2004). This negative emotional bias is evident in evaluation of amygdala reactivity even to masked stimuli, suggesting that the biases occur below the level of conscious awareness (Victor et al., 2010). Moreover, there is evidence that this biased processing of negative faces may represent a trait marker of those at risk for depression because it has been found in remitted MDD patients (e.g., Neumeister et al., 2006; Victor et al., 2010). Finally, effective treatments for depression have the effect of reducing activity in the amygdala (e.g., Mayberg et al., 2005), further evidence for the causal role of amygdala functioning in depression.

Further findings for the role of the amygdala in depressive disorders derive from other means of assessing fear-related brain circuits. Modulation of the startle blink reflex by stimulus valence (i.e., positive versus negative versus neutral) has been shown to be a sensitive marker of individual differences in fear proneness, thought to emerge from the operation of brain circuits involved in defensive reactivity. The startle blink reflex is a protective reaction that occurs upon presentation of an abrupt, intense stimulus such as a loud burst of noise. The magnitude of this protective blink can be increased if the person is simultaneously viewing an aversive stimulus (and decreased if viewing a positive stimulus). This modulation is thought to occur because the positive and aversive stimuli activate different motivational states (Lang, Greenwald, Bradley, & Hamm, 1993). If people are in a defensive motivational state (because of presentation of an aversive stimulus), their blink magnitude will be augmented upon presentation of the abrupt stimulus. Evidence from rodents (e.g., Davis, 1998) has shown that two regions of the amygdala are involved in modulation of the startle response, suggesting that individual differences in startle modulation may be a sensitive index of specific disparities in amygdala reactivity. Startle modulation, when presented with negatively valenced stimuli, is typically elevated in individuals with anxiety disorders relative to those without disorders; however, it appears to be blunted in people with unipolar depressive disorders. Startle inhibition by exposure to positive stimuli appears to be weaker in unipolar depressive disorders, particular anhedonia (Vaidyanathan, Patrick, & Cuthbert, 2009).

Finally, the amygdala is also a part of a brain circuit that interacts with the stress hormone cortisol. For example, cortisol enchances encoding of emotional memories from the amygdala to other regions of the brain (McGaugh, 2004). This may be one mechanism by which the stress system (involving cortisol) facilitates a robust stress response (by facilitating brain system responses that organize these responses).

Hippocampus. The hippocampus plays a central role in processing of emotional stimuli, specifically by encoding information about the context in which emotional stimuli are located (Phillips & LeDoux, 1992), and it is also involved in learning and long-term memory processes. Unipolar depression is associated with a decreased volume in the hippocampus (e.g., Bremner et al., 2000; Sheline, Sanghavi, Mintun, & Gado, 1999), potentially playing a role in memory deficits observed in those with depression (see Chapter 3). These structural changes may be a result of recurrent depressive episodes (Sheline et al., 1999) or chronic early stress resulting in neuronal death in the hippocampus (Campbell & MacQueen, 2004). These structural abnormalities have been linked to memory loss (Sheline, Mittler, & Mintun, 2002), but there is less evidence from functional imaging studies to demonstrate the mechanisms by which this occurs.

Reward-Related Brain Systems—Mesolimbic, Prefrontal, and Amygdala Circuits. As noted, deficits in reward-related behavior have been invoked in the etiology of depressive disorders (e.g., Depue & Iacono, 1989); consistent with this, many of the brain systems known to be involved in the processing of reward-related stimuli (e.g., the amygdala) and reward-related motivation and behavior (e.g., nucleus accumbens, ventral tegmental area) seem to be involved in depression. For example, unipolar depression is associated with weaker responses to rewarding outcomes in the nucleus accumbens and caudate (Pizzagalli et al., 2009).

Depressive disorders are associated with decreased activation of the prefrontal cortex, which is important for a number of higher order behaviors, including planning, goal-setting, anticipating affective outcomes of different behaviors, and guiding behaviors, that are commonly impaired in both mania and depression. People with MDD and BD, when actively depressed, have been shown to exhibit increased ACC activity that normalizes when they have remitted due to successful medication treatment (Drevets & Price, 2005). Moreover, there is a positive correlation between depression severity and metabolic activity in the amygdala, the ACC, and ventromedial prefrontal cortex (Drevets, Savitz, & Trimble, 2008; Hasler et al., 2008).

GENETIC INFLUENCES ON DEPRESSIVE DISORDERS

The aim of genetic research on depressive disorders is to clarify the distal causal mechanisms that lead to individual differences in risk for developing these conditions. We are far from understanding how genes are involved in the creation of biological and psychological systems that increases an individual's risk for depression, although the fact that genes do explain variation in risk for depression is not in dispute. What we do know quite clearly now is that an important reason why some people become depressed whereas others do not is because of individual variation in genes. This is broadly consistent with the diathesis–stress model outlined in Chapter 6. The same research designs that have demonstrated the importance of genes to these disorders has also revealed what aspects of the environment may be causally implicated in their development, as well as the more proximal processes that may explain the pathway by which genes exert their effect. There has been a proliferation of research attempting to identify the particular genes that are involved in these processes and, lately, attempts to understand the biological and psychological processes that underlie this pathway. However, there is a critical conundrum in this literature—twin and adoption designs have conclusively demonstrated the importance of genes in depressive disorders; however, increasingly sophisticated technologies developed to narrow the search for specific genes have generally yielded disappointing findings. Although a number of specific genes have been implicated in depressive disorders, most of these have not received sufficient replication to yield confidence in the findings.

One serious challenge to bringing clarity to this field emerges from the nature of the constructs under study. Many have pointed out that the complex nature of disorders as defined by the *Diagnostic and Statistical Manual of Mental Disorders* has limited the ability to cleanly link them to particular genes. These diagnoses involve multiple dimensions marked by diverse signs and symptoms tapping activity across numerous biological and psychological systems; thus, they do not identify processes that are likely to arise from a small number of genes. Moreover, as noted in Chapter 6, the syndromes are etiologically heterogeneous; genes may be involved only in some subgroups or dimensions of depressive syndromes; may be differentially involved in dissimilar subgroups or dimensions; or diverse genes may be involved in different subgroups or dimensions. Not knowing what these subgroups or dimensions are is obviously a serious barrier to making progress on these important questions.

Although we may be unsatisfied with the amount of progress made on identifying genetic pathways to depressive disorders, the important knowledge gained in this pursuit cannot be underestimated. First, there is indisputable evidence that these conditions are heritable. For example, first-degree relatives of those with MDD have much higher risk for the disorder than first-degree relatives of those without a history of MDD—two to four times higher (e.g., Rice, Harold, & Thapar, 2002; Sullivan, Neale, & Kendler, 2000). Thus, familial loading for the disorder is as important a risk factor as gender in identifying those at greatest likelihood of becoming depressed. Twin designs provide even stronger evidence that this elevated risk is attributable to genes. Findings from these studies indicate that there are moderate genetic influences on MDD in adolescents and adults, explaining about 30% to 40% of the variance across individuals (e.g., Rice et al., 2002; Shih, Belmonte, Zandi, 2004). Importantly, twin designs can also provide evidence for the role of environmental influences, and these studies indicate that aspects of the environment that are unique to a person (i.e., that differ across members of a twin pair) are also implicated in MDD. Adoption studies provide an important complement to family and twin designs, but there have been few focusing on depressive disorders. In an important adoption study, Tully, Iacono, and McGue (2008) found that part of the risk associated with maternal depression on children's psychiatric outcomes was attributable to environmental influences.

Second, although there are inconsistent findings, meta-analytic research indicates that the degree and nature of genetic effects on MDD are not different across men and women. This suggests that differences in genetic effects cannot account for gender differences in the prevalence of MDD.

Third, consistent with etiological heterogeneity, there is evidence that subtypes of depressive disorders may be differentiated by their heritability. Specifically, evidence from family studies suggests that early onset of MDD and recurrent cases of MDD have greater heritability than later onset MDD (typically defined as adulthood versus childhood/adolescence) and single-episode cases (Sullivan et al., 2000; Weissman et al., 1984; Zubenko et al., 2001).

Fourth, genetic effects on depressive disorders may change across the life span. In general, heritability seems consistent across adolescence and adulthood, with moderate estimates across both of these developmental periods (Rice et al., 2002). Studies of very early-onset depressive disorders—that is, in childhood— reveal somewhat different findings. Specifically, there is evidence that these cases may have less contribution of genes and greater environmental influences (e.g., Kendler, Gardner, & Lichtenstein,

2008; Scourfeld et al., 2003). Consistent with the importance of considering development, genetic effects appear to be important contributors to those aspects of depression that are stable over time, whereas environmental influences are involved in changes in depression (Lau & Eley, 2010; O'Connor, Neiderhiser, Reiss, Hetherington, & Plomin, 1998).

Fifth, whatever genes are involved in unipolar depressive disorders, their effects are not observed narrowly upon these conditions alone. Specifically, they also seem to influence other clinical syndromes and traits related to depression. Genetic influences on unipolar depression overlap considerably with those for Generalized Anxiety Disorder (GAD), as well as those for NE. This suggests that genetic influences may drive comorbidity across anxiety and depressive disorders. BD and schizophrenia have shared genetic influences, as do bipolar and unipolar depressive disorders (e.g., Huang et al., 2010). Modern molecular genetics has moved beyond the paradigm in which we expected to find common genetic variants that account for a substantial proportion of the variance in common diseases to a model in which common diseases are the result of many rare genetic variants. The risk attributable to any one variant is so small that it is unlikely to be detected independently, even in very large-scale studies with very large samples and advanced gene-mapping techniques (Gershon, Alliey-Rodriguez, & Liu, 2011). The "multiple rare variants" hypothesis proposes that each rare variant has a strong effect on the disease. Each variant is unique, so its effects are difficult to detect in an exploratory design unless one has incredibly large samples (tens or hundreds of thousand participants). However, each of these rare variants operating together produce enough cases of the disorder for the illness to be common in the population.

Sixth, the effects of genes and putative environmental factors on depressive disorders are not best understood as being independent of one another. Rather, it seems more promising to focus on the ways in which genetic and environmental influences mutually operate or interact with one another to increase risk.

These processes are collectively referred to as gene–environment correlations and interactions. First, measures of the environment that are correlated with depressive disorders are in fact now known to be influenced by genetic factors. For example, twin studies have shown that stressful life events, marital quality, parent–child relationship quality, and social support are all influenced by genetic differences across people (e.g., Kendler & Baker, 2007; Plomin & Bergeman, 1991). This suggests that the reason these factors are linked to depression may not be because they act through the environment to shape risk; rather, genetic effects that give rise to these factors may be the same as those that give rise to depression. Thus, it is possible that the same personality traits shown to be associated with depression, and to perhaps share genetic causes with depression, may also shape the environment. Genetic vulnerability may increase risk by elevating exposure to environments that facilitate risk (i.e., some genetically influenced characteristics may evoke particular reactions in others or may cause people to select into environments that are depressogenic), or by heightening some individuals' reactivity to particular environments relative to others. Finally, genes may modulate individual differences in reactivity to events. For example, it has been shown that the effects of stressors are strongest among people who are at elevated genetic risk for depression (Kendler et al., 1995; Silberg, Rutter, Neale, & Eaves, 2001). Such findings are consistent with the diathesis–stress model (see Chapter 6), suggesting that stressors are potent only among those with the diathesis for the disorder.

Specific Genetic Polymorphisms Linked to Depressive Disorders

Several specific genes have been linked in one or more studies to MDD or BD, although only a few of these have been replicated. However, among those that have been identified, several replicated findings have involved genes that are implicated in serotonergic systems. As noted, there is evidence that a functional deficit in serotonin levels is implicated in depression. Consistent with this, genes involved in serotonin transmission have been linked to depression. However, links between the two literatures—on genetic polymorphisms linked to depression and on the role of serotonin in depression—can be difficult to resolve. For example, there has been an explosion of research on the serotonin transporter gene, specifically the promoter region of this gene. This gene has several variants that can be grouped into two major variants, one which codes for low activity (i.e., fewer transporter molecules at the synapse) and the other for high activity (more transporter molecules). The low activity variant is the one that is more common among those with unipolar or bipolar depression, although with a very modest effect size (Lotrich & Pollock, 2004). However, this is somewhat surprising. The low activity variant (which produces fewer transporter molecules at the synapse) should be associated with higher levels of serotonin, which—according to the findings from studies of the efficacy of antidepressants—should be associated with lower risk of depression. Newer findings have focused on polymorphisms in genes related to BDNF. Variations in the *BDNF* gene result in variations in lower versus higher secretion of the BDNF protein; polymorphisms in this gene have been linked to MDD and BD (Schumacher et al., 2005; Sklar et al., 2002).

Over the past 10 years, there have been two major developments in psychiatric genetics. The first is the development of more powerful methods for assessing genetic variants and analyzing the resulting data, including genome-wide association studies and deep sequencing of individuals' genomes. Results from these developments have been modest to date, consistent with the conclusion that common genetic polymorphisms are unlikely to account for genetic effects on psychiatric conditions, including depressive disorders. Subsequent developments in genomics are now focusing on detection of rare genetic variants and data mining techniques for searching the genome at a more detailed level. The focus of this work is very much in the exploratory phase. The second has been a renewed concentration on

213

the role of the environment, with exciting findings demonstrating that the effects of genetic polymorphisms may depend upon exposure to particular environmental contexts (e.g., Caspi et al., 2003). In several studies, researchers showed that it was the combination of possessing a particular polymorphism and exposure to environmental stress (e.g., serious negative life events) or a particular environmental context (e.g., child abuse) that was associated with elevated risk for a psychiatric outcome, consistent with classic articulations of the diathesis–stress model. These findings were taken as evidence that common genetic variants might actually play a large role in disorders such as depression; however, their effects were not to increase risk on their own—rather, they did so only in combination with environmental factors. This argument was appealing because it suggested that we would soon make important discoveries regarding the genetic bases of depression by testing for interactions between known environmental risk factors for these disorders and genes with known effects on psychological processes, raising the possibility of conducting specific and theoretically guided tests regarding the role of particular genes. Unfortunately, the excitement of these findings outpaced their ability to be replicated (much like the earlier excitement that accompanied findings linking particular genetic polymorphisms to particular disorders). The reality of these gene–environment interactions has been hotly debated in the literature, but taken as a whole, the pattern of findings to date suggests that most gene–environment interactions that have been published are likely false positives rather than true effects (Duncan & Keller, 2011), for several reasons. Most studies with positive findings had low statistical power to detect interactions, and larger samples (which are more likely to detect significant effects) have actually produced less evidence of gene–environment interactions in psychiatric outcomes. Thus, it seems that gene–environment interactions are also unlikely to provide the final answer as to the mechanisms by which we observe significant heritability for depressive disorders.

Redefining Depressive Disorder Phenotypes to Better Define Genetic Pathways

Given the imprecision evident in our diagnostic criteria (which, after all, were not designed to facilitate uncovering the genetic bases of psychopathology), there has long been interest in the basic psychopathology literature in developing more refined targets for study. The purpose of these approaches is to define vulnerability markers in a way that (a) is more etiologically homogeneous or narrow than depressive syndromes, and (b) defines an intermediate pathway between the gene(s) and the syndromes, thus pointing to possible biological processes by which the genes may exert their effects. The resulting markers, sometimes called "endophenotypes," are meant to identify characteristics or processes that can be more clearly linked to genes, and thus have the potential to define more etiologically homogeneous subgroups. Endophenotypes can be informed by clinical research on depression or by starting with normal variations in functioning (such as basic affective processes) in the domains of neurochemistry or behavior. Underlying this approach is the assumption that it will be easier to link genes to such endophenotypes because they are presumed to lie closer in the causal chain to the genes, such as basic affective processes.

Epigenetics

An exciting and promising avenue of research aims to understand how gene functions can be shaped by the environment. Processes that regulate gene functions operate by changing the amount, timing, or location of gene outputs. It is known that hormones, cellular factors, and some environmental mechanisms are capable of affecting gene expression. Evidence from research on the rearing environment in rats (Meaney, 2001; Meaney & Szyf, 2005) demonstrates that normal variations in mothers' caring of their pups, as well as more extreme variations (such as extended separations from the mother), are associated with behavioral differences in the pups, including aberrant stress reactivity and responses to novelty. These effects of the caregiving environment on pup behavior are believed to be mediated through changes in the expression of genes implicated in stress reactivity in the hypothalamic-pituitary-adrenal (HPA) axis (Caldji, Diorio, & Meaney, 2000). There has been great interest in these findings, given evidence that chronic overactivation of the HPA axis is an outcome of chronic stress, and may be implicated in depressive disorders (e.g., McEwen, 2003).

ANIMAL MODELS OF DEPRESSION

A more direct means of isolating the biological mechanisms implicated in depressive disorders is to use nonhuman animals whose biology can be more directly mapped and manipulated. An additional advantage of these models is that they allow for a more direct test of evolutionary models of these disorders (see Chapter 5). To the extent that depression-relevant behaviors are evident in lower species, it may allow us to determine when in our evolutionary past the systems responsible for generating depression may have emerged. For example, rats and mice have been utilized in a variety of paradigms to explore these biological mechanisms. In the forced swim task, rodents are placed in an escapable cylinder filled with water. Typically, rodents initially try to escape, then develop an immobile posture; these behavioral profiles exhibit individual variability across rodents, and the behavioral effects of this test can be reduced by antidepressants. This behavior has been termed *behavioral despair* (Porsolt, Bertin, & Jalfre, 1978). This model has some analogues to the evolutionary models of depression discussed in Chapter 5. The validity of these approaches relies upon the behavioral/phenotypic similarity between the signs exhibited by these animals and the depressive syndrome in humans, as well as the sensitivity of behavior in these paradigms to known biological treatments. Specifically, an ideal animal model of depression is defined by characteristics with face validity similar to human depression; and these characteristics can be reversed with antidepressant treatment in a manner similar to that observed in humans. (Of note, most animal models have focused on the latter, rather than the former, such that they are likely better models of antidepressant action than they are of depressive disorders' etiology.) Biological manipulations can be achieved by genetic modification, selective breeding, administration of pharmacologic agents that can impact brain activity, or direct lesion of brain regions. In general, compared to other psychopathologies (such as addictions and anxiety), defining behavioral outputs in rats and mice that are analogous to depression has proven very challenging, largely owing to the heterogeneous content of depressive symptoms and the fact that many important depressive symptoms (such as suicidality, guilt/worthlessness, and so on) have no analogue in other animals. Promising paradigms involve assessment of anhedonic behaviors, as indicated by social withdrawal, lack of energy (as operationalized by swimming, running, energy expenditure, and nesting behavior), cognitive deficits (on working or spatial-memory tasks), and learned helplessness tasks. A limitation to animal models is that most have been tested only on male animals, meaning they are not useful for testing models of the well-replicated gender difference in depressive disorders. Paradoxically, many of the mice and rat models of depression that involve exposing the animal to stressors have shown that female animals are actually less reactive to these manipulations than male animals (Cryan & Mombereau, 2004).

The classic animal model of depression derived from studies of dogs exposed to repeated, uncontrollable, inescapable shocks (Overmier & Seligman, 1967). Compared to dogs subjected to shocks that were controllable (they could be ended by pressing a lever), those exposed to uncontrollable shocks later did not learn to avoid escapable shocks. Instead, they behaved passively and did not try to escape the shocks, appearing "helpless." This model was later extended to both rats and mice, demonstrating that the behavioral effects could be countered by antidepressants. Importantly, not all animals develop learned helplessness in this paradigm, suggesting there are individual differences in systems governing responses to inescapable shock. Interestingly, the effects of this paradigm appear to be stronger in male mice than in female mice (Caldarone, George, Zachariou, & Picciotto, 2000).

Other animal models of depressive disorders focus on the putative etiological factors of depression, rather than on the behavioral outputs similar to depressive symptoms. For example, there are a number of paradigms that have been developed to simulate the effects of stress that may be important to the development of mood disorders such as chronic stress. A chronic mild stress model used with rodents involves exposing the animal to a series of unpredictable, but mild, stressors over an extended period of time (usually several weeks). The effects of this manipulation extend across a number of systems in the animal, including behavioral, neuroendocrine, neurochemical, and neuroimmune changes that are observed long after the stressors have ended. Two outputs seem quite relevant to depressive disorders. Animals exposed to this treatment are observed to have lower preference for and consumption of rewarding food (sucrose), and they exhibit decreased brain-reward functioning, both indicative of possible anhedonia. These effects are also reversed by treatment with antidepressants.

Animal models hold promise for helping to potentially identify endophenotypes of depression that could be useful targets for neuroscience or genetic approaches in humans. The elegance of animal models is in their ability to directly manipulate many variables that are impossible to manipulate (or sometimes, even to measure) in humans; however, these approaches are ultimately limited in that they can only provide models of those aspects of depressive syndromes that are readily recognizable in nonhuman animals.

CONCLUSIONS

All the major theoretical models of the etiology of depressive disorders invoke mechanisms that are instantiated in biological processes (including reactivity to emotionally salient stimuli and stress reactivity). Thus, it is critical that we fit empirical knowledge of depressive disorders and risk for these conditions within our broader understanding of human biology—including the operation of neural systems that enact our most basic human tendencies and skills, as well as the genes that create individual variation in these systems. However, it is important to note that psychological mechanisms are not reducible to the action of these biological properties. Showing that a psychological process correlates with, or even that it is mediated by, a particular biological process is illuminating and important; however, it should not be taken as the ultimate explanation of the psychological process any more than we should be seeking to replace references to neural processes with references to the variables of physics. Making advances in our scientific understanding of the etiology of depression will necessarily involve continued efforts to detail the causal processes occurring at the level of biology and the level of psychological mechanisms that emerge from (but are not reducible to) biological processes.

How Can Depressive Disorders Be Treated?

The ultimate aim of applied research on depressive disorders is to stimulate the development of treatments for these conditions and to evaluate their efficacy. The role of mental health care systems is to facilitate access to these treatments—including interventions focused on ameliorating symptoms and preventive approaches intended to forestall their development—among those who could benefit from them.

PRINCIPLES GUIDING TREATMENT

What are treatments for depressive disorders designed to treat? Most therapies take as their primary aim the reduction of the symptoms of the disorder in question (e.g., Major Depressive

Disorder [MDD], Dysthymic Disorder [DD], and Bipolar Disorder [BD]). Thus, one obvious indicator of a treatment's efficacy is the degree to which the symptoms the person experienced upon entering treatment has been alleviated (entirely or reduced to a tolerable level). However, as described in Chapter 4, the impact of these disorders extends beyond symptoms to include impairment in functioning across many life domains. Accordingly, most therapies are not limited to techniques for symptom reduction, but also include those that aim to reduce the impact of symptoms on functioning, or to improve functioning directly. Most (but not all) existing treatments have an implied theoretical model of the causes of depression. This model informs targets for treatment by pointing to the presumed mechanisms that are responsible for producing the symptoms or for maintaining them. Given the recurrent nature of depression, prevention of recurrences becomes an important outcome to demonstrate for any effective intervention targeting depressive disorders. Thus, therapy may often continue well after symptom reduction has been achieved and functioning is at baseline levels—with the emphasis being on monitoring risk processes and developing strategies for dealing effectively with circumstances and psychological processes that may increase risk for another episode.

How do we know if the existing treatments are effective? The answer depends upon the scope of the question—effective for the population of persons with the disorder or effective for a particular individual? Intervention research focuses on testing which interventions are successful at treating various clinical problems in the population. For conditions such as depressive disorders, they are evaluated by the magnitude of change in symptoms and functioning measures among patients who receive the intervention, compared to patients who are exposed to some contrast condition. The contrast condition can consist of no treatment (i.e., a wait list); a theoretically inert treatment (i.e., formal meetings with a provider that do not involve the delivery of any intervention technique known or suspected to have antidepressant effects); or another active treatment thought or known to be an effective intervention for the condition (the most rigorous test, this design provides evidence for the relative efficacy or superiority of one treatment over another). Finally, some designs can also be used to isolate particular techniques that are typically combined in an efficacious treatment in order to determine which techniques are responsible for its efficacy. Efficacious treatments are those that outperform the contrast condition in research trials, with greater evidence for efficacy indicated by passing more of these tests. Effectiveness is a different (but equally important) term that describes the ability of a therapy to achieve desirable outcomes as conducted in routine clinical practice (i.e., outside of formal research studies). Efficacy does not automatically imply effectiveness because the boundary conditions under which efficacy trials are conducted may not exist in real-world clinical settings, thus resulting in diminished effects. In practice, highly efficacious treatments do not produce benefits for all patients, even in highly controlled research studies. If one wants to demonstrate that a treatment is working for a particular patient, then a single-subject research design can be utilized in which repeated measures of the outcomes of interest (e.g., manic symptoms, sleep functioning) are assessed over the course of treatment, and changes in these measures are compared before and after treatment, or before and after the introduction of therapeutic techniques.

MODALITIES OF TREATMENT FOR DEPRESSION

Treatments for unipolar and bipolar depressive disorders take many forms—including psychotherapies (delivered to individuals or to individuals in the context of their important relationships, including couple, parent–child, and family therapy) and biological interventions (such as medicines and electroconvulsive therapy). Aside from targeting similar outcomes (i.e., symptoms, functioning), these therapies can vary considerably in terms of the form of their interventions, the aspects of the disorder they target, and the structure of the therapeutic contact with the treatment provider. Moreover, most are informed (at least loosely) by a theoretical model of the factors that cause and maintain the disorder; as a result, different interventions can take very diverse approaches to depressed or manic persons. Despite these implied differences, there is good reason to believe that effective treatments may actually share some common mechanisms that contribute to their effectiveness. It is also important to note that it is possible for an intervention to be effective even if the etiological model that informed its development is inaccurate. However, the hope is that by refining our understanding of etiology, we will be able to develop new interventions that do a better job of targeting the causal mechanisms that produce the disorder. Following are descriptions of several of the most commonly employed treatments, the evidence regarding their efficacy, and the possible mechanisms by which they achieve their effects.

PSYCHOTHERAPIES

Behavioral, Cognitive, and Cognitive-Behavioral Psychotherapies

Among the most studied and best validated psychotherapies for depressive disorders are those that use behavioral and cognitive techniques to target symptoms and maintaining factors in the depressive disorders. For unipolar depressive disorders, these approaches have strong and replicated evidence for their efficacy (Butler, Chapman, Forman, & Beck, 2006; Cuijpers, Van Straten, & Warmerdam, 2007; Reineke, Ryan, & DuBois, 1998). There is evidence that their efficacy is equivalent to that of antidepressant medications in terms of reducing acute symptoms—and perhaps in terms of demonstrating longer-lasting benefits in terms of symptom reduction than do medications (Hollon, Thase, & Markowitz, 2002). However, it is also important to note that a substantial percentage of those who receive these treatments do not recover or maintain their recovery (Westen & Morrison, 2001). Because their efficacy has been demonstrated for quite some time, these interventions have had the chance to penetrate into routine clinical practice, although surveys of psychotherapy providers indicate that they most commonly use psychodynamic or eclectic approaches consisting of techniques drawn from multiple therapeutic orientations, rather than cognitive-behavioral therapies (CBTs) (e.g., Weersing, Weisz, & Donenberg, 2002). However, there is growing evidence from data collected in community samples that CBTs are effective in these settings (e.g., Stiles, Barkham, Mellor-Clark, & Connel, 2008; Weersing et al., 2006). Evidence from child samples suggests that for those treated in the community using eclectic approaches, their level of beneficial response is similar to those observed in control conditions in research comparing control conditions to CBT (Weersing & Weisz, 2002).

Cognitive Therapy for Unipolar Depression

Interventions that emphasize the importance of cognitive mechanisms in the genesis and maintenance of depressive disorders work from an etiological model of these conditions that proposes depressive symptoms emerge from patterns of negativistic thinking that impede a person's ability to cope effectively with life challenges. In Beck's influential model (Beck et al., 1987), depressed persons and those prone to depression are described as engaging in unduly negative perceptions of their world, themselves, and their future, and negative interpretations of stimuli and events in their environment. These negativistic ways of thinking dominate the person's subjective experience, thus contributing to the maintenance and escalation of negative affect (including depressive symptoms). They also increase the likelihood that negative or even ambiguous events and stimuli will elicit a negative response, and they reduce the likelihood that positive events can elicit a decrease in negative mood or an increase in positive mood. Furthermore, these negative patterns of thinking and processing information result in patterns of behavior that do little to ameliorate conditions that may be generating or maintaining the depressive syndrome—in fact, they may even worsen these conditions. For example, people who ruminate about how unlikable they are to others will be less likely to reach out to friends and family, thus preventing them from accessing an important source of support that might improve their mood. In cognitive therapy, negative cognitions can be targeted at the level of specific cognitions or at the level of organized systems of beliefs and assumptions called *schemas* that are presumed to underlie the more specific cognitions. It is important to note that the traditional cognitive model of psychotherapy for depression focuses primarily on the *content* of individuals' cognitions, rather than the *mechanisms* of their cognitions. However, more recent developments in cognitive science and greater integration of findings from cognitive science into intervention research (see Chapter 4) have led clinical researchers to propose and develop novel interventions that target the mechanisms potentially underlying negative information processing. To illustrate, in cognitive bias modification, patients are taught to correct negative attentional and interpretive biases through computerized training in responses to negative and positive stimuli (e.g., Mathews & Mackintosh, 2000).

The primary presumed mechanism by which traditional cognitive therapy facilitates change in depressive symptoms is by correcting negative schemas and cognitions. This correction is achieved through a didactic and Socratic process wherein therapists help clients to recognize the presence and impact of their negative cognitions; to examine thoughtfully and then critically evaluate the validity of these cognitions; and to enact more positive cognitions that will help them cope more effectively with challenges in their lives. Therapy involves clients learning new skills from therapists that they can practice applying independently outside of the therapeutic sessions to counteract negative thoughts as they occur and to engage proactively in more positive ways of thinking. Therapy begins with exercises designed to uncover clients' particular patterns of negative beliefs and interpretations of themselves, their worlds, and the future. By drawing out these core beliefs and assumptions, therapists help patients to articulate more clearly and consciously the meaning they make of their lives and the world. Once these patterns are clearly and specifically articulated, clients and therapists can then begin to critically examine these cognitions. This process involves elucidating the evidence for and against these beliefs; generating alternative explanations or interpretations that could be offered for the situations described by the beliefs; and the consequences of the negative cognitions and their alternatives.

Cognitive techniques are intended to draw out the connection between patients' thoughts and feelings and their depressive symptoms. Clients and therapists work together to draw links between negative cognitions and the feelings and behaviors that result from them, and to evaluate the consequences and desirability of these feelings and behaviors. Finally, therapists encourage the clients to test out their beliefs and the alternatives generated in therapy by engaging in experiments designed to test these various beliefs. For example, a person with a schema that they will fail if they take on more difficult tasks at work will be encouraged to test out this belief by taking the behavioral risk of trying these new tasks.

In general, cognitive therapy is designed to be a short-term treatment that is primarily focused on the present (i.e., the here and now of a person's life). For uncomplicated cases, this might mean 10 to 20 sessions focused primarily on current problems and symptoms a person is facing. However, for clients who have more long-standing, rigid patterns of negativistic thinking (either because their depression is chronic or because they have personality characteristics associated with trait-like negative thinking), a short course of treatment may be insufficient.

Some cognitive therapy theorists have modified cognitive therapy to address these more severe cases, particularly those that serious personality difficulties and/or early home environment adversity hypothesized to produce more resistant patterns of negative schemas. Beck and colleagues (Beck, Freeman, & Davis, 2006) have described an elaborated version that includes an examination of the historical antecedents of clients' beliefs/meaning systems, as well as how these beliefs are made evident in their interactions with therapists. This is thought to be particularly useful when negative beliefs are so long-standing and entrenched that clients cannot easily generate alternative ways of thinking about themselves and the world. The aim of these interventions is to clarify for people how these beliefs, with their past origins, are operating in the here and now to maintain depressive symptoms.

Cognitive therapy fares well in comparison to minimal treatment controls and other psychotherapies (DeRubeis & Crits-Cristoph, 1998), and its efficacy is similar to that of medications (DeRubeis et al., 2005; Hollon et al., 1992; Jarrett et al., 1999; Murphy, Simons, Wetzel, & Lustman, 1984). There is also evidence that cognitive therapy may lead to changes that persist even after therapy has ended. Five studies have shown that those in cognitive therapy who achieve remission by the end of therapy are less likely to relapse than those who achieve remission when treated only with medications (Blackburn, Eunson, & Bishop, 1986; Evans et al., 1992; Hollon et al., 2005; Kovacs, Rush, Beck, & Hollon, 1981; Simons, Murphy, Levine, & Wetzel, 1986). Cognitive therapy's efficacy outpaces its effectiveness, which is true of any therapy. Evidence from treatment efficacy studies in which cognitive therapy was compared to another form of psychotherapy has shown that even knowledgeable therapists who learn cognitive therapy anew may have difficulty achieving the same outcomes as therapists who are experienced in the use of cognitive therapy and are more aligned with those groups that developed these techniques (Hollon & Dimidjian, 2009).

Behavioral Therapy for Unipolar Depression

Several psychotherapies are characterized by a greater emphasis on behavioral techniques than cognitive strategies. These
include problem-solving therapy and self-control therapy, as
well as approaches given the more general label of behavioral
therapy. In problem-solving therapy, therapists help clients to
clarify the problems in their lives in a specific way, and then
to generate a list of possible solutions to these problems and
select among them. The therapist and client develop a plan for
implementing the solution, the client enacts the plan, and then
the plan is evaluated as to how well it resolved the problem.
Although there are far fewer studies of this approach compared
to cognitive therapy, the evidence does suggest that it is efficacious (Mynors-Wallis, Gath, Day, & Baker, 2000; Nezu, 1986;
Nezu & Perri, 1989). This approach focuses more on behavioral solutions in that the emphasis is on patients' enactment
and monitoring of the effectiveness of new behaviors to address
their ongoing problems, rather than their interpretations of
those problems. In self-control therapy, patients learn to attend
to, monitor, and then evaluate their behaviors in a more positive
way, and to systematically reward themselves for meeting certain
standards (Rehm, 1977).

The most commonly employed behavioral treatment for
depression is Lewinsohn's Coping with Depression course
(CWD; Lewinsohn, Hoberman, Teri, & Hautzinger, 1985). It
involves clients developing a "toolbox" of skills, including
cognitive restructuring and social skills, meant to help cope
with and to replace depressive emotions and behaviors. It also
encompasses behavioral activation in the form of positive activity scheduling. The aim of these strategies is to increase clients'
feelings of self-efficacy for dealing with depression and situations in their lives they find aversive. Social skills are employed to
help the person develop more effective interpersonal behaviors
and to resolve interpersonal stressors; positive activity scheduling involves drawing up a list of pleasant activities and then

engaging in these behaviors in order to increase positive mood and to combat the withdrawal and amotivation that characterize depression.

It is important to note that cognitive and behavioral techniques are often integrated with one another—many cognitive therapies involve behavioral techniques and vice versa. There is growing evidence that the behavioral components of these well-studied interventions may in fact be critical for understanding their effects. An important study by Jacobson and colleagues (1996) dismantled a cognitive-behavioral package by comparing a condition in which patients received only the behavioral activation component—monitoring daily activities and the pleasure elicited by these activities; engaging in increasingly difficult tasks that might produce a sense of pleasure of mastery; rehearsing these activities to problem-solve potential obstacles to enacting them; and social skills training—to one in which they received full cognitive therapy (including behavioral activation techniques). The researchers found that the behavioral activation component alone was as equivalently effective as the full cognitive therapy package. Behavioral activation derives from Lewinsohn and Armenson's (1978) theories regarding the role of reinforcement in depression. Specifically, they propose that depression is generated and maintained by the subjective sense of being infrequently reinforced. They are maintained by the avoidance and withdrawal tendencies that result. The intervention attempts to change the person's avoidance and withdrawal by encouraging new ways of behaving that reengage the person with reinforcing experiences. Therapists and clients work together to develop assignments in which individuals will engage in experiences that require them to approach rewarding situations—in which they have a high likelihood of experiencing mastery and positive affect/pleasure. Thus, clients are encouraged to commit themselves to action, replacing avoidance behaviors with approach-oriented behaviors. There is now evidence that behavioral activation alone may be an effective psychotherapy for unipolar depression. For more severely depressed persons, it resulted in outcomes comparable to phar-macotherapy and outperformed cognitive therapy (Dimidgian et al., 2006). Other studies show behavioral activation may pre-vent relapse (Dobson et al., 2008).

Mindfulness-Based Cognitive Therapy for Unipolar Depression

This psychotherapy involves incorporating mindfulness tech-niques developed in the context of meditation practice within cognitive therapy. Mindfulness involves clients learning to observe—rather than engage with—their thoughts, with the aim of reducing the affective charge of the thoughts. There is prom-ising evidence suggesting that this approach may be efficacious for treating depression and reducing relapse (e.g., Ma & Teasdale, 2004; Teasdale et al., 2000).

Interpersonal Therapy (IPT) for Unipolar Depression

IPT was articulated by Klerman and Weissman in the 1980s (Klerman, Weissman, Rounsaville, & Chevron, 1984), although it was first developed in the 1970s as an offshoot of psychody-namically informed approaches that incorporated a present focus and structured approach from CBT. Its theoretical model emphasizes that regardless of their etiologies, all cases of depres-sion occur in interpersonal contexts that are influenced by and in turn influence depression. IPT consists of a first phase of psy-choeducation about depression and its symptoms, followed by a period in which the therapist and client explore the client's inter-personal life and then make connections between these contexts and the client's depressive symptoms. The interpersonal context can be characterized as fitting one of several foci identified in IPT as common elicitors of depression: complicated grief following the loss of a loved one, role transitions (challenges that accom-pany changes in one's relationship[s] or life circumstances), interpersonal conflict, or interpersonal deficits (often leading to social isolation). IPT has demonstrated efficacy for MDD (e.g., Cuijpers et al., 2011; Klerman et al., 1984).

Cognitive Behavioral Analysis System of Psychotherapy (CBASP)

CBASP was developed by James McCullough as a specific intervention for those with chronic forms of depression. It incorporates techniques from cognitive and behavioral approaches along with an understanding of the early home environment and early learning experiences that may have contributed to rigid, maladaptive patterns of thinking and behavior that characterize chronic depression. In McCullough's model (2003), chronic depression is seen as emerging from an inability to adequately perceive and interpret present circumstances in a realistic manner. Rather, patients are disconnected from the actual consequences of their behavior and therefore unable to achieve the outcomes they desire (e.g., better relationships, success). Techniques are included that specifically focus on addressing the lack of motivation for change that characterizes many chronically depressed persons. CBASP therapists set up contingencies in sessions that help patients learn the associations between their own behaviors and their negative affect and see how changing their behaviors will result in a decrease in negative affect. Techniques include situational analysis in which patients select a problematic interpersonal event from the recent past in order to describe it in the present tense in a highly specific way. Therapists help patients to describe the actual outcomes of situations (e.g., "my friend hung up on me") and patients' desired outcomes (e.g., "my friend invites me to hang out"), and to see how their own behaviors produced the discrepancy between the actual and desired outcomes. Problem solving is used to identify alternative behaviors that might achieve desired outcomes, with the goal being to help patients develop new patterns of behavior that result in getting more of the things they want in their lives.

CBASP is an effective form of psychotherapy, as demonstrated in multiple trials of patients with chronic depression, with benefits in reducing the acute symptoms of a depressive episode and in the prevention of recurrence. It also has demonstrated effectiveness among those who failed to improve on medication (e.g., Keller et al., 2000; Klein et al., 2004; Schatzberg et al., 2005).

COUPLE AND FAMILY TREATMENTS FOR UNIPOLAR DEPRESSIVE DISORDERS

Given replicated findings that depressive disorders are associated with significant difficulty in interpersonal functioning (see Chapter 4), including close relationships, it is possible that interventions targeting these domains might be an effective strategy for treating these conditions. Three studies have compared couple therapy (intervention with both partners addressing aspects of a couple's interpersonal interactions) to individual psychotherapy (such as cognitive therapy) for depression, with most focusing on depressed women. Evidence from these three studies (Beach & O'Leary, 1992; Emanuels-Zuurveen & Emmelkamp, 1996; Jacobson, Dobson, Fruzzetti, Schmaling, & Salusky, 1991) indicates that couple therapy and individual psychotherapy were equivalent in their effect on depressive symptoms, whereas couple therapy had a specific benefit in terms of improving patients' marital functioning. Findings from the first two studies showed that couple therapy was effective to the extent that it improved marital functioning because changes in depressive symptoms were driven by changes in marital functioning among those receiving couple treatment.

There is also evidence that treatments aimed at improving parenting can be effective for reducing depressive symptoms in parents. Interventions targeting parenting and parent–child interactions among parents of young children with behavior problems are associated with reductions in parents' depressive symptoms (e.g., Beach et al., 2008; Gallart & Matthey, 2005; Gelfand, Teti, Seiner, & Jameson, 1996; Hutchings, Lane, & Kelly, 2004). Moreover, there are data that reductions in depressive symptoms may be driven by the extent to which these interventions are successful at improving parents' efficacy and parenting abilities (Beach et al., 2008). By contrast, the evidence that parent–child interventions reduce depressive symptoms in youngsters is mixed at best (Restifo & Bogels, 2009).

PSYCHOTHERAPY FOR BIPOLAR DISORDER

Psychoeducation

Psychoeducation includes techniques to increase awareness and knowledge about the disorder and to encourage patients to maintain compliance with their ongoing treatment regimen (e.g., medication, psychotherapy). It may also include aspects such as stress management, understanding the negative impact of substance abuse on the disorder, promoting a regular lifestyle, coping with residual and/or subsyndromal symptoms, and dealing with the psychosocial consequences of previous and future episodes (e.g., Basco & Rush, 1996). There is evidence that psychoeducation employed in a group format can reduce relapse, recurrence, and hospitalization rates among those with BD (e.g., Colom et al., 2003).

Cognitive and Behavioral Psychotherapy for Bipolar Disorder

Traditionally, psychosocial interventions have been viewed as useful for maintenance (i.e., prevention of relapse; support for treatment adherence) in BD, not frontline treatments for acute manic episodes. However, there is growing evidence that psychotherapy may be helpful for treating acute episodes of depression among those with BD. Cognitive-behavioral treatments for BD are similar to those developed for MDD. Thus, they include behavioral activation components, techniques to modify dysfunctional thinking (particularly the excessively positive cognitions that typify manic episodes). They also incorporate monitoring of daily activities to reduce engagement in those that may be overstimulating (and thus increase risk for mania), and targeting cognitions that reduce likelihood of adhering to treatment recommendations. There is evidence that adding CBT to pharmacotherapy (compared to usual care) is effective for reducing relapse (Lam, Hayward, Watkins, Wright, & Sham, 2005), but these effects may be limited to those in the earlier phases of the disorder (Scott et al., 2006). In the Scott and colleagues' (2006) study, self-reports of hyperpositive thinking predicted higher risk of relapse, suggesting that therapeutic techniques addressing this cognitive style might be an important adjunct to other interventions.

Interpersonal Psychotherapy for Bipolar Disorder

Interpersonal and social rhythm therapy (IPSRT) is an extension of IPT originally developed for use with unipolar mood disorders. IPSRT for BD involves assisting clients with problem solving in their interpersonal contexts, clarifying their interpersonal issues, and enacting solutions to these issues. In addition to the traditional IPT foci of role conflicts, role transitions, grief, and interpersonal skills deficits, IPSRT adds a focus on dysregulation in social and circadian rhythms that may be particularly important for treating BD. This focus is based on work by Ehlers, Kupfer, Frank, and Monk (1993), who described the critical functions of social timekeepers (social zeitgebers) and social time disturbers (social zeitstorers). The former are thought to stabilize moods, whereas the latter do the opposite. For example, a spouse may help a patient to maintain healthy sleep patterns (a social zeitgeber); loss of this spouse may disrupt sleep, a known risk factor for the emergence of mania in those with BD (e.g., Leibenluft, Albert, Rosenthal, & Wehr, 1996). By contrast, some role changes (such as the arrival of a newborn) may introduce elements that disrupt social rhythms. There is evidence that social rhythm disruption may play a role in the onset of manic episodes but not depressive episodes (Malkoff-Schwartz et al., 1998). Thus, IPSRT aims to help patients reduce influences that disrupt their social and biological rhythms and strengthen those that stabilize these rhythms. One study showed that the addition of IPSRT to pharmacotherapy during the maintenance phase of treatment reduced time to relapse (Frank et al., 2005).

Family Therapy for Bipolar Disorder

Family-focused therapy, developed by Miklowitz (2004), is an intervention developed specifically to stabilize and prevent relapse among those with BD. Patients attend along with their immediate family members, which can include spouses, parents, or siblings. Elements of the treatment include psychoeducation about BD and its treatment, and training in problem solving and communication. In this treatment, therapists attempt to help family members understand the signs, symptoms, and impact of manic and depressive episodes, as well as the likelihood that patients will experience another episode of the disorder. They also learn how to identify the early signs of recurrences and to distinguish those from personality traits that may typify patients but not be an impending sign of a manic or depressive episode that necessitates intervention. Family members learn about the role that stressors can play in precipitating episodes, and how best to help patients cope with these stressors effectively. Techniques are employed to increase the likelihood that patients will adhere to medication regimens, and to shore up the protective role that family members may play in stabilizing the patients' functioning. Considering data from several studies, family-focused therapy reduces recurrence across 2 years by 35% to 40% (Miklowitz, 2009). There is some evidence that family-focused therapy may be particularly useful for those patients from families with high levels of expressed emotion (EE; see Chapter 8).

One large-scale study, the Systematic Treatment Enhancement Program for Bipolar Disorder (STEP-BD) study, was conducted to compare different psychosocial interventions for bipolar spectrum disorders. Patients who were experiencing a depressive episode were randomly assigned to one of three psychotherapies that were relatively intensive in their duration (9 months): cognitive-behavioral therapy, family-focused therapy, or interpersonal social rhythm therapy. All patients also received medications delivered according to best practices. These three groups were contrasted to a control condition called collaborative care in which the patients received three therapy sessions spread over 6 weeks during which they focused on developing a plan for addressing relapse prevention. All three treatments were associated with greater likelihood of recovery and a more rapid recovery from the index depressive episode compared to the collaborative care condition (Miklowitz, Otto, Frank, Reilly-Harrington, Wisniewski et al., 2007). Moreover, the intensive treatments were also associated with better functioning overall, as well as better relationship functioning (Miklowitz, Otto, Frank, Reilly-Harrington, Kogan et al., 2007). These data suggest that psychotherapy is a beneficial adjutant to psychopharmacology for bipolar spectrum disorders.

BIOLOGICAL TREATMENTS

Psychopharmacology for Unipolar Depressive Disorders

Medicines for unipolar depressive disorders come from several different drug classes (see Table 10.1). The first generation of medicines to be developed, the tricyclic antidepressants (TCAs)

TABLE 10.1 **ANTIDEPRESSANT MEDICINES**

Primary Neurotransmitter Target	Drug Class	Generic Name	Trade Name
Serotonin	SSRIs	Citalopram	Celexa
		Escitalopram	Lexapro
		Fluoxetine	Prozac
		Paroxetine	Paxil
		Fluvoxamine	Luvox
		Sertraline	Zoloft
Serotonin	Serotonin modulators	Nefazodone	Serzone
		Trazodone	Desyrel
Serotonin and norepinephrine	SNRIs	Venlafaxine	Effexor
Dopamine and norepinephrine		Bupropion	Wellbutrin
	MAOIs	Isocarboxazid	Marplan
		Phenelzine	Nardil
	TCAs	Amitriptyline	Elavil
		Clomipramine	Anafranil
		Imipramine	Tofranil

Note: MAOIs = monoamine oxidase inhibitors; SNRIs = serotonin and norepinephrine reuptake inhibitors; SSRIs = selective serotonin reuptake inhibitors; TCAs = tricyclic antidepressants.

and the monoamine oxidase inhibitors (MAOIs), are less routinely prescribed than medications from the three modern antidepressant drug classes: selective serotonin reuptake inhibitors (SSRIs); serotonin and norepinephrine reuptake inhibitors (SNRIs); and bupropion (a norepinephrine-dopamine reuptake inhibitor).

There is little empirical evidence to guide the clinical decision as to which of these medicines to try first, and only about one half of the time does the first medication result in an adequate response (Thase & Denko, 2008). Failure to respond to one medicine does not indicate that the person cannot have a response to a different medicine. Most psychopharmacologists begin with an SSRI because they are typically well tolerated and effective (e.g., Cipriani et al., 2009; Thase & Kupfer, 1996). One SNRI, venlafaxine (trade name Effexor), has also received considerable support for its efficacy, including evidence it may be more effective than certain SSRIs (Thase, Entsuah, & Rudolph, 2001). It is typically recommended that those who respond to a medication continue on that regimen for several months after remission because discontinuing in the first one half to three fourths of a year after remission doubles the chances for relapse (Geddes et al., 2003).

Psychopharmacology for Bipolar Disorder

There is supportive evidence for the use of several different kinds of psychoactive medicines for BD, including lithium, anticonvulsants, and atypical antipsychotic medicines. Currently, 11 medications from various classes (lithium, anticonvulsants, atypical antipsychotics, and antidepressants) have been approved for adult patients with BD. Fewer have been approved for youngsters with BD. Unfortunately, even the effective treatments leave much to be desired. In particular, existing treatments are ineffective for treating depressive episodes among those with BD. In a large study that involved patients across 22 different research sites, only one fourth of the patients taking optimal doses of mood-stabilizing medications recovered from their depressive episodes (Sachs et al., 2007). Given the remitting course of BDs (see Chapter 4), the need for flexible and multimodal treatments for these conditions has become increasingly evident. Treating depressive episodes among those with BD is complicated by evidence that administration of antidepressant medications to individuals with the disorder who are in the midst of a major depressive episode (MDE) may precipitate a "switch" to a manic episode or accelerate cycling between episodes. This is most problematic for those who have yet to experience a manic episode, and may be misdiagnosed as MDD rather than BD.

There are few findings that newer medications— anticonvulsants or atypical antipsychotics—are more effective than the traditional agent, lithium, which was the first effective medicine discovered for BD. Lithium is associated with remission of manic symptoms in approximately 60% to 70% of cases (Keck & McElroy, 2004). It is also effective at preventing relapses of manic episodes, but less so for depressive episodes (Geddes, Burgess, Hawton, Jamison, & Goodwin, 2004). Newer medications have similar results in that they are more effective for treating manic episodes than depressive episodes (Moller, Grunze, & Broich, 2006). Importantly, lithium use is also associated with a lower risk of suicide attempts or completions (Goodwin et al., 2003). However, newer medications generally have fewer side effects than lithium—this is important, given that many individuals with BD may discontinue their maintenance medication regimens because they find the side effects intolerable. Lithium is associated with feelings of sleepiness, gastrointestinal distress, weight gain, acne, tremors, hypothyroidism, and cognitive dulling. Currently, the first-line treatment for BD is generally the combination of an antidepressant along with a medicine from the mood-stabilizing class. However, the empirical evidence for the effectiveness of this strategy is mixed (Sachs et al., 2007).

Treatment adherence is a serious issue among those with BDs. Failure to adhere to recommended medications is quite high among those with these conditions, with estimates ranging from 50% to 65% (e.g., Sajatovic, Valenstein, Blow, Ganoczy, & Ignacio, 2006; Strakowski et al., 1998). There are known predictors of nonadherence, including younger ages, having more severe symptoms of the disorder, and the presence of comorbid substance or personality disorders (Colom et al., 2000).

OTHER BIOLOGICAL INTERVENTIONS

Electroconvulsive Therapy

Electroconvulsive therapy (ECT) is an intervention that has particular efficacy for those with severe depression that is nonresponsive to other interventions and for patients for whom medication may be contraindicated (older adults and pregnant women). ECT involves electrically inducing mild seizures while the patient is under anesthesia. Two meta-analyses found that ECT was more effective for the treatment of severe depression than placebo, simulated ECT, or antidepressants (Janicak et al., 1985; Pagnin, de Queiroz, Pini, & Cassano, 2004). The mechanisms by which ECT exerts antidepressant effects remain unknown. The use of ECT has long been controversial, with the most common (and serious) concerns focusing on memory impairments following the use of ECT. It is not unusual for patients to experience confusion immediately following treatment and some degree of memory loss for events in the weeks or months prior to treatment, with a smaller proportion reporting longer term effects on their memories (e.g., Rose, Fleischmann, Wykes, Leese, & Bindman, 2003; Squire & Slater, 1983).

Transcranial Magnetic Stimulation

Transcranial magnetic stimulation therapy (TMS) is a biological intervention that involves noninvasively inducing intracerebral currents in the brain in order to modulate activity across different cortical regions and their neural circuits. A magnetic pulse is delivered to the cerebral cortex by applying a stimulating coil to the head of the patient, resulting in an electrical current in the underlying brain tissue (Hallet, 2000). Modern applications of this approach often involve multiple applications during a single session. There is evidence from numerous studies that a round of daily application of TMS to the left prefrontal cortex is an effective treatment for depression (e.g., George et al., 2010; Holtzheimer, Russo, & Avery, 2001). One advantage of TMS over

241

other biological interventions, such as antidepressant medications or ECT, is that it may achieve symptom reduction in a shorter period of time (2 to 3 weeks vs. typically 6 to 8 weeks, or 3 to 4 weeks for medications or ECT, respectively).

TREATMENTS FOR SPECIAL POPULATIONS

There is far less evidence for making treatment decisions for youngsters with depressive disorders (both unipolar and bipolar). For bipolar spectrum disorders, there is evidence that lithium, atypical antipsychotics, and anticonvulsants may be effective for treating mania in adolescents. Treatment guidelines for adolescents (Kowatch et al., 2005) propose that clinicians should begin with a mood-stabilizing medication either alone or in combination with an atypical antipsychotic. If this approach leads to an insufficient response, a suggestion is to add a second mood stabilizer or atypical antipsychotic medication. For unipolar depression, a relatively small (in comparison to adults) literature suggests that medications, psychosocial treatments, and combinations of these two are effective for youngsters (Kaslow, Davis, & Smith, 2009). However, the degree of effectiveness appears to be lower for youngsters than for adults. For example, a meta-analysis of studies of psychotherapies for depression in youngsters showed that they have a small effect (Weisz, McCarty, & Valeri, 2006).

Prescriptions of antidepressant medications for depressive disorders in youngsters have increased greatly since the mid-1990s (Ma, Lee, & Stafford, 2005; Vitiello, Zuvekas, & Norquist, 2006). Clinical use of these medicines has largely outpaced evidence for their safety and efficacy. Although larger scale treatment studies have begun to be developed to test the safety and efficacy of these medications, the evidence base is much smaller than for adults and existing evidence suggests that conclusions drawn from studies of adults may not hold for youngsters. In general, newer classes of antidepressants, such as the SSRIs, are safer and more effective than the older classes of tricyclic antidepressants but still have only mixed evidence for their safety (Kaslow et al., 2009). In the late 2000s, there was increased focus on the possibility that SSRIs are associated with elevated risk of suicidality in youth. A task force of the American College of Neuropsychopharmacology issued a report (Mann et al., 2006) reviewing adverse effects of SSRIs on youth. They concluded that only one antidepressant could be considered efficacious for youngsters (Prozac), and that antidepressants are associated with a small increase in risk for suicidal ideation or attempts. The researchers argued that evidence is inconclusive regarding whether elevated suicidality is caused by antidepressants or is an artifact of the greater severity of depression evident among youngsters who receive such treatment. It is important to keep in mind that failure to treat depression among young people is also associated with some risk of negative outcomes, such that the risks and benefits associated with any treatment (including antidepressant medications) must be weighed against the risks and benefits of no treatment or alternative treatments.

Psychotherapies for depression in children and adolescents are not as well established as those for adults with these conditions, with far fewer specific therapies exhibiting sufficient evidence to be characterized as empirically supported—although there have been promising findings for particular packages, including many using behavioral and cognitive-behavioral techniques and theories. Much more evidence is available for adolescents, for whom the CWD package has been modified for use with teenagers (CWD-A; Clarke et al., 2002; Clarke, Rohde, Lewinsohn, Hops, & Seeley, 1999; Rohde, Clarke, Mace, Jorgensen, & Seeley, 2004). This approach has received support in several empirical studies (Clarke et al., 1995, 2002, 1999; Lewinsohn, Clarke, Rohde, Hops, & Seeley, 1996; Rohde et al., 2004). An interpersonally oriented approach adapted from IPT for adults has also received some support in two samples (Mufson et al., 2004; Mufson, Weissman, Moreau, & Garfinkel, 1999). Modifications to the traditional IPT focus include helping teenagers understand and cope with interpersonal challenges that are heightened during (or unique to) the adolescent period, including changes in the parent–child relationship associated with this developmental time.

The Treatment for Adolescents with Depression Study (TADS) (March et al., 2004) was designed to evaluate the relative effectiveness of CBT alone, Prozac alone, Prozac plus CBT, and placebo alone. In this 12-week study, 71% of the patients fell below the diagnostic cutoff for MDD at the end of treatment; 50% had residual symptoms; and 23% achieved remission. CBT was disappointing in that it did not outperform placebo. It was outperformed by Prozac; and the combination of Prozac plus CBT resulted in improvements over either alone only for youths whose depression was mild to moderate in severity (as opposed to those with the most severe initial levels of depression). However, on average, the combined treatment achieved the best results in terms of reducing clinician ratings of depressive symptoms and patients' reports of suicidal ideation. The latter finding is important because youths in the Prozac-alone group experienced twice as many suicidal events as those in the combined or CBT-alone groups. One other study also reported that the combination of CBT with an antidepressant was more effective than an antidepressant alone (Clarke et al., 2005); however, two other studies did not find an added benefit of incorporating CBT with an antidepressant (Goodyer et al., 2007; Melvin et al., 2006). Thus, the existing evidence indicates that we have much further to go in terms of developing effective interventions that can address the needs of depressed youngsters.

TREATMENT MATCHING AND PREDICTORS OF TREATMENT RESPONSE

Treatment efficacy would be enhanced if we were able to predict which of the various efficacious treatments for depressive disorders are likely to work best for particular patients. In fact, many treatments are developed with specific client characteristics or specific depressive phenomena in mind. Unfortunately, there is little evidence that certain types of patients respond better to particular forms of treatment. For example, some have argued that melancholic depression is associated with better response to medications than to psychotherapies, or that those with comorbid personality disorders may respond better to psychotherapy than to medications. In the NIMH (National Institute of Mental Health) Treatment of Depression Collaborative Research Program (Elkin et al., 1985), which compared interpersonal therapy, CBT, placebo, and antidepressant medications, predictors of response to the different arms of treatment did not necessarily map onto theoretical predictions. For example, surprisingly, *low* levels of social dysfunction predicted better response to IPT, and *low* cognitive dysfunction predicted better response to CBT.

Treatment responsivity does seem to be moderated by depressive severity, however. For example, drug response (i.e., the difference between antidepressant and placebo) is smaller in those with milder variants of MDD (Elkin et al., 1989), including minor depressive disorder (Ackerman & Williams, 2002), suggesting that watchful waiting (or even placebos) may be an effective strategy for addressing milder forms of depression. Larger drug effects are observed in severe, as opposed to moderate, depression (e.g., Khan, Brodhead, Kolts, & Brown, 2005). Finally, response to both medication and psychotherapy is lower in those with chronic as opposed to nonchronic depression (Hamilton & Dobson, 2002; Kocsis, 2003). Taken together, this evidence suggests that intervention research targeting more chronic and/or severe cases is critical for addressing the burden of depressive disorders in the population.

PREVENTION

Interventions can be described as addressing health and disease at one of four levels: treatment, maintenance, prevention, and promotion. Treatments are the focus of almost all intervention research and most intervention that occurs in the community; the focus of treatment is to reduce the total number of individuals who have the disorder. Treatment does so by targeting mechanisms that reduce the symptoms of the disorder. Maintenance treatments occur after treatment and are aimed at encouraging compliance with ongoing treatment or aftercare plans, and aim to reduce the number of individuals who experience relapses or recurrences of the disorder. Prevention efforts occur before the onset of a clinical episode, and are targeted at reducing the incidence of the disorder (i.e., the number of new cases of the disorder that onset). Prevention can be universal, selective, or indicated. Universal preventive interventions target the entire population; selective interventions target groups from the population sharing characteristics that mark those individuals as being at elevated risk for the disorder; and indicated preventions are delivered to those who already have early signs or symptoms of the disorder. Finally, promotion interventions are not designed to reduce the development of the disorder per se, but rather to encourage the development and expression of adaptive aspects of functioning thought to promote a more general sense of resilience. Thus, they may prevent the disorder but are not designed specifically to do so.

Prevention for depressive disorders is much less fully developed than is treatment science (as is true for most psychiatric disorders). There are particular challenges to prevention work that have hindered its progress, despite great interest in the potentially large societal benefits that could accrue given efficacious prevention strategies. First—because showing that a prevention works requires demonstrating that individuals in a prevention condition develop the disorder at a lower rate than those in the comparison condition over the observation period—it is necessary to enroll sufficient numbers of people who will develop the disorder over that period so that there are enough cases to compare across the two groups. The identification and enrollment of a truly high-risk group is thus essential to the enterprise. Ideally, the more valid the risk factor(s) (i.e., the more likely they are part of or closely linked to the actual causal processes implicated in the disorder), the more informative that sample will be. Much risk-factor research focuses on identifying which individuals will ever develop a depressive disorder. The factors uncovered using this approach will not be terribly useful if they do not also predict risk over a shorter time interval. Unfortunately, given the likely effect sizes of most preventive interventions, the sample sizes required are quite large, raising issues of cost and feasibility. Consistent with this low power, most studies of universal preventions have failed to show an effect on reduced incidence of depressive disorders (Munoz, Cuijpers, Smit, Barrera, & Leykin, 2010). Indicated preventions have a greater likelihood of showing an effect because more people will be expected to develop the disorder over the course of the study.

Evidence regarding the empirical basis for prevention approaches to depressive disorders is stronger in terms of showing that these programs do increase purported protective factors, such as social or problem-solving skills, but there is less evidence that they actually reduce the incidence of MDEs (Munoz et al., 2010). A meta-analysis of prevention studies of depressive disorders found that they reduced the risk of onset of new cases by 22%, in comparison to the control group (Cuijpers, Van Straten, Smit, Mihalopoulos, & Beekman, 2008). Several different types of therapy, including Lewinsohn's CWD course and IPT, have been shown to have preventive effects in at least one study.

Although prevention science is in its infancy, the relatively high prevalence of depressive disorders, our knowledge of risk factors for these conditions (including evidence that subthreshold symptoms are a good predictor of relatively imminent risk), and the existence of several empirically supported approaches for treating these conditions make it possible to use this knowledge in cost-effective ways to substantially reduce the societal burden of these conditions. Munoz and colleagues (2010) made several recommendations. First, public awareness of these disorders, their symptoms, means of dealing with subthreshold manifestations, and how to seek help when these efforts fail, should be increased through outreach and education efforts. Second, applying effective screening measures in settings (such as medical facilities) that already include some assessment may be helpful. Third, large-scale prevention efforts may be most beneficial if delivered to populations, such as adolescents, in which there is a high incidence of the disorders. Preventing first episodes may also be particularly important because of the chronic and recurrent nature of these conditions. Forestalling even the first onset may result in improved functioning and outcome among these individuals. Fourth, efforts should be directed at developing effective approaches for preventing relapse and recurrence. Fifth, more cost-effective strategies are needed that make less use of highly trained personnel time. Self-help interventions delivered via bibliotherapy or the Internet can penetrate the population much more readily and more cheaply than face-to-face interventions between a single client and a single therapist, or even group formats.

WHO RECEIVES TREATMENT?

Although we might be disappointed that efficacious treatments for unipolar and bipolar disorders do not guarantee improvement or maintenance of gains for all patients, an even more troubling fact is that many people with these conditions do not receive existing effective treatment for their symptoms. First, few of the empirically supported treatments are commonly deployed in the community. Second, the generalizability of treatment effects from more controlled research settings to treatment as it occurs in the community is unclear. Third, access to treatment is limited. For example, retrospective data comparing reported age of onset to reported age at first presentation for treatment for MDE indicate that the gap is commonly many years and often more than a decade in length (Olfson, Kessler, Berglund, & Lin, 2008). More recent cohorts seem to have shorter gaps, but early-onset cases tend to have longer gaps than late-onset cases (Kessler, Olfson, & Berglund, 1998; Olfson et al., 2008). This delay may be due to the fact that early-onset cases (in childhood or adolescence) occur among individuals who cannot present themselves for treatment. In the National Comorbidity Survey-Replication (NCS-R) sample, data showed that in 2001–2002, only about one half of people with a depressive disorder received treatment in the prior 12 months. This estimate is similar to those from European samples (Wittchen & Pittrow, 2002). Moreover, the NCS-R data indicate that when depression is treated in the community, the majority of cases receive substandard care. Thus, from a public health perspective we have far to go in terms of translating knowledge from clinical science into efforts that will help those who suffer from depression.

11

How Can We Integrate Our Knowledge of Depressive Disorders to Improve Our Understanding and Treatment of These Conditions?

s is hopefully clear from the preceding chapters, considerable progress has been made in describing depressive disorders across the life span—their impact on behavior and functioning; their relationship to broader psychological systems (such as cognition and personality); and identifying some of the processes within people and their environmental circumstances that may be involved in the etiologies of these disorders. The past 20 years have seen important advances in the measurement of stress and biological systems, as well as a more concerted effort to understand depressive disorders in their developmental context—all of which has generated much more sophisticated research questions and informed new research designs for illuminating the etiology of depression and mania. However, what we can say definitively about these disorders and their causes is still rather descriptive in nature—we know quite a lot about what correlates with depression and mania, but we are still far from being able to provide a mechanistic account of the processes that cause them. In addition, organizing even the correlational findings into a coherent framework can be challenging, given the wide variety of constructs that have been linked to depressive disorders and the various levels at which they may be measured and analyzed. The following is offered: (a) a summary of some of the important findings about depression that will likely be a critical part of any such framework; (b) notes on how we might think about connecting findings generated using different measures or levels of analysis; and (c) some directions for further research currently being explored by psychopathologists that may prove important for deepening our understanding of the causes of depression and mania.

THE KNOWNS

First, there is great variability in presentation of mood disorders. Some of this variability can be systematically explained by developmental factors and some may be influenced by personality traits or cultural factors. Nonetheless, not all of the variability evident is equally important to understand from a scientific perspective. Underlying the various symptom presentations that can occur across the many depressive disorders identified in the *Diagnostic and Statistical Manual of Mental Disorders, fifth edition (DSM-5)*

(American Psychiatric Association, 2013), or even across individuals who all meet diagnostic criteria for the same depressive disorder, are likely a smaller number of critical dimensions that reflect the action of important etiological factors. The two most obvious are chronicity and severity. Other dimensions that may prove important concern comorbidity with other psychiatric conditions (such as anxiety and substance use disorders) because these may indicate the action of broader etiological factors that contribute to multiple problems (not just depression). Certain symptoms may cluster together into meaningful dimensions, or particular kinds of impairment (e.g., in relationship functioning) may represent processes that cut across different diagnostic categories but share similar causes. Future progress in understanding depressive syndromes may in fact emerge from considering variations in these dimensions as the target for empirical research, rather than comparing different diagnostic groups or people with one diagnosis to control participants. This approach would be consistent with important evidence showing that subthreshold symptoms of depressive disorders have the same correlates as categorical diagnoses.

Second, depressive disorders are etiologically heterogeneous. Grouping individuals on the basis of their symptom presentation does not appear to be a successful strategy for identifying people who share the same etiological pathways. Refining constructs or dimensions of interest may be a better solution, as may be redirecting our target toward studying the putative etiological processes and their origins and outcomes themselves.

Third, although depressive disorders appear more continuously distributed in the population than is implied by the categorical model utilized in the *DSM*, the bulk of the burden of depressive disorders (in terms of suffering and cost) lies in a small group of people who are the most severely afflicted. Thus, there are practical reasons for identifying and studying these people. It may be the case that there are unique factors (or patterns of factors) that are important etiological agents for these people, but not for individuals with less-serious forms of depressive disorders. Thus, as much as research may advance by considering normal band dimensions of functioning, it must also consider emergent properties that can occur among those with very extreme levels of these dimensions.

Fourth, depression and mania are distinct on some dimensions but not on others. There are obviously causal factors that are unique to mania; however, the distinction between depressive episodes in unipolar and bipolar disorders and their causes is not currently well understood. More work that simultaneously considers predictors of both poles of depressive disorders will be important in this respect.

Fifth, depressive disorders vary in their prevalence as a function of age and gender, and their impact on functioning and outcome over time can vary according to these factors as well. Etiological models must offer an explanation of the causes of gender differences and the developmental forces that increase and decrease risk over time.

CONNECTING THE DOTS

A full consideration of depressive disorders requires theoretical models that incorporate both the broad views of these conditions—why they exist and why they manifest as they do; the basic psychological systems that give rise to their symptoms; how these systems may vary across people; and how these differences across individuals operate in the context of broader developmental processes and interact with aspects of the environment. There is no single study that could possibly address all of these pieces simultaneously. Moreover, there are many instances in which a rather narrow focus on a small set of possible etiological processes is absolutely crucial for providing a detailed account of the action of these processes and the nature of their association with depression or mania. When one considers all of the possible causal processes that have been linked to risk for depression (e.g., information-processing biases, stress reactivity, changes in neurotransmitter receptor density), the sheer breadth of factors and the very different ways in which they are measured produce a research literature in which some domains of study share very little overlap with others, although each is ostensibly trying to explain the same phenomena. However, there are a number of core ideas that come to the fore when one considers all of these disparate lines of research and which suggest a broad model for understanding the psychology of depression.

First, evolutionary models provide the basic context for understanding how human organisms are constructed in terms of their goals, capabilities, and means of processing and manipulating their environment. Our brains evolved in a social, biological, and environmental context to accomplish a small set of tasks—each highly complex—providing us with a general blueprint for behavior. These evolutionary pressures resulted in brain systems that incorporate motivation, cognition, and emotion to serve goals that were defined by our history as social animals; and, importantly, there are individual differences in the action of these brain systems, producing individual differences in core systems related to feeling, thinking, and doing.

Second, these individual differences partially explain why some people and not others are more likely to fall victim to depression or mania. Thus, the by-product of the variability generated through evolutionary processes is that some people are predisposed to experience maladaptive states of depression or mania. The origin of this variability is genetic in nature, and we may eventually be able to identify the variety of genes that contribute to this variability across people. Risk attributable to differences in the action of these core systems should be present very early in life, well before a person ever experiences symptoms of a depressive disorder. These traits can be assessed at the level of self-perceptions, but also by behavior and psychophysiological indices.

Third, depression and mania are often episodic and, even when chronic, wax and wane in their severity over time. Many people who are at elevated risk for these conditions never develop symptoms. Thus, aspects of our human context must play a role in when these conditions appear in the life span—likely due to maturation, the occurrence of events, and the challenges of particular developmental periods—and how they evolve. Environmental contexts may shape core psychological systems that give rise to symptoms, or individual differences in these systems may shape how people select and respond to their environments. In turn, the repercussions of manic and depressive episodes may profoundly alter a person's environment.

Fourth, all of the processes detailed here are filtered through the constraints of the brain, which mediates between our goals, feelings, and perceptions of the world and the behaviors we enact on the basis of that understanding. The brain also develops and changes over time as a result of maturation and the influence of events, relationships, and learning. However, even if we could offer a fully mechanistic account of the circuits and neurochemistry involved in the development of a manic or depressive episode, we could never fully understand these processes without also comprehending the psychological output of these brain systems—the thoughts, feelings, and behaviors that accompanied this transition and, more importantly, the narrative by which individuals apprehend their experiences. As we move closer and closer to understanding links between constructs defined at the psychological level (such as depressive disorders) and brain and biological measures, true progress results from concerted efforts to refine our understanding at multiple levels of analysis, such that biological mechanisms do not replace psychological mechanisms. Rather, we develop more sophisticated and precise descriptions of both that detail how they relate to one another.

MOVING FORWARD

The next decades of research on unipolar and bipolar mood disorders seem likely to focus much more explicitly on making connections across evidence derived from very different lines of research in order to provide more direct evidence for the mechanisms that underlie risk for and expression of depression and mania. For example, important achievements would be: understanding how a stressful experience is interpreted (cognitively); how this interpretation influences homeostatic physiological systems; and how these biological changes influence brain functioning and structure. Other research will detail the characteristics of people that put some, in the first place, at greater risk for experiencing stress. Basic psychological science focused on understanding brain mechanisms will likely generate many new hypotheses regarding the roles of different brain/cognitive/behavioral mechanisms in the origin and maintenance of depression and mania.

Some areas of research on depression will necessarily become increasingly technological and specialized (e.g., genomics). The challenge for psychopathologists will be to define the psychological and clinical constructs that are the most promising targets for exploration using these new technologies.

Finally, further research on the basic processes underlying depression and mania will potentially suggest new avenues for treatment. For example, psychological dimensions that underlie depression and can be linked to a brain mechanism/circuit may suggest novel medicines, therapeutic techniques, or behavioral strategies. Continued work on identifying those at highest risk will be critical for optimizing delivery of prevention and intervention services across the population; and rich descriptions of the interpersonal and psychological characteristics of depressive disorders will inform our attempts to connect with those who are suffering, to help them understand their circumstances, and to support and guide them as they recover.

References

Achenbach, T. M., & Howell, C. T. (1993). Are American children's problems getting worse? A 13-year comparison. *Journal of the American Academy of Child and Adolescent Psychiatry, 32*(6), 1145–1154.

Ackerman, R. T., & Williams, J. Q. (2002). Rational treatment choices for non-major depressions in primary care. *Journal of General Internal Medicine, 17*(4), 293–301.

Akiskal, H. S. (1983). The bipolar spectrum: New concepts in classification and diagnosis. In L. Grinspoon (Ed.), *Psychiatry update: The American Psychiatric Association annual review* (Vol. 2, pp. 271–292). Washington, DC: American Psychiatric Press.

Akiskal, H. S., Bourgeois, M. L., Angst, J., Post, R., Moller, H.-J., & Hirschfeld, R. (2000). Re-evaluating the prevalence of and diagnostic composition within the broad clinical spectrum of bipolar disorders. *Journal of Affective Disorders, 59*, S5–S30.

Akiskal, H. S., & Mallya, G. (1987). Criteria for the "soft" bipolar spectrum: Treatment implications. *Psychopharmacology Bulletin, 23*(1), 68–73.

Akiskal, H. S., Maser, J. D., Zeller, P. J., Endicott, J., Coryell, W., Keller, M., . . . Goodwin, F. K. (1995). Switching from "unipolar" to bipolar II: An 11-year prospective study of clinical and temperamental predictors in 559 patients. *Archives of General Psychiatry, 52*, 114–123.

Akiskal, H. S., & McKinney Jr, W. T. (1973). Depressive disorders: Toward a unified hypothesis. *Science, 182*(4107), 20–29.

Akiskal, H. S., Placidi, G. F., Maremmani, I., Signoretta, S., Liguori, A., Gervasi, R., . . . Puzantian, V. R. (1998). TEMPS-I: Delineating the most discriminant traits of the cyclothymic, depressive, hyperthymic and irritable temperaments in a nonpatient population. *Journal of Affective Disorders, 51*, 7–19.

Akiskal, H. S., Walker, P., Puzantian, V. R., King, D., Rosenthal, T. L., & Dranon, M. (1983). Bipolar outcome in the course of depressive illness: Phenomenologic, familial, and pharmacologic predictors. *Journal of Affective Disorders, 5*(2), 115–128.

Allen, N. B., & Badcock, P. B. (2003). The social risk hypothesis of depressed mood: Evolutionary, psychosocial, and neurobiological perspectives. *Psychological Bulletin, 129*(6), 887–913.

Allgood-Merton, B., Lewinsohn, P. M., & Hops, H. (1990). Sex differences and adolescent depression. *Journal of Abnormal Psychology, 99*, 55–63.

Alloy, L. B., & Abramson, L. Y. (1979). Judgment of contingency in depressed and nondepressed students: Sadder but wiser? *Journal of Experimental Psychology: General, 108*(4), 441.

Alloy, L. B., Abramson, L. Y., & Rusoff, R. (1981). Depression and the generation of complex hypotheses in the judgment of contingency. *Behavior Research and Therapy, 19*(1), 35–45.

Alpert, J. E., Fava, M., Uebelacker, L. A., Nierenberg, A. A., Pava, J. A., Worthington, J. R., & Rosenbaum, J. F. (1999). Patterns of axis I comorbidity in early-onset versus late-onset major depressive disorder. *Biological Psychiatry, 46*(2), 202–211.

American Psychiatric Association. (2000). *Diagnostic and statistical manual of mental disorders* (4th ed., text rev.). Washington, DC: Author.

American Psychiatric Association. (2013). *Diagnostic and statistical manual of mental disorders* (5th ed.). Washington, DC: Author.

Anderson, J. C., Williams, S., McGee, R., & Silva, P. (1987). DSM-III-R disorders in preadolescent children. *Archives of General Psychiatry, 44*, 69–76.

Anderson, J. R. (2011). A primatological perspective on death. *American Journal of Primatology, 73*(5), 410–414.

Andrade, L., Caraveo-Anduaga, J. J., Berglund, P., Bijl, R. V., deGraaf, R., Volleberg, W., ... Wittchen, H.-U. (2003). The epidemiology of major depressive episodes: Results from the International Consortium of Psychiatric Epidemiology (ICPE) surveys. *International Journal of Methods in Psychiatric Research, 12*(1), 3–21.

Angold, A., & Costello, E. J. (1993). Depressive comorbidity in children and adolescents: Empirical, theoretical, and methodological issues. *American Journal of Psychiatry, 150*, 1779–1791.

Angold, A., Costello, E. J., Erkanli, A., & Worthman, C. M. (1999). Pubertal change in hormone levels and depression in girls. *Psychological Medicine, 29*(5), 1043–1053.

Angold, A., Costello, E. J., & Worthman, C. M. (1998). Puberty and depression: The roles of age, pubertal status and pubertal timing. *Psychological Medicine, 28*(1), 51–61.

Angst, J. (1986). The course of major depression, atypical bipolar disorder, and bipolar disorder. In H. Hippius, G. L. Klerman, & N. Matussek (Eds.), *New results in depression research* (pp. 26–35). Berlin, Germany: Springer.

Angst, J. (1987). Switch from depression to mania, or from mania to depression. *Journal of Psychopharmacology, 1*, 13–19.

Angst, J. (1998). The emerging epidemiology of hypomania and bipolar II disorder. *Journal of Affective Disorders, 50*(2/3), 143–151.

Angst, J., Gamma, A., Sellaro, R., Zhang, H., & Merikangas, K. (2002). Toward validation of atypical depression in the community: Results of the Zurich cohort study. *Journal of Affective Disorders, 72*, 125–138.

Angst, J., & Preisig, M. (1995). Outcome of a clinical cohort of unipolar, bipolar and schizoaffective patients: Results of a prospective study from 1959 to 1985. *Schweizer Archiv fur Neurologie und Psychiatrie, 146*(1), 17–23.

Angst, J., & Sellaro, R. (2000). Historical perspectives and natural history of bipolar disorder. *Biological Psychiatry, 48*(6), 445–457.

Bagby, R. M., Bindseil, K. K, Schuller, D. R., Rector, N. A., Young, L. T., et al. (1997). Relationship between the five-factor model of personality and unipolar, bipolar and schizophrenic patients. *Psychiatry Research, 70*(2), 83–94.

Baldassano, C. F., Marangell, L. B., Gyulai, L., Ghaemi, S. N., Joffe, H., et al. (2005). Gender differences in bipolar disorder: Retrospective data from the first 500 STEP-BP participants. *Bipolar Disorders, 7*(5), 465–470.

Barrio, C. (2000). The cultural relevance of community support programs. *Psychiatric Services, 51*(7), 879–884.

Basco, M. R., & Rush, A. J. (1996). *Cognitive-behavioral therapy for bipolar disorder.* New York, NY: Guilford Press.

Basco, M. R., & Rush, A. J. (2005). *Cognitive-behavioral therapy for bipolar disorder.* New York, NY: Guilford Press.

Beach, S. R., Kogan, S. M., Brody, G. H., Chen, Y. F., Lei, M. K., & Murry, V. M. (2008). Change in caregiver depression as a function of the Strong African American Families Program. *Journal of Family Psychology, 22*(2), 241–252.

Beach, S. R., & O'Leary, K. (1992). Treating depression in the context of marital discord: Outcome and predictors of response of marital therapy versus cognitive therapy. *Behavior Therapy, 23*(4), 507–528.

Beck, A. T. (1987). Cognitive models of depression. *Journal of Cognitive Psychotherapy, 1*(1), 5–37.

Beck, A. T., Freeman, A., & Davis, P. D. D. (2006). *Cognitive therapy of personality disorders.* New York, NY: Guilford Press.

Beck, A. T., Rush, A. J., Shaw, B. F., & Emery, G. (1987). *Cognitive therapy of depression.* New York, NY: Guilford Press.

Bender, R. E., & Alloy, L. B. (2011). Life stress and kindling in bipolar disorder: Review of the evidence and integration with emerging biopsychosocial theories. *Clinical Psychology Review, 31*, 383–398.

Bhangoo, R., Dell, M. L., Towbin, K., Meyers, F. S., Lowe, C. L., Pine, D. S., & Leibenluft, E. (2003). Clinical correlates of episodicity in juvenile mania. *Journal of Child and Adolescent Psychopharmacology, 13*(4), 507–514.

Birmaher, B., Axelson, D., Strober, M., Gill, M. K., Valeri, S., et al. (2006). Clinical course of children and adolescents with bipolar spectrum disorders. *Archives of General Psychiatry, 63*(2), 175–183.

Birmaher, B., Ryan, N. D., Williamson, D. E., Brent, D. A., Kaufman, J., Dahl, R. W., . . . Nelson, B. (1996). Childhood and adolescent depression: A review of the past 10 years. Part I. *Journal of the American Academy of Child and Adolescent Psychiatry, 35*(11), 1427–1439.

Birnbaum, H. G., Leong, S. A., & Greenberg, P. E. (2003). The economics of women and depression: An employer's perspective. *Journal of Affective Disorders, 74*(1), 15–22.

Blackburn, I. M., Eunson, K. M., & Bishop, S. (1986). A two-year naturalistic follow-up of depressed patients treated with cognitive therapy, pharmacotherapy, and a combination of both. *Journal of Affective Disorders, 10*, 67–75.

Blair, M. J., Robinson, R. L., Katon, W., & Kroenke, K. (2003). Depression and pain comorbidity: A literature review. *Archives of Internal Medicine, 163*, 2433–2445.

Blazer, D. G., & Hybels, C. F. (2005). Origins of depression in later life. *Psychological Medicine, 35*, 1–12.

Blazer, D. G., Kessler, R. C., McGonagle, K. A., & Swartz, M. S. (1994). The prevalence and distribution of major depression in a national community sample: The National Comorbidity Survey. *American Journal of Psychiatry, 151,* 979–986.

Blonigen, D. M., Carlson, M. D., Hicks, B. M., Krueger, R. F., & Iacono, W. G. (2008). Stability and change in personality traits from late adolescence to early adulthood: A longitudinal twin study. *Journal of Personality, 76*(2), 229–266.

Bolger, N., & Schilling, E. A. (1991). Personality and the problems of everyday life: The role of neuroticism in exposure and reactivity to daily stressors. *Journal of Personality, 59*(3), 355–386.

Booker, J. M., & Hellekson, C. J. (1992). Prevalence of seasonal affective disorder in Alaska. *American Journal of Psychiatry, 149*(9), 1176–1182.

Bostwick, J. M., & Pankratz, V. S. (2000). Affective disorders and suicide risk: A reexamination. *American Journal of Psychiatry, 157*(12), 1925–1932.

Bremner, J. D., Narayan, M., Anderson, E. R., Staib, K. H., Miller, H. L., & Charney, D. S. (2000). Hippocampal volume reduction in major depression. *American Journal of Psychiatry, 157*(1), 115–118.

Brent, D., Oquendo, M., Birmaher, B., Greenhill, L., Kolko, K., et al. (2002). Familial pathways to early-onset suicide attempt: Risk for suicidal behavior in offspring of mood-disordered suicide attempters. *Archives of General Psychiatry, 59*(9), 801–807.

Brittlebank, A. D., Scott, J., Williams, J. M., & Ferrier, I. N. (1993). Autobiographical memory in depression: State or trait marker? *British Journal of Psychiatry, 162*(1), 118–121.

Brotman, M. A., Schmajuk, M., Rich, B. A., Dickstein, D. P., Guyer, A. E., Costello, E. J., . . . Leibenluft, E. (2006). Prevalence, clinical correlates, and longitudinal course of severe mood dysregulation in children. *Biological Psychiatry, 60,* 991–997.

Brown, G. W. (1993). Life events and affective disorder: Replications and limitations. *Psychosomatic Medicine, 55,* 248–259.

Brown, G. W., Bifulco, A., & Harris, T. O. (1987). Life events, vulnerability and onset of depression: Some refinements. *British Journal of Psychiatry, 150*(1), 30–42.

Brown, G. W., & Harris, T. (1978). Social origins of depression: A reply. *Psychological Medicine, 8*(4), 577–588.

Brown, G. W., Lemyre, L., & Bifulco, A. (1992). Social factors and recovery from anxiety and depressive disorders: A test of specificity. *British Journal of Psychiatry, 161*(1), 44–54.

Brown, G. W., & Moran, P. (1994). Clinical and psychosocial origins of chronic depressive episodes. I: A community survey. *British Journal of Psychiatry, 165*(4), 447–456.

Burke, K. C., Burke, J. D., Rae, D. S., & Regier, D. A. (1991). Comparing age of onset of major depression and other psychiatric disorders by birth cohorts in five U.S. community populations. *Archives of General Psychiatry, 48*(9), 789–795.

Burton, R. (2001). *The anatomy of melancholy* (New York Review Book Classics). J. Holbrook (Ed.). New York, NY: New York Review Books.

Buss, D. M., Haselton, M. G., Shackleford, T. K., Bleske, A. L., & Wakefield, J. C. (1998). Adaptations, exaptations, and spandrels. *American Psychologist, 53*(5), 533–548.

Butler, A. C., Chapman, J. E., Forman, E. M., & Beck, A. T. (2006). The empirical status of cognitive-behavioral therapy: A review of meta-analyses. *Clinical Psychology Review, 26*(1), 17–31.

Butzlaff, R. L., & Hooley, J. M. (1998). Expressed emotion and psychiatric relapse: A meta-analysis. *Archives of General Psychiatry, 55*(6), 547–552.

Caldarone, B. J., George, T. P., Zachariou, V., & Picciotto, M. R. (2000). Gender differences in learned helplessness behavior are influenced by genetic background. *Pharmacology, Biochemistry, and Behavior, 66*(4), 811–817.

Caldji, C., Diorio, J., & Meaney, M. J. (2000). Variations in maternal care in infancy regulate the development of stress reactivity. *Biological Psychiatry, 48*(12), 1164–1174.

Campbell, S., & MacQueen, G. (2004). The role of the hippocampus in the pathophysiology of major depression. *Journal of Psychiatry and Neuroscience, 29*(6), 417–426.

Cannon, W. B. (1929). Organization for physiological homeostasis. *Physiological Reviews, 9*, 399–431.

Cannon, W. B. (1932). *The wisdom of the body.* New York, NY: Norton.

Capaldi, D. M., & Stoolmiller, M. (1999). Co-occurrence of conduct problems and depressive symptoms in early adolescent boys: III. Prediction to young-adult adjustment. *Development and Psychopathology, 11*(1), 59–84.

Cardno, A. G., Marshall, E. J., Coid, B., Macdonald, A. M., Ribchester, T. R., Davies, N. J., . . . Murray, R. M. (1999). Heritability estimates for psychotic disorders: The Maudsley twin psychosis series. *Archives of General Psychiatry, 56*, 162–168.

Carlson, G. A. (2007). Who are the children with severe mood dysregulation, a.k.a., "rages"? *American Journal of Psychiatry, 164*, 1140–1142.

Carlson, G. A., Bromet, E. J., & Sievers, S. (2000). Phenomenology and outcome of subjects with early- and adult-onset psychotic mania. *American Journal of Psychiatry, 157*(2), 213–219.

Carlson, G. A., & Cantwell, D. P. (1980). Unmasking masked depression in children and adolescents. *American Journal of Psychiatry, 137*(4), 445–449.

Carstensen, L. L., & Mikels, J. A. (2005). At the intersection of emotion and cognition: Aging and the positivity effect. *Current Directions in Psychological Science, 14*(3), 117–121.

Carver, C. S., Johnson, S. L., & Joorman, J. (2008). Serotonergic function, two-mode models of self-regulation, and vulnerability to depression: What depression has in common with impulsive aggression. *Psychological Bulletin, 134*(6), 912–943.

Carver, C. S., & Miller, C. J. (2006). Relations of serotonin function to personality: Current views and a key methodological issue. *Psychiatry Research, 144*(1), 1–15.

Carver, C. S., & Scheier, M. F. (1990). Origins and functions of positive and negative affect: A control-process view. *Psychological Review, 97*(1), 19–35.

Caspi, A., Moffitt, T. E., Newman, D. L., & Silva, P. A. (1996). Behavioral observations at age 3 years predict adult psychiatric disorders: Longitudinal evidence from a birth cohort. *Archives of General Psychiatry, 53*(11), 1033–1039.

Caspi, A., Roberts, B. W., & Shiner, R. L. (2005). Personality development: Stability and change. *Annual Review of Psychology, 56*, 453–484.

Caspi, A., Sugden, K., Moffitt, T. E., Taylor, A., Craig, I. W., et al. (2003). Influence of life stress on depression: Moderation by a polymorphism in the 5-HTT gene. *Science, 301*(5631), 386–389.

Cassano, G. B., Rucci, P., Frank, E., Fagiolini, A., Dell'Osso, L., Shear, K., & Kupfer, D. J. (2004). The mood spectrum in unipolar and bipolar disorder: Arguments for a unitary approach. *American Journal of Psychiatry, 161*, 1264–1269.

Cavanagh, J. T., Carson, A. J., Sharpe, M., & Lowrie, S. M. (2003). Psychological autopsy studies on suicide: A systematic review. *Psychological Medicine, 33*, 395–405.

Champion, L. A., Goodall, G., & Rutter, M. (1995). Behavior problems in childhood and stressors in early adult life: I. A 20-year follow-up of London school children. *Psychological Medicine, 25*(2), 231–246.

Charles, S. T., Mather, M., & Carstensen, L. L. (2003). Aging and emotional memory: The forgettable nature of negative images for older adults. *Journal of Experimental Psychology: General, 132*(2), 310–324.

Chengappa, K. N. R., Kupfer, D. J., Frank, E., Houck, P. R., Grochocinski, V. J., Cluss, P. A., & Stapf, D. A. (2003). Relationship of birth cohort and early age of onset of illness in a bipolar disorder case registry. *American Journal of Psychiatry, 160*, 1636–1642.

Chentsova-Dutton, Y. E., & Tsai, J. L. (2009). In I. H. Gotlib & C. L. Hammens (Eds.), *Handbook of depression* (2nd ed., pp. 363–385). New York, NY: Guilford Press.

Cipriani, A., Furukawa, T. A., Salanti, G., Geddes, J. R., Higgins, J., Churchill, R., et al. (2009). Comparative efficacy and acceptability of 12 new-generation antidepressants: A multiple-treatments meta-analysis. *Lancet, 373*(9665), 746–758.

Clark, L. A. (2005). Temperament as a unifying basis for personality and psychopathology. *Journal of Abnormal Psychology, 114*(4), 505–521.

Clark, L. A., & Watson, D. (1991). Tripartite model of anxiety and depression: Psychometric evidence and taxonomic implications. *Journal of Abnormal Psychology, 100*(3), 316–336.

Clark, L. A., Watson, D., & Mineka, S. (1994). Temperament, personality, and the mood and anxiety disorders. *Journal of Abnormal Psychology, 103*, 103–116.

Clarke, G., Debar, L., Lynch, F., Powell, J., Gale, J., O'Connor, E., et al. (2005). A randomized effectiveness trial of brief cognitive-behavioral therapy for depressed adolescents receiving antidepressant medication. *Journal of the American Academy of Child & Adolescent Psychiatry, 44*(9), 888–898.

Clarke, G. N., Hawkins, W., Murphy, M., Sheeber, L. B., Lewinsohn, P. M., & Seeley, J. R. (1995). Targeted prevention of unipolar depressive disorder in an at-risk sample of high school adolescents: A randomized trial of a group cognitive intervention. *Journal of the American Academy of Child & Adolescent Psychiatry, 34*(3), 312–321.

Clarke, G. N., Hornbrook, M., Lynch, F., Polen, M., Gale, J., O'Connor, E., et al. (2002). Group cognitive-behavioral treatment for depressed adolescent offspring of depressed parents in a health maintenance organization. *Journal of the American Academy of Child & Adolescent Psychiatry, 41*(3), 305–313.

Clarke, G. N., Rohde, P., Lewinsohn, P. M., Hops, H., & Seeley, J. R. (1999). Cognitive-behavioral treatment of adolescent depression: Efficacy of acute group treatment and booster sessions. *Journal of the American Academy of Child & Adolescent Psychiatry, 38*(3), 272–279.

Cole, D. A., Peeke, L. G., Martin, J. M., Truglio, R., & Seroczynski, A. D. (1998). A longitudinal look at the relation between depression and anxiety in children and adolescents. *Journal of Consulting and Clinical Psychology, 66*(3), 451–460.

Colom, F., Vieta, E., Martinez-Aran, A., Reinares, M., Benabarre, A., & Casto, C. (2000). Clinical features associated with treatment noncompliance in euthymic bipolar patients. *Journal of Clinical Psychiatry, 61,* 549–555.

Colom, F, Vieta, E., Martinez-Aran, A., Reinares, M., Goikolea, J. M., et al. (2003). A randomized trial on the efficacy of group psychoeducation in the prophylaxis of recurrences in bipolar patients whose disease is in remission. *Archives of General Psychiatry, 60*(4), 402–407.

Compas, B. E., Connor-Smith, J., & Jaser, S. S. (2004). Temperament, stress reactivity, and coping: Implications for depression in childhood and adolescence. *Journal of Clinical Child and Adolescent Psychology, 33*(1), 21–31.

Compton, W. S., Conway, K. P., Stinson, F. S., & Grant, B. F. (2006). Changes in the prevalence of major depression and comorbid substance use disorders in the United States between 1991–1992 and 2001–2002. *American Journal of Psychiatry, 163,* 2141–2147.

Copeland, W. E., Shanahan, L., Costello, E. J., & Angold, A. (2009). Childhood and adolescent psychiatric disorders as predictors of young adult disorders. *Archives of General Psychiatry, 66*(7), 764–772.

Coryell, W., Endicott, J., & Keller, M. B. (1990). Outcomes of patients with chronic affective disorder: A five-year follow-up. *American Journal of Psychiatry, 147*(12), 1627–1633.

Coryell, W., & Tsuang, M. T. (1985). Major depression with mood-congruent or mood-incongruent psychotic features: Outcome after 40 years. *American Journal of Psychiatry, 142*(4), 479–482.

Coryell, W., Winokur, G., Shea, T., Maser, J. D., Endicott, J., & Akiskal, H. S. (1994). The long-term stability of depressive subtypes. *American Journal of Psychiatry, 151*(2), 199–204.

Costa, P. T., Terracciano, A., & McCrae, R. R. (2001). Gender differences in personality traits across cultures: Robust and surprising findings. *Journal of Personality and Social Psychology, 81*(2), 322–331.

Costello, E. J., Erklani, A., & Angold, A. (2006). Is there an epidemic of child or adolescent depression? *Journal of Child Psychology and Psychiatry, 47*(12), 1263–1271.

Costello, E. J., Erklani, A., Fairbank, J. A., & Angold, A. (2002). The prevalence of potentially traumatic events in childhood and adolescence. *Journal of Traumatic Stress, 15*(2), 99–112.

Cousins, D. A., Butts, K., & Young, A. H. (2009). The role of dopamine in bipolar disorder. *Bipolar Disorders, 11*, 787–806.

Coyne, J. C. (1976). Depression and the response of others. *Journal of Abnormal Psychology, 85*, 186–193.

Cryan, J. F., & Mombereau, C. (2004). In search of a depressed mouse: Utility of models for studying depression-related behavior in genetically modified mice. *Molecular Psychiatry, 9*, 326–357.

Cuellar, A. K., Johnson, S. L., & Winters, R. (2005). Distinctions between bipolar and unipolar depression. *Clinical Psychology Review, 25*, 307–339.

Cuijpers, P., Geraedts, A. S., Van Oppen, P., Andersson, G., Markowitz, J. C., & Van Straten, A. (2011). Interpersonal psychotherapy for depression: A meta-analysis. *American Journal of Psychiatry, 168*(6), 581–592.

Cuijpers, P., Van Straten, A., Smit, F., Mihalopoulos, C., & Beekman, A. (2008). Preventing the onset of depressive disorders: A meta-analytic review of psychological interventions. *American Journal of Psychiatry, 165*(10), 1272–1280.

Cuijpers, P., Van Straten, A., & Warmerdam, L. (2007). Behavioral activation treatments of depression: A meta-analysis. *Clinical Psychology Review, 27*(3), 318–326.

Cutler, S. E., & Nolen-Hoeksema, S. (1991). Accounting for sex differences in depression through female victimization: Childhood sexual abuse. *Sex Roles, 24*(7/8), 425–439.

Cyranowski, J. M., Frank, E., & Shear, M. K. (2000). Adolescent onset of the gender difference in lifetime rates of major depression: A theoretical model. *Archives of General Psychiatry, 57*(1), 21–27.

Dalgleish, T., Spinks, H., Yiend, J., & Kuyken, W. (2001). Autobiographical memory style in seasonal affective disorder and its relationship to future symptom remission. *Journal of Abnormal Psychology, 110*, 335–340.

Davidson, K. W., Burg, M. M., Kronish, I. M., Shimbo, D., Dettenborn, L., Mehran, R., et al. (2010). Association of anhedonia with recurrent major adverse cardiac events and mortality 1 year after acute coronary syndrome. *Archives of General Psychiatry, 67*(5), 480–488.

Davila, J. (2001). Refining the association between excessive reassurance seeking and depressive symptoms: The role of related interpersonal constructs. *Journal of Social and Clinical Psychology, 20*(4), 538–559.

Davila, J., Bradbury, T. N., Cohen, C. L., & Tochluk, S. (1997). Marital functioning and depressive symptoms: Evidence for a stress generation model. *Journal of Personality and Social Psychology, 73*, 849–861.

Davila, J., Karney, B. R., Hall, T. W., & Bradbury, T. N. (2003). Depressive symptoms and marital satisfaction: Within-subject associations and the moderating effects of gender and neuroticism. *Journal of Family Psychology, 17*(4), 557–570.

Davila, J., Stroud, C. B., & Starr, L. R. (2009). Depression in couples and families. In I. H. Gotlib & C. L. Hammen (Eds.), *Handbook of depression* (Vol 2., pp. 467–491). New York, NY: Guilford Press.

Davis, M. (1998). Are different parts of the extended amygdala involved in fear versus anxiety? *Biological Psychiatry, 44*(12), 1239–1247.

Davis, M. C., Matthews, K. A., & Twamley, E. W. (1999). Is life more difficult on Mars or Venus? A meta-analytic review of sex differences in major and minor life events. *Annals of Behavioral Medicine, 21*(1), 83–97.

Depue, R. A., & Iacono, W. G. (1989). Neurobehavioral aspects of affective disorders. *Annual Review of Psychology, 40*(1), 457–492.

Depue, R. A., & Monroe, S. M. (1978). The unipolar-bipolar distinction in the depressive disorders. *Psychological Bulletin, 85*(5), 1001–1029.

DeRoma, V. M., Leach, J. B., & Leverett, J. P. (2009). The relationship between depression and college academic performance. *College Student Journal, 43*(2), 325–334.

DeRubeis, R. J., & Crits-Cristoph, P. (1998). Empirically supported individual and group psychological treatments for adult mental disorders. *Journal of Consulting and Clinical Psychology, 66*(1), 37–52.

DeRubeis, R. J., Hollon, S. D., Amsterdam, J. D., Shelton, R. C., Young, P. R., Salomon, R. M., et al. (2005). Cognitive therapy vs medications in the treatment of moderate to severe depression. *Archives of General Psychiatry, 62*(4), 409–416.

Diener, E., & Suh, E. M. (2000). *Culture and subjective well-being.* New York, NY: MIT Press.

Dienes, K. A., Hammen, C., Henry, R. M., Cohen, A. N., & Daley, S. E. (2006). The stress sensitization hypothesis: Understanding the course of bipolar disorder. *Journal of Affective Disorders, 95,* 43–49.

Dimidjian, S., Hollon, S. D., Dobson, K. S., Schmaling, K. B., Kohlenberg, R. J., Addis, M. E., et al. (2006). Randomized trial of behavioral activation, cognitive therapy, and antidepressant medication in the acute treatment of adults with major depression. *Journal of Consulting and Clinical Psychology, 74*(4), 658–670.

Dobson, K. S., Hollon, S. D., Dimidjian, S., Schmaling, K. B., Kohlenberg, R. J., Gallop, R., et al. (2008). Randomized trial of behavioral activation, cognitive therapy, and antidepressant medication in the prevention of relapse and recurrence in major depression. *Journal of Consulting and Clinical Psychology, 76*(3), 468–477.

Donohue, J. M., & Pincus, H. A. (2007). Reducing the social burden of depression: A review of economic costs, quality of care and effects of treatment. *Pharmacoeconomics, 25*(1), 7–24.

Downey, G., & Coyne, J. C. (1990). Children of depressed parents: An integrative review. *Psychological Bulletin, 108*(1), 50–76.

Drevets, W. C., & Price, J. L. (2005). Neuroimaging and neuropathological studies of mood disorders. In J. W. M. Licinio (Ed.), *Biology of depression: From novel insights to therapeutic strategies* (pp. 427–466). Weinheim, Germany: Wiley-VCH Verlag GmbH.

Drevets, W. C., & Raichle, M. E. (1992). Neuroanatomical circuits in depression: Implications for treatment mechanisms. *Psychopharmacology Bulletin, 28*(3), 261.

Drevets, W. C., Savitz, J., & Trimble, M. (2008). The subgenual anterior cingulate cortex in mood disorders. *CNS Spectrums, 13*(8), 663.

Druss, B. G., Schlesinger, M., & Allen, H. M. (2001). Depressive symptoms, satisfaction with health care, and 2-year work outcomes in an employed population. *American Journal of Psychiatry, 158*(5), 731–734.

Duggan, C. F., Sham, P., Lee, A. S., & Murray, R. M. (1991). Does recurrent depression lead to a change in neuroticism? *Psychological Medicine, 21,* 985–990.

Duncan, L. E., & Keller, M. C. (2011). A critical review of the first 10 years of candidate gene-by-environment interaction research in psychiatry. *American Journal of Psychiatry, 168,* 1041–1049.

Dunlop, B. Q., & Nemeroff, C. B. (2007). The role of dopamine in the patho-physiology of depression. *Archives of General Psychiatry, 64*, 327–337.

Durbin, C. E., Hicks, B. M., Blonigen, D. M., Johnson, W., Iacono, W. G., & McGue, M. (under review). *Personality trait change across late childhood to young adulthood: Evidence for nonlinearity and sex differences in change.*

Eaton, W. W., Anthony, J. C., Gallo, J. J., et al. (1997). Natural history of Diagnostic Interview Schedule/DSM-IV major depression. The Baltimore Epidemiologic Catchment Area follow-up. *Archives of General Psychiatry, 54*, 993–999.

Eaton, W. W., Shao, H., Nestadt, G., Lee, B. H., Bienvenu, J., & Zandi, P. (2008). Population-based study of first onset and chronicity in major depressive disorder. *Archives of General Psychiatry, 65*(5), 513–520.

Egger, H. L., & Angold, A. (2006). Common emotional and behavioral disorders in preschool children: Presentation, nosology, and epidemiology. *Journal of Child Psychology and Psychiatry, 47*, 313–337.

Ehlers, C. L., Kupfer, D. J., Frank, E., & Monk, T. H. (1993). Biological rhythms and depression: The role of zeitgebers and zeitstorers. *Depression, 1*(6), 285–293.

Eid, M., & Diener, E. (2001). Norms for experiencing emotions in different cultures: Inter- and intranational differences. *Journal of Personality and Social Psychology, 81*(5), 869–885.

Elkin, I., Parloff, M., Hadley, S., et al. (1985). The National Institute of Mental Health Treatment of Depression Collaborative Research Program: Background and research plan. *Archives of General Psychiatry, 42*, 305–316.

Elkin, I., Shea, M. T., Watkins, J. T., et al. (1989). The National Institute of Mental Health Treatment of Depression Collaborative Research Program: General effectiveness of treatments. *Archives of General Psychiatry, 46*(11), 971–982.

Ellis, H. C., & Ashbrook, P. W. (1988). Resource allocation model of the effects of depressed mood states on memory. In K. Fiedler & J. Forgas (Eds.), *Affect, cognition, and social behavior* (pp. 25–42). Toronto, Canada: Hogrefe.

Else-Quest, N. M., Hyde, J. S., Goldsmith, H. H., & VanHulle, C. A. (2006). Gender differences in temperament: A meta-analysis. *Psychological Bulletin, 132*(1), 33–72.

Emanuels-Zuurveen, L., & Emmelkamp, P. M. (1996). Individual behavioural-cognitive therapy v. marital therapy for depression in maritally distressed couples. *British Journal of Psychiatry, 169*(2), 181–188.

Ernst, C., & Angst, J. (1995). Depression in old age. *European Archives of Psychiatry and Clinical Neuroscience, 245*(6), 272–287.

Ernst, C. L., & Goldberg, J. F. (2004). Clinical features related to age of onset in bipolar disorder. *Journal of Affective Disorders, 82*(1), 21–27.

Essau, C. A., Lewinsohn, P. M., Seeley, J. R., & Sasagawa, S. (2010). Gender differences in the developmental course of depression. *Journal of Affective Disorders, 127,* 185–190.

Evans, M. D., Hollon, S. D., DeRubeis, R. J., Piasecki, J. M., Grove, W. M., Garvey, M. J., & Tuason, V. B. (1992). Differential relapse following cognitive therapy and pharmacotherapy for depression. *Archives of General Psychiatry, 49*(10), 802–808.

Fanous, A., Gardner, C. O., Prescott, C. A., Cancro, R., & Kendler, K. S. (2002). Neuroticism, major depression and gender: A population-based twin study. *Psychological Medicine, 32*(4), 719–728.

Fanous, A. H., Neale, M. C., Aggen, S. H., & Kendler, K. S. (2007). A longitudinal study of personality and major depression in a population-based sample of male twins. *Psychological Medicine, 37,* 1163–1172.

Fergusson, D. M., Boden, J. M., & Horwood, J. (2009). Tests of causal links between alcohol abuse or dependence and major depression. *Archives of General Psychiatry, 66*(3), 260–266.

Fergusson, D. M., Horwood, J., Ridder, E. M., & Beautrais, A. L. (2005). Subthreshold depression in adolescence and mental health outcomes in adulthood. *Archives of General Psychiatry, 62*(1), 66–72.

Fincham, F. D., Beach, S. R., Harold, G. T., & Osborne, L. N. (1997). Marital satisfaction and depression: Different causal relationships for men and women? *Psychological Science, 8*(5), 351–356.

Finkelhor, D., & Baron, L. (1986). Risk factors for child sexual abuse. *Journal of Interpersonal Violence, 1*(1), 43–71.

Fombonne, E. (1994). Increased rates of depression: Update of epidemiological findings and analytical problems. *Acta Psychiatrica Scandinavica, 90,* 144–156.

Frank, E., Kupfer, D. J., Thase, M. E., Mallinger, A. G., Swartz, H. A., Fagiolini, A. M., . . . Monk, T. (2005). Two-year outcomes for interpersonal and social rhythm therapy in individuals with bipolar I disorder. *Archives of General Psychiatry, 62*(9), 996.

Fredrickson, B. L. (2001). The role of positive emotions in positive psychology: The broaden-and-build theory of positive emotions. *The American Psychologist, 56*(3), 218–226.

Frodl, T. S., Koutsouleris, N., Bottlender, R., Born, C., Jager, M., Scupin, I., . . . Meisenzahl, E. M. (2008). Depression-related variation in brain morphology over 3 years. *Archives of General Psychiatry, 65*(10), 1156–1165.

Furman, W. (2002). The emerging field of adolescent romantic relationships. *Current Directions in Psychological Science, 11*(5), 177–180.

Gallart, S. C., & Matthey, S. (2005). The effectiveness of Group Triple P and the impact of the four telephone contacts. *Behavior Change, 22*(2), 71–80.

Garno, J. L., Goldberg, J. R., Hamen, P. M., & Hitzler, B. A. (2005). Impact of childhood abuse on the clinical course of bipolar disorder. *British Journal of Psychiatry, 186*(2), 121–125.

Gartstein, M. A., & Rothbart, M. K. (2003). Studying infant temperament via the Revised Infant Behavior Questionnaire. *Infant Behavior and Development, 26*(1), 64–86.

Gavin, N. I., Gaynes, B. N., Lohr, K. N., Meltzer-Brody, S., Gartlehner, G., & Swinson, T. (2005). Perinatal depression: A systematic review of prevalence and incidence. *Obstetrics & Gynecology, 106*(5), 1071–1083.

Ge, X., Conger, R. D., & Elder, G. H. (1996). Coming of age too early: Pubertal influences on girls' vulnerability to psychological distress. *Child Development, 67*(6), 3386–3400.

Geddes, J. R., Burgess, S., Hawton, K., Jamison, K., & Goodwin, G. M. (2004). Long-term lithium therapy for bipolar disorder: Systematic review and meta-analysis of randomized controlled trials. *American Journal of Psychiatry, 161*(2), 217–222.

Geddes, J. R., Carney, S. M., Davies, C., Furukawa, T. A., Kupfer, D. J., Frank, E., & Goodwin, G. M. (2003). Relapse prevention with antidepressant drug treatment in depressive disorders: A systematic review. *Lancet, 361*(9358), 653–661.

Gelfand, D. M., Teti, D. M., Seiner, S. A., & Jameson, P. B. (1996). Helping mothers fight depression: Evaluation of a home-based intervention program for depressed mothers and their infants. *Journal of Clinical Child Psychology, 25*(4), 406–422.

Geller, B., & Luby, J. (1997). Child and adolescent bipolar disorder: A review of the past 10 years. *Journal of the American Academy of Child and Adolescent Psychiatry, 36*(9), 1168–1176.

Geller, B., Tillman, R., Bolhofner, K., & Zimmerman, B. (2008). Child bipolar I disorder: Prospective continuity with adult bipolar I disorder; characteristics of second and third episodes; predictors of 8-year outcome. *Archives of General Psychiatry, 65*(10), 1125–1133.

Geller, B., Tillman, R., Craney, J. L., & Bolhofner, K. (2004). Four-year prospective outcome: A natural history of mania in children with a prepubertal and early adolescent bipolar disorder phenotype. *Archives of General Psychiatry, 61*(5), 459–467.

George, M. S., Lisanby, S. H., Avery, D., McDonald, W. M., Durkalski, C., Pavlicova, M., . . . Sackheim, H. A. (2010). Daily left prefrontal transcranial magnetic stimulation therapy for major depressive disorder. *Archives of General Psychiatry, 67*(5), 507–516.

Gershon, E. S., Alliey-Rodriguez, N., & Liu, C. (2011). After GWAS: Searching for genetic risk for schizophrenia and bipolar disorder. *American Journal of Psychiatry, 168*, 253–256.

Gershon, E. S., Hamovit, J. H., Gurhoff, J. J., & Nurnberger, J. I. (1987). Birth-cohort changes in manic and depressive disorders in relatives of bipolar and schizoaffective patients. *Archives of General Psychiatry, 44*(4), 314–319.

Giesler, R. B., Josephs, R. A., & Swann, W. B. (1996). Self-verification in clinical depression: The desire for negative evaluation. *Journal of Abnormal Psychology, 105*, 358–368.

Gilliom, M., & Shaw, D. S. (2004). Codevelopment of externalizing and internalizing problems in early childhood. *Development and Psychopathology, 16*, 313–333.

Gilman, S. E., Breslau, J., Trinh, N.-H., Fava, M., Murphy, J. M., & Smoller, J. W. (2012). Bereavement and the diagnosis of major depressive episode in the National Epidemiologic Survey on Alcohol and Related Conditions. *Journal of Clinical Psychiatry, 73*(2), 208–215.

Gilman, S. E., Kawachi, I., Fitzmaurice, G. M., & Buka, S. L. (2003). Socio-economic status, family disruption and residential stability in childhood: Relation to onset, recurrence and remission of major depression. *Psychological Medicine, 33*, 1341–1355.

Gjone, H., & Stevenson, J. (1997). A longitudinal twin study of temperament and behavior problems: Common genetic or environmental influences? *Journal of the American Academy of Child and Adolescent Psychiatry, 36*(10), 1448–1456.

Glaser, K. (1967). Masked depression in children and adolescents. *American Journal of Psychotherapy, 21*(3), 565–574.

Gold, P. W., & Chrousos, G. P. (1999). The endocrinology of melancholic and atypical depression: Relation to neurocircuitry and somatic consequences. *Proceedings of the Association of American Physicians, 111*(1), 22–34.

Gold, P. W., & Chrousos, G. P. (2002). Organization of the stress system and its dysregulation in melancholic and atypical depression: High vs low CRH/NE states. *Molecular Psychiatry, 7,* 254–275.

Goldberg, J., Harrow, M., & Whiteside, J. E. (2001). Risk for bipolar illness in patients initially hospitalized for unipolar depression. *American Journal of Psychiatry, 158*(8), 1265–1270.

Goodwin, F. K., Fireman, B., Simon, G. E., Hunkeler, E. M., Lee, J., & Revicki, D. (2003). Suicide risk in bipolar disorder during treatment with lithium and divalproex. *JAMA, 290*(11), 1467–1473.

Goodyer, I., Dubicka, B., Wilkinson, P., Kelvin, R., Roberts, C., Byford, S., . . . Harrington, R. (2007). Selective serotonin reuptake inhibitors (SSRIs) and routine specialist care with and without cognitive behaviour therapy in adolescents with major depression: Randomised controlled trial. *British Medical Journal, 335*(7611), 142–146.

Gotlib, I. H., & Joorman, J. (2010). Cognition and depression: Current status and future directions. *Annual Review of Clinical Psychology, 6,* 285–312.

Gotlib, I. H., Lewinsohn, P. M., & Seeley, J. R. (1995). Symptoms versus a diagnosis of depression: Differences in psychosocial functioning. *Journal of Consulting and Clinical Psychology, 63,* 90–100.

Gotlib, I. H., Whiffen, V. E., Wallace, P. M., & Mount, J. H. (1991). Prospective investigation of postpartum depression: Factors involved in onset and recovery. *Journal of Abnormal Psychology, 100*(2), 122–132.

Graber, J. A., Lewinsohn, P. M., Seeley, J. R., & Brooks-Gunn, J. (1997). Is psychopathology associated with the timing of pubertal development? *Journal of the American Academy of Child and Adolescent Psychiatry, 36*(12), 1768–1776.

Granger, D. A., Shirtcliff, E. A., Zahn-Waxler, C., Usher, B., Klimes-Dougan, B., & Hastings, P. (2003). Salivary testosterone diurnal variation and psychopathology in adolescent males and females: Individual differences and developmental effects. *Development and Psychopathology, 15,* 431–449.

Grant, B. F., Stinson, F. S., Hasin, D. S., Dawson, D .S., Chou, P., Ruan, W. J., & Huang, B. (2005). Prevalence, correlates, and comorbidity of bipolar I disorder and axis I and II disorders: Results from the National Epidemiologic Survey on Alcohol and Related Conditions. *Journal of Clinical Psychiatry, 66*(10), 1205–1215.

Green, E. K., Grozeva, D., Jones, I., Jones, L., Kirov, G., Caesar, S., et al. (2010). The bipolar disorder risk allele at CACNA1C also confers risk of recurrent major depression and of schizophrenia. *Molecular Psychiatry, 15*, 1016–1022.

Green, E. K., Raybould, R., Macgregor, S., Hyde, S., Young, A. H., et al. (2006). Genetic variation of brain-derived neurotrophic factor (BDNF) in bipolar disorder: Case control study of over 3000 individuals from the UK. *British Journal of Psychiatry, 188*(1), 21–25.

Greenberg, P., Corey-Lisle, P. K., Marynchenko, M., & Claxton, A. (2004). Economic implications of treatment-resistant depression among employees. *Pharmacoeconomics, 22*(6), 363–373.

Greenberg, P. E., Kessler, R. C., Birnbaum, H. G., Leong, S. A., Lowe, S. W., Berglund, P. A., & Corey-Lisle, P. K. (2003). The economic burden of depression in the United States: How did it change between 1990 and 2000? *Journal of Clinical Psychiatry, 64*(12), 1465–1475.

Griffith, J. W., Zinbarg, R. E., Craske, M. G., Mineka, S., Rose, R. D., Waters, A. M., & Sutton, J. M. (2010). Neuroticism as a common dimension in the internalizing disorders. *Psychological Medicine, 40*(7), 1125.

Gruber, J., Eidelman, P., Johnson, S. L., Smith, B., & Harvey, A. G. (2011). Hooked on a feeling: Rumination about positive and negative emotion in interepisode bipolar disorder. *Journal of Abnormal Psychology, 120*(4), 956.

Haddjeri, N., Blier, P., & DeMontigny, C. (1998). Long-term antidepressant treatments result in a tonic activation of forebrain 5-HT1A receptors. *Journal of Neuroscience, 18*(23), 10150–10156.

Hagnell, O., & Grasbeck, A. (1990). Comorbidity of anxiety and depression in the Lundby 25-year prospective study: The pattern of subsequent episodes. In J. D. Maser & C. R. Cloninger (Eds.), *Comorbidity of mood and anxiety disorders* (pp. 139–152). Arlington, VA: American Psychiatric Association.

Hallett, M. (2000). Transcranial magnetic stimulation and the human brain. *Nature, 406*(6792), 147–150.

Hamilton, K. E., & Dobson, K. S. (2002). Cognitive therapy of depression: Pretreatment patient predictors of outcome. *Clinical Psychology Review, 22*(6), 875–893.

Hammen, C. (1991). Generation of stress in the course of unipolar depression. *Journal of Abnormal Psychology, 100*(4), 555–561.

Hammen, C. (2005). Stress and depression. *Annual Review of Clinical Psychology, 1*, 293–319.

Hammen, C., & Brennan, P. (2001). Depressed adolescents of depressed and nondepressed mothers: Tests of an interpersonal impairment hypothesis. *Journal of Consulting and Clinical Psychology, 69*(2), 284–292.

Hammen, C., Henry, R., & Daley, S. E. (2000). Depression and sensitization to stressors among young women as a function of childhood adversity. *Journal of Consulting and Clinical Psychology, 68,* 782–787.

Hankin, B. L., & Abramson, L. Y. (2001). Development of gender differences in depression: An elaborated cognitive vulnerability-transactional stress theory. *Psychological Bulletin, 27*(6), 773–796.

Hankin, B. L., Abramson, L. Y., Moffitt, T. E., Silva, P. A., McGee, R., & Angell, K. E. (1998). Development of depression from preadolescence to young adulthood: Emerging gender differences in a 10-year longitudinal study. *Journal of Abnormal Psychology, 107*(1), 128–140.

Harkness, K. L., Bruce, A. E., & Lumley, M. N. (2006). The role of childhood abuse and neglect in the sensitization to stressful life events in adolescent depression. *Journal of Abnormal Psychology, 115*(4), 730–741.

Harkness, K. L., & Monroe, S. M. (2006). Severe melancholic depression is more vulnerable than non-melancholic depression to minor precipitating life events. *Journal of Affective Disorders, 91,* 257–263.

Harper, P. S., Harley, H. G., Reardon, W., & Shaw, D. J. (1992). Anticipation in myotonic dystrophy: New light on an old problem. *American Journal of Human Genetics, 51,* 10–16.

Harrington, R. C., Fudge, H., Rutter, M. L., Pickles, A., & Hill, J. (1990). Adult outcomes of childhood and adolescent depression: I. Psychiatric status. *Archives of General Psychiatry, 47,* 465–473.

Harris, E. C., & Barraclough, B. (1997). Suicide as an outcome for mental disorders. A meta-analysis. *The British Journal of Psychiatry, 170*(3), 205–228.

Hartlage, S., Alloy, L. B., Vázquez, C., & Dykman, B. (1993). Automatic and effortful processing in depression. *Psychological Bulletin, 113*(2), 247.

Hasler, G., Fromm, S., Carlson, P. J., Luckenbaugh, D. A., Waldeck, T., Geraci, M., . . . Drevets, W. C. (2008). Neural response to catecholamine depletion in unmedicated subjects with major depressive disorder in remission and healthy subjects. *Archives of General Psychiatry, 65*(5), 521–531.

Heidrich, A., Schleyer, M., Spingler, H., Albert, P., Knoche, A. M., & Lanczik, M. (1994). Postpartum blues: Relationship between non-protein bound steroid hormones in plasma and postpartum mood changes. *Journal of Affective Disorders, 30*(2), 93–98.

Heim, C., & Nemeroff, C. B. (2001). The role of childhood trauma in the neurobiology of mood and anxiety disorders: Preclinical and clinical studies. *Biological Psychiatry, 49*(12), 1023–1039.

Hendrick, V., Altshuler, L. L., Gitlin, M. J., Delrahim, S., & Hammen, C. (2000). Gender and bipolar illness. *Journal of Clinical Psychiatry, 61*(5), 393–396.

Hendrick, V., Altshuler, L. L., & Suri, R. (1998). Hormonal changes in the postpartum and implications for postpartum depression. *Psychosomatics, 39*(2), 93–101.

Hettema, J. M., Prescott, C. A., & Kendler, K. S. (2004). Genetic and environmental sources of covariation between generalized anxiety disorder and neuroticism. *American Journal of Psychiatry, 161*(9), 1581–1587.

Higgins, E. T. (1997). Beyond pleasure and pain. *American Psychologist, 52*, 1280–1300.

Hill, J., Pickles, A., Rollinson, L., Davies, R., & Byatt, M. (2004). Juvenile- versus adult-onset depression: Multiple differences imply different pathways. *Psychological Medicine, 34*, 1483–1493.

Hirschfeld, R., Montgomery, S. A., Keller, M. B., Kasper, S., Schatzberg, A. F., Möller, H. J., et al. (2000). Social functioning in depression: A review. *Journal of Clinical Psychiatry, 61*(4), 268–275.

Hollon, S. D., DeRubeis, R. J., Evans, M. D., Wiemer, M. J., Garvey, M. J., Grove, W. M., & Tuason, V. B. (1992). Cognitive therapy and pharmacotherapy for depression: Singly and in combination. *Archives of General Psychiatry, 49*(10), 774–781.

Hollon, S. D., DeRubeis, R. J., Shelton, R. C., Amsterdam, J. D., Salomon, R. M., O'Reardon, J. P., et al. (2005). Prevention of relapse following cognitive therapy vs medications in moderate to severe depression. *Archives of General Psychiatry, 62*(4), 417–422.

Hollon, S. D., & Dimidjian, S. (2009). Cognitive and behavioral treatment of depression. In I. H. Gotlib & C. L. Hammen (Eds.), *Handbook of depression* (2nd ed., pp. 586–603). New York, NY: Guilford Press.

Hollon, S. D., Thase, M. E., & Markowitz, J. C. (2002). Treatment and prevention of depression. *Psychological Science in the Public Interest, 3*(2), 39–77.

Holtzheimer, P. E., Russo, J., & Avery, D. (2001). A meta-analysis of repetitive transcranial magnetic stimulation in the treatment of depression. *Psychopharmacology Bulletin, 35*(4), 149–169.

Hooley, J. M., Richters, J. E., Weintraub, S., & Neale, J. M. (1987). Psychopathology and marital distress: The positive side of positive symptoms. *Journal of Abnormal Psychology, 96*(1), 27–33.

Howland, R. H. (1993). General health, health care utilization, and medical comorbidity in dsythymia. *International Journal of Psychiatry in Medicine, 23*(3), 211–238.

Huang, B., Grant, B. F., Dawson, D. A., Stinson, F. S., Chou, P. S., et al. (2006). Race-ethnicity and the prevalence and co-occurrence of *Diagnostic and Statistical Manual of Mental Disorders, Fourth Edition,* alcohol and drug use disorders and axis I and II disorders: United States, 2001 to 2003. *Comprehensive Psychiatry, 47*(4), 252–257.

Huang, J., Perlis, R. H., Lee, P. H., Rush, A. J., Fava, M., et al. (2010). Cross-disorder genomewide analysis of schizophrenia, bipolar disorder, and depression. *American Journal of Psychiatry, 167,* 1254–1263.

Hutchings, J., Lane, E., & Kelly, J. (2004). Comparison of two treatments for children with severely disruptive behaviors. *Behavioural and Cognitive Psychotherapy, 32*(1), 15–30.

Hyde, J .S., Mezulis, A. H., & Abramson, L. Y. (2008). The ABCs of depression: Integrating affective, biological, and cognitive models to explain the emergence of the gender difference in depression. *Psychological Review, 115*(2), 291–313.

Iacono, W. G. (2004). Major depression and conduct disorder in youth: Associations with parental psychopathology and parent-child conflict. *Journal of Child Psychology and Psychiatry, 45*(2), 377–386.

Insel, T. R. (2010). The challenge of translation in social neuroscience: A review of oxytocin, vasopressin, and affiliative behavior. *Neuron, 65*(6), 768–779.

Jacobson, N. S., Dobson, K., Fruzzetti, A. E., Schmaling, K. B., & Salusky, S. (1991). Marital therapy as a treatment for depression. *Journal of Consulting and Clinical Psychology, 59*(4), 547–557.

Jacobson, N. S., Dobson, K. S., Truax, P. A., Addis, M. E., Koerner, K., Gollan, J. K., et al. (1996). A component analysis of cognitive-behavioral treatment for depression. *Journal of Consulting and Clinical Psychology, 64,* 295–304.

Jaffee, S. R., Moffitt, T. E., Caspi, A., Fombonne, E., Poulton, R., & Martin, J. (2002). Differences in early childhood risk factors for juvenile-onset and adult-onset depression. *Archives of General Psychiatry, 59*(3), 215–222.

Janicak, P. G., Davis, J. M., Gibbons, R. D., Ericksen, S., Chang, S., & Gallagher, P. (1985). Efficacy of ECT: A meta-analysis. *American Journal of Psychiatry, 142*(3), 297–302.

Jarrett, R. B., Schaffer, M., McIntire, D., Witt-Browder, A., Kraft, D., & Risser, R. C. (1999). Treatment of atypical depression with cognitive therapy or phenelzine: A double-blind, placebo-controlled trial. *Archives of General Psychiatry, 56*(5), 431–437.

Johnson, J., Horwath, E., & Weissman, M. W. (1991). The validity of major depression with psychotic features based on a community study. *Archives of General Psychiatry, 48*(12), 1075–1081.

Johnson, S. L. (2005). Life events in bipolar disorder: Towards more specific models. *Clinical Psychology Review, 25*(8), 1008–1027.

Johnson, S. L., Edge, M. D., Holmes, M. K., & Carver, C. S. (2012). The behavioral activation system and mania. *Annual Review of Clinical Psychology, 8*, 243–267.

Johnson, S. L., & Miller, I. (1997). Negative life events and time to recovery from episodes of bipolar disorder. *Journal of Abnormal Psychology, 106*(3), 449–457.

Johnson, S. L., Murray, G., Fredrickson, B., Youngstrom, E. A., Hinshaw, S., Bass, J. M., . . . Salloum, I. (2012). Creativity and bipolar disorder: Touched by fire or burning with questions? *Clinical Psychology Review, 32*, 1–12.

Joiner, T. E., Metalsky, G. I., Katz, J., & Beach, S. R. (1999). Depression and excessive reassurance-seeking. *Psychological Inquiry, 10*(3), 269–278.

Jorm, A. F. (2000). Does old age reduce the risk of anxiety and depression? A review of epidemiological studies across the adult life span. *Psychological Medicine, 30*(1), 11–22.

Joyce, P. R. (1984). Age of onset in bipolar affective disorder and misdiagnosis as schizophrenia. *Psychological Medicine, 14*(1), 145–149.

Judd, L. L., Akiskal, H. S., Schettler, P. J., Endicott, J., Maser, J., Solomon, D. A., . . . Keller, M. B. (2002). The long-term natural history of the weekly symptomatic status of bipolar I disorder. *Archives of General Psychiatry, 59*(6), 530–537.

Judd, L. L., Paulus, M. D., & Zeller, P. (1999). The role of residual subthreshold depressive symptoms in early episode relapse in unipolar major depressive disorder (letter). *Archives of General Psychiatry, 56,* 764–765.

Judd, L. L., Paulus, M. J., Schettler, P. J., Akiskal, H. S., Endicott, J., et al. (2000). Does incomplete recovery from first lifetime major depressive episode herald a chronic course of illness? *American Journal of Psychiatry, 157*(9), 1501–1504.

Judd, L. L., Schettler, P. J., Akiskal, H. S., Coryell, W., Leon, A. C., Maser, J. D., & Solomon, D. A. (2008). Residual symptom recovery from major affective episodes in bipolar disorders and rapid episode relapse/recurrence. *Archives of General Psychiatry, 65*(4), 386–394.

Kalibatseva, Z., & Leong, F. T. L. (2011). Depression among Asian Americans: Review and recommendations. *Depression Research and Treatment,* 1–9.

Kaltiala-Heino, R., Kosunen, E., & Rimpela, M. (2003). Pubertal timing, sexual behaviour and self-reported depression in middle adolescence. *Journal of Adolescence, 26*(5), 531–545.

Karney, B. R. (2001). Depressive symptoms and marital satisfaction in the early years of marriage: Narrowing the gap between theory and research. In S. R. H. Beach (Ed.), *Marital and family processes in depression: A scientific foundation for clinical practice* (pp. 45–68). Washington, DC: American Psychological Association.

Kaslow, N. J., Davis, S. P., & Smith, C. O. (2009). Biological and psychosocial interventions for depression in children and adolescents. In I. H. Gotlib & C. L. Hammen (Eds.), *Handbook of depression* (2nd ed., pp. 642–672). New York, NY: Guilford Press.

Keck, P. E., & McElroy, S. L. (1996). Outcome in the pharmacologic treatment of bipolar disorder. *Journal of Clinical Psychopharmacology, 16*(Suppl. 2), 15S–23S.

Keck, P. E., & McElroy, S. L. (2004). Treatment of bipolar disorder. In A. F. Schatzberg & C. B. Nemeroff (Eds.) *Psychopharmacology.* Washington, DC: Psychiatric Publishing.

Keck, P. E., McElroy, S. L., Strakowski, S. M., West, S. A., Sax, K. W., Hawkins, J. M., . . . Haggard, P. (2003). 12-month outcome of patients with bipolar disorder following hospitalization for a manic or mixed episode. *Focus, 1*(1), 44–52.

Keller, M. B., & Boland, R. J. (1998). Implications of failing to achieve successful long-term maintenance of recurrent unipolar major depression. *Biological Psychiatry, 44*(5), 348–360.

Keller, M. B., Lavori, P. W., Coryell, W., Endicott, J., & Mueller, T. I. (1993). Bipolar I: A five-year prospective follow-up. *Journal of Nervous and Mental Disease, 181*(4), 238–245.

Keller, M. B., Lavori, P. W., Rice, J., Coryell, W., & Hirschfeld, R. M. A. (1986). The persistent risk of chronicity in recurrent episodes of nonbipolar major depressive disorder: A prospective follow-up. *American Journal of Psychiatry, 143,* 24–28.

Keller, M. B., McCullough, J. P., Klein, D. N., Arnow, B., Dunner, D. L., Gelenberg, A. J., . . . Zajecka, J. (2000). A comparison of nefaza-done, the cognitive-behavioral analysis system of psychotherapy, and their combination for the treatment of chronic depression. *The New England Journal of Medicine, 342*(20), 1462–1470.

Keller, M. B., Shapiro, R. W., Lavori, P. W., et al. (1982). Relapse in major depressive disorder: Analysis with the life table. *Archives of General Psychiatry, 39,* 911–915.

Keller, M. C., Neale, M. C., & Kendler, K. S. (2007). Association of different adverse life events with distinct patterns of depressive symptoms. *Archives of General Psychiatry, 164,* 1521–1529.

Kempton, M. J., Geddes, J. R., Ettinger, U., Williams, S. C. R., & Grasby, P. M. (2008). Meta-analysis, database, and meta-regression of 98 structural imaging studies in bipolar disorder. *Archives of General Psychiatry, 65*(9), 1017–1032.

Kempton, M. J., Salvador, Z., Munafo, M. R., Geddes, J. R., Simmons, A., Frangou, S., & Williams, S. C. R. (2011). Structural neuroim-aging studies in major depressive disorder. *Archives of General Psychiatry, 68*(7), 675–690.

Kendler, K. S. (1997). The diagnostic validity of melancholic major depression in a population-based sample of female twins. *Archives of General Psychiatry, 54,* 299–304.

Kendler, K. S., & Baker, J. H. (2007). Genetic influences on measures of the environment: A systematic review. *Psychological Medicine, 37*(5), 615–626.

Kendler, K. S., & Gardner, C. O. (1998). Boundaries of major depres-sion: An evaluation of *DSM-IV* criteria. *American Journal of Psychiatry, 155,* 172–177.

Kendler, K. S., & Gardner, C. O. (2010). Dependent stressful life events and prior depressive episodes in the prediction of major depres-sion. *Archives of General Psychiatry, 67*(11), 1120–1127.

Kendler, K. S., Gardner, C. O., Fiske, A., & Gatz, M. (2009). Major depression and coronary artery disease in the Swedish twin registry: Phenotypic, genetic, and environmental sources of comorbidity. *Archives of General Psychiatry, 66*(8), 857–863.

Kendler, K. S., Gardner, C. O., & Lichtenstein, P. (2008). A developmental twin study of symptoms of anxiety and depression: Evidence for genetic innovation and attenuation. *Psychological Medicine, 38*(11), 1567–1575.

Kendler, K. S., Gardner, C. O., & Prescott, C. A. (2003). Personality and the experience of environmental adversity. *Psychological Medicine, 33*(7), 1193–1202.

Kendler, K. S., Gatz, M., Gardner, C. O., & Pedersen, N. L. (2006). Personality and major depression: A Swedish longitudinal, population-based twin study. *Archives of General Psychiatry, 63*(10), 1113–1120.

Kendler, K. S., Karkowski, L. M., & Prescott, C. A. (1999). Causal relationship between stressful life events and the onset of major depression. *American Journal of Psychiatry, 156*(6), 837–841.

Kendler, K. S., & Karkowski-Shuman, L. (1997). Stressful life events and genetic liability to major depression: Genetic control of exposure to the environment? *Psychological Medicine, 27*(3), 539–547.

Kendler, K. S., Kessler, R. C., Walters, E. E., MacLean, C., Neale, M. C., Heath, A. C., & Eaves, L. J. (1995). Stressful life events, genetic liability, and onset of an episode of major depression in women. *American Journal of Psychiatry, 152*(6), 833–842.

Kendler, K. S., Kuhn, J., & Prescott, C. A. (2004). The interrelationship of neuroticism, sex, and stressful life events in the prediction of episodes of major depression. *American Journal of Psychiatry, 161*(4), 631–636.

Kendler, K. S., Myers, J., & Prescott, C. A. (2005). Sex differences in the relationship between social support and risk for major depression: A longitudinal study of opposite-sex twin pairs. *American Journal of Psychiatry, 162*(2), 250–256.

Kendler, K. S., Myers, J., & Zisook, S. (2008). Does bereavement-related major depression differ from major depression associated with other stressful life events? *American Journal of Psychiatry, 165*(11), 1449–1455.

Kendler, K. S., Neale, M. C., Kessler, R. C., & Heath, A. C. (1993). A longitudinal twin study of personality and major depression in women. *Archives of General Psychiatry, 50*(11), 853–862.

Kendler, K. S., Neale, M. C., Kessler, R. C., Heath, A. C., & Eaves, L. J. (1992). Major depression and generalized anxiety disorder: Same genes, (partly) different environments? *Archives of General Psychiatry, 49*(9), 716–722.

Kendler, K. S., Pedersen, N., Johnson, L., Neale, M. C., & Mathe, A. A. (1993). A pilot Swedish twin study of affective illness, including hospital and population-ascertained subsamples. *Archives of General Psychiatry, 50*, 699–700.

Kendler, K. S., Thornton, L. M., & Prescott, C. A. (2001). Gender differences in the rates of exposure to stressful life events and sensitivity to their depressogenic effects. *American Journal of Psychiatry, 158*(4), 587–593.

Kennedy, N., Boydell, J., Kalindi, S., Fearon, P., Jones, P. B., Van Os, J., & Murray, R. M. (2005). Gender differences in incidence and age of onset of mania and bipolar disorder over a 35-year period in Camberwell, England. *American Journal of Psychiatry, 162*(2), 257–262.

Kessing, L. V. (2008). The prevalence of mixed episodes during the course of illness in bipolar disorder. *Acta Psychiatrica Scandinavica, 117*(3), 216–224.

Kessing, L. V., Agerbo, E., & Mortensen, P. B. (2004). Major stressful life events and other risk factors for first admission with mania. *Bipolar Disorders, 6*(2), 122–129.

Kessler, R. C., Akiskal, H. S., Ames, M., Birnbaum, H., Greenberg, P., Hirschfeld, R. M. A., . . . Wang, P. S. (2006). The prevalence and effects of mood disorders on work performance in a nationally representative sample of US workers. *American Journal of Psychiatry, 163*(9), 1561–1568.

Kessler, R. C., Avenevoli, S., & Merikangas, K. R. (2001). Mood disorders in children and adolescents: An epidemiologic perspective. *Biological Psychiatry, 49*(12), 1002–1014.

Kessler, R. C., Berglund, P., Demier, O., Jin, R., Merikangas, K. R., & Walters, E. E. (2005a). Lifetime prevalence and age-of-onset distributions of DSM-IV disorders in the National Comorbidity Survey Replication. *Archives of General Psychiatry, 62*(6), 593–602.

Kessler, R. C., Birnbaum, H., Bromet, E., Hwang, I., Sampson, N., & Shahly, V. (2010). Age differences in major depression: Results from the National Comorbidity Survey Replication (NCS-R). *Psychological Medicine, 40,* 225–237.

Kessler, R. C., Chiu, W. T., Demler, O., & Walters, E. E. (2005b). Prevalence, severity, and comorbidity of 12-month DSM-IV disorders in the National Comorbidity Survey Replication. *Archives of General Psychiatry, 62*(6), 617–627.

Kessler, R. C., & Frank, R. G. (1997). The impact of psychiatric disorders on work loss days. *Psychological Medicine, 27*(4), 861–873.

Kessler, R. C., McGonagle, K. A., Swartz, M., Blazer, D. G., & Nelson, C. B. (1993). Sex and depression in the National Comorbidity Survey I: Lifetime prevalence, chronicity and recurrence. *Journal of Affective Disorders, 29,* 85–96.

Kessler, R. C., McGonagle, K. A., Zhao, S., Nelson, C. B., Hughes, M., Eshleman, S., . . . Kendler, K. S. (1994). Lifetime and 12-month prevalence of DSM-III-R psychiatric disorders in the United States. *Archives of General Psychiatry, 51,* 8–19.

Kessler, R. C., & McRae, J. A. (1984). A note on the relationship of sex and marital status to psychological distress. *Research in Community and Mental Health, 4,* 109–130.

Kessler, R. C., Merikangas, K. R., & Wang, P. S. (2007). Prevalence, comorbidity, and service utilization for mood disorders in the United States at the beginning of the twenty-first century. *Annual Review of Clinical Psychology, 3,* 137–158.

Kessler, R. C., Olfson, M., & Berglund, P. A. (1998). Patterns and predictors of treatment contact after first onset of psychiatric disorders. *American Journal of Psychiatry, 155*(1), 62–69.

Kessler, R. C., Rubinow, D. R., Holmes, C., Abelson, J. M., & Zhao, S. (1997). The epidemiology of DSM-III-R bipolar I disorders in a general population survey. *Psychological Medicine, 27*(5), 1079–1089.

Kessler, R. C., & Wang, P. S. (2009). Epidemiology of depression. In I. H. Gotlib & C. L. Hammens (Eds.), *Handbook of depression* (2nd ed., pp. 5–22). New York, NY: Guilford Press.

Khan, A., Brodhead, A. E., Kolts, R. L., & Brown, W. A. (2005). Severity of depressive symptoms and response to antidepressants and placebo in antidepressant trials. *Journal of Psychiatric Research, 39*(2), 145–150.

Killgore, W. D., & Yurgelun-Todd, D. A. (2004). Activation of the amygdala and anterior cingulate during nonconscious processing of sad versus happy faces. *Neuroimage, 21*(4), 1215–1223.

Kiloh, L. G., & Garside, R. F. (1963). The independence of neurotic depression and endogenous depression. *British Journal of Psychiatry, 109*, 451–463.

King, S. M., Iacono, W. G., & McGue, M. (2004). Childhood externalizing and internalizing psychopathology in the prediction of early substance use. *Addiction, 99*(12), 1548–1559.

Kinkelin, M. (1954). Verlauf und prognose des manisch-depressiven irreseins. *Schweizer Archiv fur Neurologie, Neurochirurgie, und Psychiatrie, 73*, 100–146.

Klein, D. N. (1990). Depressive personality: Reliability, validity, and relation to dysthymia. *Journal of Abnormal Psychology, 99*, 412–421.

Klein, D. N. (1999). Depressive personality disorder in the relatives of outpatients with dysthymic disorder and episodic major depressive disorder and normal controls. *Journal of Affective Disorders, 55*(1), 19–27.

Klein, D. N. (2008). Classification of depressive disorders in *DSM-V*: Proposal for a two-dimension system. *Journal of Abnormal Psychology, 117*(3), 552–560.

Klein, D. N., Depue, R. A., & Slater, J. F. (1986). Inventory identification of cyclothymia IX: Validation in offspring of Bipolar I patients. *Archives of General Psychiatry, 43*(5), 441–445.

Klein, D. N., Durbin, C. E., & Shankman, S. (2009). Personality and mood disorders. In I. H. Gotlib & C. L. Hammen (Eds.), *Handbook of depression* (2nd ed., pp. 93–112). New York, NY: Guilford Press.

Klein, D. N., Kotov, R., & Bufferd, S. (2011). Personality and depression: Explanatory models and review of the evidence. *Annual Review of Clinical Psychology, 7*, 269–295.

Klein, D. N., & Miller, G. A. (1993). Depressive personality in a nonclinical sample. *American Journal of Psychiatry, 150*, 1718–1724.

Klein, D. N., Santiago, N. J., Vivian, D., Blalock, J. A., Kocsis, J. H., Markowitz, J. C., et al. (2004). Cognitive-behavioral analysis system of psychotherapy as a maintenance treatment for chronic depression. *Journal of Consulting and Clinical Psychology, 72*(4), 681–688.

Klein, D. N., Schatzberg, A. F., McCullough, J. P., Dowling, F., Goodman, D., et al. (1999). Age of onset in chronic major depression: Relation to demographic and clinical variables, family history, and treatment response. *Journal of Affective Disorders, 55*(2/3), 149–157.

Klein, D. N., Shankman, S. A., Lewinsohn, P. M., & Seeley, J. R. (2009). Subthreshold depressive disorder in adolescents: Predictors of escalation to full-syndrome depressive disorders. *Journal of the American Academy of Child and Adolescent Psychiatry, 48*(7), 703–710.

Klein, D. N., Shankman, S., & Rose, S. (2006). Ten-year prospective follow-up study of the naturalistic course of dysthymic disorder and double depression. *American Journal of Psychiatry, 163*(5), 872–880.

Klein, D. N., & Shih, J. H. (1998). Depressive personality disorder: Associations with DSM-III-R mood and personality disorders and negative and positive affectivity, 30-month stability, and prediction of course of axis I depressive disorders. *Journal of Abnormal Psychology, 107*(2), 319–327.

Kleinman, A., & Good, B. J. (1985). *Culture and depression: Studies in the anthropology and cross-cultural psychiatry of affect and disorder.* Berkeley: University of California Press.

Klerman, G. L. (1974). Treatment of depression by drugs and psychotherapy. *American Journal of Psychiatry, 131*(2), 186–191.

Klerman, G. L., Weissman, M. M., Rounsaville, B. J., & Chevron, E. S. (1984). *Interpersonal psychotherapy of depression.* New York, NY: Basic Books.

Kocsis, J. H. (2003). Pharmacotherapy for chronic depression. *Journal of Clinical Psychology, 59*(8), 885–892.

Kotov, R., Gamez, W., Schmidt, F., & Watson, D. (2010). Linking "big" personality traits to anxiety, depressive, and substance use disorders: A meta-analysis. *Psychological Bulletin, 136*(5), 768–821.

Kovacs, M., Feinberg, T. L., Crouse-Novack, M., Paulauskas, S. L., Pollock, M., & Finkelstein, R. (1984). Depression disorders in childhood. II: A longitudinal study of the risk for a subsequent major depression. *Archives of General Psychiatry, 41*(7), 643–649.

Kovacs, M., Rush, A. J., Beck, A. T., & Hollon, S. D. (1981). Depressed outpatients treated with cognitive therapy or pharmacotherapy: A one-year follow-up. *Archives of General Psychiatry, 38*(1), 33–39.

Kowatch, R. A., Fristad, M., Birmahr, B., Wagner, K. D., Findling, R. L., & Hellander, M. (2005). Treatment guidelines for children and adolescents with bipolar disorder. *Journal of the American Academy of Child and Adolescent Psychiatry, 44*(3), 213–235.

Kraemer, H. C., Kazdin, A. E., Offord, D. R., Kessler, R. C., Jensen, P. S., & Kupfer, D. J. (1997). Coming to terms with the terms of risk. *Archives of General Psychiatry, 54*(4), 337.

Kraepelin, E. (1921). *Manic depressive insanity and paranoia.* Bristol, England: Thoemmes Press.

Krishnan, K. R. R. (2005). Psychiatric and medical comorbidities of bipolar disorder. *Psychosomatic Medicine, 67*(1), 1–8.

Krueger, R. F., & Markon, K. E. (2006). Reinterpreting comorbidity: A model-based approach to understanding and classifying psychopathology. *Annual Review of Clinical Psychology, 2*, 111–133.

Kuma, H., Miki, T., Matsumoto, Y., Gu, H., Li, H. P., Kusaka, T., et al. (2004). Early maternal deprivation induces alterations in brain-derived neurotrophic factor expression in the developing rat hippocampus. *Neuroscience Letters, 372*(1), 68–73.

Kupka, R. W., Luckenbaugh, D. A., Post, R. M., Suppes, T., & Altshuler, L. L. (2005). Comparison of rapid-cycling and non-rapid-cycling bipolar disorder based on prospective mood ratings in 530 outpatients. *American Journal of Psychiatry, 162*(7), 1273–1280.

Kwapil, T. R., Miller, M. B., Zinser, M. C., Chapman, L. J., Chapman, J., & Eckblad, M. (2000). A longitudinal study of high scorers on the hypomanic personality scale. *Journal of Abnormal Psychology, 109*(2), 222–226.

Kwon, J. S., Kim, Y.-M., Chang, C.-G., Park, B.-J., & Kim, L. (2000). Three-year follow-up of women with the sole diagnosis of depressive personality disorder: Subsequent development of dysthymia and major depression. *American Journal of Psychiatry, 157*, 1966–1972.

Lam, D. H., Hayward, P., Watkins, E. R., Wright, K., & Sham, P. (2005). Relapse prevention in patients with bipolar disorder: Cognitive therapy outcome after 2 years. *American Journal of Psychiatry, 162*(2), 324–329.

Lang, P. J., Greenwald, M. K., Bradley, M. M., & Hamm, A. O. (1993). Looking at pictures: Affective, facial, visceral, and behavioral reactions. *Psychophysiology, 30*(3), 261–273.

Lang, U. E., Hellweg, R., Kalus, P., Bajbouj, M., Lenzen, K. P., Sander, T., et al. (2005). Association of a functional BDNF polymorphism and anxiety-related personality traits. *Psychopharmacology, 180*(1), 95–99.

Laptook, R., Klein, D., & Dougherty, L. (2006). Ten-year stability of depressive personality disorder in depressed outpatients. *American Journal of Psychiatry, 163*(5), 865–871.

Lara, M. E., Leader, J., & Klein, D. N. (1997). The association between social support and course of depression: Is it confounded with personality? *Journal of Abnormal Psychology, 106*(3), 478–482.

Lasch, K., Weissman, M., Wickramaratne, P., & Burce, M. L. (1990). Birth-cohort changes in the rates of mania. *Psychiatry Research, 33*(1), 31–37.

Lau, J. Y. F., & Eley, T. C. (2010). The genetics of mood disorders. *Annual Review of Clinical Psychology, 6,* 313–337.

Laursen, B., Coy, K. C., & Collins, W. A. (1998). Considering changes in parent-child conflict across adolescence: A meta-analysis. *Child Development, 69*(3), 817–832.

Leckman, J. F., Weissman, M. M., Prusoff, B. A., Caruso, K. A., Merikangas, K. R., Pauls, D. L., & Kidd, K. K. (1984). Subtypes of depression. *Archives of General Psychiatry, 41,* 833–838.

Leibenluft, E. (2011). Severe mood dysregulation, irritability, and the diagnostic boundaries of bipolar disorder in youths. *American Journal of Psychiatry, 168*(2), 129–142.

Leibenluft, E., Albert, P. S., Rosenthal, N. E., & Wehr, T. A. (1996). Relationship between sleep and mood in patients with rapid-cycling bipolar disorder. *Psychiatry Research, 63*(2), 161–168.

Lenzenweger, M. F., Lane, M. C., Loranger, A. W., & Kessler, R. C. (2007). DSM-IV personality disorders in the National Comorbidity Survey Replication. *Biological Psychiatry, 62,* 553–564.

Leverich, G. S., McElroy, S. L., Suppes, T., Keck, P. E., Denicoff, K. S., Nolen, W. A., et al. (2002). Early physical and sexual abuse associated with an adverse course of bipolar illness. *Biological Psychiatry, 51*(4), 288–297.

Lewinsohn, P. M., & Amenson, C. S. (1978). Some relations between pleasant and unpleasant mood-related events and depression. *Journal of Abnormal Psychology, 87*(6), 644–654.

Lewinsohn, P. M., Clarke, G. N., Rohde, P., Hops, H., & Seeley, J. R. (1996). A course in coping: A cognitive-behavioral approach to the treatment of adolescent depression. In E. D. Hibbs & P. S. Jensen (Eds.), *Psychosocial treatments for child and adolescent disorders: Empirically based strategies for clinical practice* (pp. 109–135). Washington, DC: American Psychological Association.

Lewinsohn, P. M., Clarke, G. N., Seeley, J. R., & Rohde, P. (1994). Major depression in community adolescents: Age at onset, episode duration, and time to recurrence. *Journal of the American Academy of Child and Adolescent Psychiatry, 33*(6), 809–818.

Lewinsohn, P. M., Gotlib, I. H., Lewinsohn, M., Seeley, J. R., & Allen, N. B. (1998). Gender differences in anxiety disorders and anxiety symptoms in adolescents. *Journal of Abnormal Psychology, 107*(1), 109–117.

Lewinsohn, P. M., Hoberman, H., Teri, L., & Hautzinger, M. (1985). An integrative theory of depression. In S. Reiss & R. R. Bootzin (Eds.), *Theoretical issues in behavior therapy* (pp. 313–359). New York, NY: Academic Press.

Lewinsohn, P. M., Klein, D. N., Durbin, C. E., Seeley, J. R., & Rohde, P. (2003). Family study of subthreshold depressive symptoms: Risk factor for MDD? *Journal of Affective Disorders, 77,* 149–157.

Lewinsohn, P. M., Klein, D. N., & Seeley, J. R. (1995). Bipolar disorders in a community sample of older adolescents: Prevalence, phenomenology, comorbidity, and course. *Journal of the American Academy of Child and Adolescent Psychiatry, 34*(4), 454–463.

Lewinsohn, P. M., Rohde, P., & Seeley, J. R. (1994). Psychosocial risk factors for future adolescent suicide attempts. *Journal of Consulting and Clinical Psychology, 62*(2), 297–305.

Lewinsohn, P. M., Rohde, P., Seeley, J. R., & Fischer, S. A. (1993). Age-cohort changes in the lifetime occurrence of depression and other mental disorders. *Journal of Abnormal Psychology, 102*(1), 110–120.

Lewinsohn, P. M., Shankman, S. A., Gau, J. M., & Klein, D. N. (2004). The prevalence and comorbidity of subthreshold psychiatric conditions. *Psychological Medicine, 34*(4), 613–622.

Lewinsohn, P. M., Solomon, A., Seeley, J. R., & Zeiss, A. (2000). Clinical implications of "subthreshold" depressive symptoms. *Journal of Abnormal Psychology, 109,* 345–351.

Lewis, A. J. (1934). Melancholia: A clinical survey of depressive states. *The British Journal of Psychiatry, 80*(329), 277–378.

Liebowitz, M. R., Quitkin, F. M., Stewart, J. W., McGrath, P. J., Harrison, W. M., Rabkin, J. G., . . . Klein, D. F. (1988). Antidepressant specificity in atypical depression. *Archives of General Psychiatry, 45,* 129–137.

Lish, J. D., Dime-Meenan, S., Whybrow, P. C., Price, R. A., & Hirschfeld, R. M. A. (1994). The national depressive and manic-depressive association (DMDA) survey of bipolar members. *Journal of Affective Disorders, 31*(4), 281–294.

Loeber, R., & Keenan, K. (1994). Interaction between conduct disorder and its comorbid conditions: Effects of age and gender. *Clinical Psychology Review, 14*(6), 497–523.

Lonigan, C. J., Phillips, B. M., & Hooe, E. S. (2003). Relations of positive and negative affectivity to anxiety and depression in children: Evidence from a latent variable longitudinal study. *Journal of Consulting and Clinical Psychology, 71*(3), 465–481.

Lotrich, F. E., & Pollock, B. G. (2004). Meta-analysis of serotonin transporter polymorphisms and affective disorders. *Psychiatric Genetics, 14*(3), 121–129.

Lovejoy, M. C., Graczyk, P. A., O'Hare, E., & Neuman, G. (2000). Maternal depression and parenting behavior: A meta-analytic review. *Clinical Psychology Review, 20*(5), 561–592.

Luby, J. L., Si, X., Belden, A. C., Tandon, M., & Spitznagel, E. (2009). Preschool depression: Homotypic continuity and course over 24 months. *Archives of General Psychiatry, 66*(8), 897–905.

Luppino, F. S., de Wit, L. M., Bouvy, P. F., Stijnen, T., Cuijpers, P., Penninx, B. W., & Zitman, F. G. (2010). Overweight, obesity, and depression: A systematic review and meta-analysis of longitudinal studies. *Archives of General Psychiatry, 67*(3), 220–229.

Ma, J., Lee, K. V., & Stafford, R. S. (2005). Depression treatment during outpatient visits by US children and adolescents. *Journal of Adolescent Health, 37*(6), 434–442.

Ma, S. H., & Teasdale, J. D. (2004). Mindfulness-based cognitive therapy for depression: Replication and exploration of differential relapse prevention effects. *Journal of Consulting and Clinical Psychology, 72*(1), 31–40.

Magnus, K., Diener, E., Fugita, F., & Pavot, W. (1993). Extraversion and neuroticism as predictors of objective life events: A longitudinal analysis. *Journal of Personality and Social Psychology, 65*(5), 1046–1053.

Mahmood, T., & Silverstone, T. (2001). Serotonin and bipolar disorder. *Journal of Affective Disorders, 66*(1), 1–11.

Malkoff-Schwartz, S., Frank, E., Anderson, B. P., Hlastala, S. A., Luther, J. F., Sherrill, J. T., et al. (2000). Social rhythm disruption and stressful life events in the onset of bipolar and unipolar episodes. *Psychological Medicine, 30*(5), 1005–1016.

Malkoff-Schwartz, S., Frank, E., Anderson, B., Sherrill, J. T., Siegel, L., Patterson, D., & Kupfer, D. J. (1998). Stressful life events and social rhythm disruption in the onset of manic and depressive bipolar episodes: A preliminary investigation. *Archives of General Psychiatry, 55*(8), 702–707.

Mann, J. J., Emslie, G., Baldessarini, R. J., Beardslee, W., Fawcett, J. A., Goodwin, F. K., . . . Wagner, K. (2006). ACNP task force report on SSRIs and suicidal behavior in youth. *Neuropsychopharmacology, 31,* 473–492.

March, J., Silva, S., Petrycki, S., Curry, J., Wells, K., Fairbank, J., et al. (2004). Fluoxetine, cognitive-behavioral therapy, and their combination for adolescents with depression: Treatment for Adolescents with Depression Study (TADS) randomized controlled trial. *JAMA, 292*(7), 807–820.

Markon, K. E., Krueger, R. F., & Watson, D. (2005). Delineating the structure of normal and abnormal personality: An integrative hierarchical approach. *Journal of Personality and Social Psychology, 88*(1), 139–157.

Marks, N. F., & Lambert, J. D. (1998). Marital status continuity and change among young and midlife adults. *Journal of Family Issues, 19,* 652–688.

Markus, H. R., & Kitayama, S. (1991). Culture and the self: Implications for cognition, emotion, and motivation. *Psychological Review, 98*(2), 224–253.

Martínez-Arán, A., Vieta, E., Colom, F., Torrent, C., Sánchez-Moreno, J., Reinares, M., et al. (2004). Cognitive impairment in euthymic bipolar patients: Implications for clinical and functional outcome. *Bipolar Disorders, 6*(3), 224–232.

Mathews, A., & Mackintosh, B. (2000). Induced emotional interpretation bias and anxiety. *Journal of Abnormal Psychology, 109*(4), 602–615.

Mathews, A., & MacLeod, C. (2005). Cognitive vulnerability to emotional disorders. *Annual Review of Clinical Psychology, 1,* 167–195.

Mathews, C. A., & Reus, V. I. (2001). Assortative mating in the affective disorders: A systematic review and meta-analysis. *Comprehensive Psychiatry, 42*(4), 257–262.

Matza, L. S., Revicki, D. A., Davidson, J. R., & Stewart, J. W. (2003). Depression with atypical features in the National Comorbidity Survey: Classification, description, and consequences. *Archives of General Psychiatry, 60,* 817–826.

Mayberg, H. S., Lozano, A. M., Voon, V., et al. (2005). Deep brain stimulation for treatment-resistant depression. *Neuron, 45,* 651–660.

McAdams, D. P., & Pals, J. L. (2006). A new Big Five. *American Psychologist, 61*(3), 204–217.

McCauley, E., Myers, K., Mitchell, J., Calderon, R., Schloredt, K., & Treder, R. (1993). Depression in young people: Initial presentation and clinical course. *Journal of the American Academy of Child and Adolescent Psychiatry, 32*(4), 714–722.

McCrae, R. R., & Costa Jr., P. T. (1999). A five-factor theory of personality. In L. Pervin & O. John (Eds.), *Handbook of personality: Theory and research* (pp. 139–153). New York, NY: Guilford Press.

McCullough, J. P. (2003). *Treatment for chronic depression: Cognitive behavioral analysis system of psychotherapy (CBASP).* New York, NY: Guilford Press.

McEwen, B. S. (1998). Protective and damaging effects of stress mediators. *New England Journal of Medicine, 338,* 171–179.

McEwen, B. S. (2003). Mood disorders and allostatic load. *Biological Psychiatry, 54*(3), 200–207.

McGaugh, J. L. (2004). The amygdala modulates the consolidation of memories of emotionally arousing experiences. *Annual Review Neuroscience, 27,* 1–28.

McGonagle, K. A., & Kessler, R. C. (1990). Chronic stress, acute stress, and depressive symptoms. *American Journal of Community Psychology, 18*(5), 681–706.

McGuffin, P., Katz, R., & Bebbington, P. (1988). The Camberwell Collaborative Depression Study. III. Depression and adversity in the relatives of depressed probands. *The British Journal of Psychiatry, 152*(6), 775–782.

McGuffin, P., Katz, R., Watkins, S., & Rutherford, J. (1996). A hospital-based twin register of the heritability of DSM-IV unipolar depression. *Archives of General Psychiatry, 53,* 129–136.

McGuffin, P., Rijsdijk, F., Andrew, M., Sham, P., Katz, R., & Cardno, A. (2003). The heritability of bipolar affective disorder and the genetic relationship to unipolar depression. *Archives of General Psychiatry, 60,* 497–502.

McInnis, M. G., McMahon, F .J., Chase, G. A., Simpson, S. G., Ross, C. A., & DePaulo, J. R. (1993). Anticipation in bipolar affective disorder. *American Journal of Human Genetics, 53*(2), 385–390.

McIntosh, J. L., & Drapeau, C. W. (for the American Association of Suicidology). (2012, November 28). *USA suicide 2010: Official final data*. Washington, DC: American Association of Suicidality. Retrieved from http://www.suicidality.org

McLaughlin, K. A., Green, J. G., Gruber, M. J., Sampson, N. A., Zaslovsky, A. M., & Kessler, R. C. (2010). Childhood adversities and adult psychiatric disorders in the National Comborbidity Survey Replication II. *Archives of General Psychiatry, 67*(2), 124–132.

McLeod, B. D., Weisz, J. R., & Wood, J. J. (2007). Examining the association between parenting and childhood depression: A meta-analysis. *Clinical Psychology Review, 27,* 986–1003.

Meaney, M. J. (2001). Maternal care, gene expression, and the transmission of individual differences in stress reactivity across generations. *Annual Review of Neuroscience, 24*(1), 1161–1192.

Meaney, M. J., & Szyf, M. (2005). Environmental programming of stress responses through DNA methylation: Life at the interface between a dynamic environment and a fixed genome. *Dialogues in Clinical Neuroscience, 7*(2), 103.

Meehl, P.E. (1962). Schizotaxia, schizotypy, schizophrenia. *American Psychologist, 17,* 827–838.

Melvin, G. A., Tonge, B. J., King, N. J., Heyne, D., Gordon, M. S., & Klimkeit, E. (2006). A comparison of cognitive-behavioral therapy, sertraline, and their combination for adolescent depression. *Journal of the American Academy of Child and Adolescent Psychiatry, 45*(10), 1151–1161.

Merikangas, K. R. (1984). Divorce and assortative mating among depressed patients. *American Journal of Psychiatry, 141*(1), 74–76.

Merikangas, K. R., Akiskal, H. S., Angst, J., Greenberg, P. E., Hirschfeld, R. M. A., Petukhova, M., & Kessler, R. C. (2007). Lifetime and 12-month prevalence of bipolar spectrum disorder in the National Comorbidity Survey Replication. *Archives of General Psychiatry, 64*(5), 543–552.

Merikangas, K. R., He, J.-P., Burstein, M., Swanson, S. A., Avenevoli, S., Cui, K., . . . Swendsen, J. (2010). Lifetime prevalence of mental disorders in U.S. adolescents: Results from the National Comorbidity Survey Replication–Adolescent supplement (NCS-A). *Journal of the American Academy of Child and Adolescent Psychiatry, 49*(10), 980–989.

Merikangas, K. R., Zhang, H., Avenevoli, S., Acharyya, S., Neuenschwander, M., & Angst, J. (2003). Longitudinal trajectories of depression and anxiety in a prospective community study: The Zurich Cohort Study. *Archives of General Psychiatry, 60*(10), 993–1000.

Meyer, T. D. (2002). The Hypomanic Personality Scale, the Big Five, and their relationship to depression and mania. *Personality and Individual Differences, 32*(4), 649–660.

Miklowitz, D. J. (2010). *Bipolar disorder: A family-focused treatment approach.* New York, NY: Guilford Press.

Miklowitz, D. J., Otto, M. W., Frank, E., Reilly-Harrington, N. A., Kogan, J. N., Sachs, G. S., et al. (2007). Intensive psychosocial intervention enhances functioning in patients with bipolar depression: Results from a 9-month randomized controlled trial. *American Journal of Psychiatry, 164*(9), 1340–1347.

Miklowitz, D. J., Otto, M. W., Frank, E., Reilly-Harrington, N. A., Wisniewski, S. R., Kogan, J. N., et al., (2007). Psychosocial treatments for bipolar depression: A 1-year randomized trial from the Systematic Treatment Enhancement Program. *Archives of General Psychiatry, 64*(4), 419–426.

Miklowitz, D. J., & Scott, J. (2009). Psychosocial treatments for bipolar disorder: Cost-effectiveness, mediating mechanisms, and future directions. *Bipolar Disorders, 11*(Suppl. 2), 110S–122S.

Mineka, S., & Sutton, S. K. (1992). Cognitive biases and the emotional disorders. *Psychological Science, 3*(1), 65–69.

Moffitt, T. E., Caspi, A., Taylor, A., Kokaua, J., Milne, B. J., Polanczyk, G., et al. (2010). How common are common mental disorders? Evidence that lifetime prevalence rates are doubled by prospective versus retrospective ascertainment. *Psychological Medicine, 40*(6), 899–909.

Moller, H. J., Grunze, H., & Broich, K. (2006). Does recent efficacy data on the drug treatment of acute bipolar depression support the position that drugs other than antidepressants are the treatment of choice? *European Archives of Psychiatry and Clinical Neuroscience, 256*(1), 116.

Mongeau, R., Blier, P., & DeMontigny, C. (1997). The serotonergic and noradrenergic systems of the hippocampus: Their interactions and the effects of antidepressant treatments. *Brain Research Reviews, 23*(3), 145–195.

Monroe, S. M. (2008). Modern approaches to conceptualizing and measuring human life stress. *Annual Review of Clinical Psychology, 4*, 33–52.

Monroe, S. M., Torres, L. D., Guillamot, J., Harkness, K. L., Roberts, J. E., Frank, E., & Kupfer, D. (2006). Life stress and the long-term treatment course of recurrent depression: III. Nonsevere life events predict recurrence for medicated patients over 3 years. *Journal of Consulting and Clinical Psychology, 74*(1), 112–120.

Moore, M. T., & Fresco, D. M. (2012). Depressive realism: A meta-analytic review. *Clinical Psychology Review, 32*(6), 496–509.

Moreno, C., Laje, G., Blanco, C., Jiang, H., Schmidt, A. B., & Olfson, M. (2007). National trends in the outpatient diagnosis and treatment of bipolar disorder in youths. *Archives of General Psychiatry, 64*(9), 1032–1039.

Mufson, L., Dorta, K. P., Wickramaratne, P., Nomura, Y., Olfson, M., & Weissman, M. M. (2004). A randomized effectiveness trial of interpersonal psychotherapy for depressed adolescents. *Archives of General Psychiatry, 61*(6), 577–584.

Mufson, L., Weissman, M. M., Moreau, D., & Garfinkel, R. (1999). Efficacy of interpersonal psychotherapy for depressed adolescents. *Archives of General Psychiatry, 56*(6), 573–579.

Munoz, R. F., Cuijpers, P., Smit, F., Barrera, A. Z., & Leykin, Y. (2010). Prevention of major depression. *Annual Review of Clinical Psychology, 6*, 181–212.

Muris, P., & Ollendick, T. H. (2005). The role of temperament in the etiology of child psychopathology. *Clinical Child and Family Psychology Review, 8*(4), 271–289.

Murphy, G. E., Simons, A. D., Wetzel, R. D., & Lustman, P. J. (1984). Cognitive therapy and pharmacotherapy: Singly and together in the treatment of depression. *Archives of General Psychiatry, 41*(1), 33–41.

Murphy, J. M., Laird, N.-M., Monson, R. R., Sobol, A. M., & Leighton, A. H. (2000). A 40-year perspective on the prevalence of depression. *Archives of General Psychiatry, 57*, 209–215.

Murray, C. J. L., & Lopez, A. D. (1996). Evidence-based health policy— Lessons from the Global Burden of Disease study. *Science, 274*, 740–743.

Mynors-Wallis, L. M., Gath, D. H., Day, A., & Baker, F. (2000). Randomised controlled trial of problem solving treatment, antidepressant medication, and combined treatment for major depression in primary care. *British Medical Journal, 320*(7226), 26–30.

Naragon-Gainey, K., Watson, D., & Markon, K. E. (2009). Differential relations of depression and social anxiety symptoms to the facets of extraversion/positive emotionality. *Journal of Abnormal Psychology, 118*(2), 299–310.

Nazroo, J. Y., Edwards, A. C., & Brown, G. W. (1997). Gender differences in the onset of depression following a shared life event: A study of couples. *Psychological Medicine, 27*(1), 9–19.

Nesse, R. M. (2000). Is depression an adaptation? *Archives of General Psychiatry, 57*(1), 14–20.

Nettle, D. (2004). Evolutionary origins of depression: A review and reformulation. *Journal of Affective Disorders, 81*, 91–102.

Nettle, D. (2008). An evolutionary model of low mood states. *Journal of Theoretical Biology, 257*(1), 100–103.

Neumeister, A., Drevets, W. C., Belfer, I., Luckenbaugh, D. A., Henry, S., Bonne, O., . . . Charney, D. S. (2006). Effects of an alpha 2C-adrenoreceptor gene polymorphism on neural responses to facial expressions in depression. *Neuropsychopharmacology, 31*, 1750–1756.

Newton-Howes, G., Tyrer, P., & Johnson, T. (2006). Personality disorder and the outcome of depression: Meta-analysis of published studies. *British Journal of Psychiatry, 188*, 13–20.

Nezu, A. M. (1986). Efficacy of a social problem-solving therapy approach for unipolar depression. *Journal of Consulting and Clinical Psychology, 54*(2), 196–202.

Nezu, A. M., & Perri, M. G. (1989). Social problem-solving therapy for unipolar depression: An initial dismantling investigation. *Journal of Consulting and Clinical Psychology, 57*(3), 408–413.

Nibuya, M., Morinobu, S., & Duman, R. S. (1995). Regulation of BDNF and trkB mRNA in rat brain by chronic electroconvulsive seizure and antidepressant drug treatments. *Neuroscience, 15*(11), 7539–7547.

Nock, M. K., Green, J. G., Hwang, I., McLaughlin, K. A., Sampson, N. A., Zaslavsky, A. M., & Kessler, R. C. (2013). Prevalence, correlates, and treatment of lifetime suicidal behavior among adolescents. *Journal of the American Medical Academy: Psychiatry, 70*(3), 300–310.

Nolen-Hoeksema, S. (1990). *Sex differences in depression.* Stanford, CA: Stanford University Press.

Nolen-Hoeksema, S. (1991). Responses to depression and their effects on the duration of depressive episodes. *Journal of Abnormal Psychology, 100*(4), 569.

Nolen-Hoeksema, S., & Girgus, J. S. (1994). The emergence of gender differences in depression during adolescence. *Psychological Bulletin, 115*(3), 424–443.

Nolen-Hoeksema, S., Girgus, J., & Seligman, M. E. P. (1992). Predictors and consequences of childhood depressive symptoms: A 5-year longitudinal study. *Journal of Abnormal Psychology, 101*, 405–422.

Nolen-Hoeksema, S., Wisco, B. E., & Lyubomirsky, S. (2008). Rethinking rumination. *Perspectives on Psychological Science, 3*(5), 400–424.

Novick, J. S., Stewart, J. W., Wisniewski, S. R., Cook, I. A., Manev, R., Nierenberg, A. A., . . . Star*D Investigators. (2005). Clinical and demographic features of atypical depression in outpatients with major depressive disorder: Preliminary findings from STAR*D. *Journal of Clinical Psychiatry, 66*(8), 1002–1011.

O'Connor, T. G., McGuire, S., Reiss, D., Hetherington, E. M., & Plomin, R. (1998). Co-occurrence of depressive symptoms and antisocial behavior in adolescents: A common genetic liability. *Journal of Abnormal Psychology, 107*(1), 27–37.

O'Connor, T. G., Neiderhiser, J. M., Reiss, D., Hetherington, E. M., & Plomin, R. (1998). Genetic contributions to continuity, change, and co-occurrence of antisocial and depressive symptoms in adolescence. *Journal of Child Psychology and Psychiatry, 39*(3), 323–336.

O'Hara, M. W. (2009). Postpartum depression: What we know. *Journal of Clinical Psychology, 65*(12), 1258–1269.

O'Hara, M. W., Neunaber, D. J., & Zekoski, E. M. (1984). Prospective study of postpartum depression: Prevalence, course, and predictive factors. *Journal of Abnormal Psychology, 93*(2), 158–171.

O'Hara, M. W., Schlechte, J. A., Lewis, D. A., & Varner, M. W. (1991). Controlled prospective study of postpartum mood disorders: Psychological, environmental, and hormonal variables. *Journal of Abnormal Psychology, 100*(1), 63–73.

Olfson, M., Kessler, R. C., Berglund, P. A., & Lin, E. (2008). Psychiatric disorder onset and first treatment contact in the United States and Ontario. *American Journal of Psychiatry, 155*(10), 1415–1422.

Olino, T. M., Durbin, C. E., Klein, D. N., Hayden, E. P., & Dyson, M. W. (2013). Gender differences in young children's temperament traits: A multi-method analysis. *Journal of Personality, 81*(2), 119–129.

Olino, T. M., Shankman, S. A., Klein, D. N., Seeley, J. R., Pettit, J. W., Farmer, R. F., & Lewinsohn, P. M. (2012). Lifetime rates of psychopathology in single versus multiple diagnostic assessments: Comparison in community sample of probands and siblings. *Journal of Psychiatric Research, 46*(9), 1217–1222.

Ormel, J., Rosmalen, J., & Farmer, A. (2004). Neuroticism: A noninformative marker of vulnerability to psychopathology. *Social Psychiatry and Psychiatric Epidemiology, 39*(11), 906–912.

Orstavik, R., Kendler, K. S., Czajkowski, N., Tambs, K., & Reichborn-Kjennerud, T. (2007). The relationship between depressive personality disorder and major depressive disorder: A population-based twin study. *American Journal of Psychiatry, 164*, 1866–1872.

Overmier, J. B., & Seligman, M. E. (1967). Effects of inescapable shock upon subsequent escape and avoidance responding. *Journal of Comparative and Physiological Psychology, 63*(1), 28–33.

Pagnin, D., de Queiroz, V., Pini, S., & Cassano, G. B. (2004). Efficacy of ECT in depression: A meta-analytic review. *Journal of ECT, 20*(1), 13–20.

Papolos, D. F., & Papolos, J. D. (1999). *The bipolar child: The definitive and reassuring guide to one of childhood's most misunderstood disorders.* New York, NY: Broadway Books.

Parker, G., Roy, K., Mitchell, P., Wilhelm, K., Malhi, G., & Hadzi-Pavlovic, D. (2002). A typical depression: A reappraisal. *American Journal of Psychiatry, 159*, 1470–1479.

Parrish, C. L., & Radomsky, A. S. (2010). Why do people seek reassurance and check repeatedly? An investigation of factors involved in compulsive behavior in OCD and depression. *Journal of Anxiety Disorders, 24*(2), 211–222.

Paulson, J. F., & Bazemore, S. D. (2010). Prenatal and postpartum depression in fathers and its association with maternal depression. *Journal of the American Medical Association, 303*(19), 1961–1969.

Paykel, E. S. (2003). Life events and affective disorders. *Acta Psychiatrica Scandinavica, 108*, 61–66.

Peluso, M. A., Hatch, J. P., Glahn, D. C., Monkul, E. S., Sanches, M., Najt, P., et al. (2007). Trait impulsivity in patients with mood disorders. *Journal of Affective Disorders, 100*(1–3), 227–231.

Perlis, R. H., Ostacher, M. J., Patel, J. K., Marangell, L. B., Zhang, H., et al. (2006). Predictors of recurrence in bipolar disorder: Primary outcomes from the Systematic Treatment Enhancement Program for Bipolar Disorder (STEP-BD). *Focus, 4*, 553–561.

Perugi, G., Akiskal, H. S., Lattanzi, L., Cecconi, D., Mastrocinque, C., Patronelli, A., . . . Bemi, E. (1998). The high prevalence of 'soft' bipolar (II) features in atypical depression. *Comprehensive Psychiatry, 39*(2), 63–71.

Pescosolido, B. A., Martin, J. K., Long, S., Medina, T. R., Phelan, J. C., & Link, B. G. (2010). "A disease like any other"? A decade of change in public reactions to schizophrenia, depression, and alcohol dependence. *American Journal of Psychiatry, 167*(11), 1321–1330.

Phillips, R. G., & LeDoux, J. E. (1992). Differential contribution of amygdala and hippocampus to cued and contextual fear conditioning. *Behavioral Neuroscience, 106*(2), 274–285.

Pine, D. P., Cohen, P., Gurley, D., Brook, J., & Ma, Y. (1998). The risk for early-adulthood anxiety and depressive disorders in adolescents with anxiety and depressive disorders. *Archives of General Psychiatry, 55*(1), 56–64.

Pine, D. S., Cohen, E., Cohen, P., & Brook, J. (1999). Adolescent depressive symptoms as predictors of adult depression: Moodiness or mood disorder? *American Journal of Psychiatry, 156*, 133–135.

Pizzagalli, D. A., Holmes, A. J., Dillon, D. G., Goetz, E. L., Birk, J. L., Bogdan, R., . . . Fava, M. (2009). Reduced caudate and nucleus accumbens response to rewards in unmedicated individuals with major depressive disorder. *American Journal of Psychiatry, 166*(6), 702–710.

Plomin, R., & Bergeman, C. S. (1991). The nature of nurture: Genetic influence on "environmental" measures. *Behavioral and Brain Sciences, 14*(3), 373–386.

Pogge, D. L., Wayland-Smith, D., Zacchario, M., Borgaro, S., Stokes, J., & Harvey, P. D. (2001). Diagnosis of adolescent inpatients: Structured diagnostic procedures compared to clinical chart diagnoses. *Psychiatry Research, 101*(1), 47–54.

Porsolt, R. D., Bertin, A., & Jalfre, M. (1978). "Behavioural despair" in rats and mice: Strain differences and the effects of imipramine. *European Journal of Pharmacology, 51*(3), 291–294.

Post, R. M. (1992). Transduction of psychosocial stress into the neurobiology of recurrent affective disorder. *American Journal of Psychiatry, 149*, 999–1010.

Post, R. M. (2007). Role of BDNF in bipolar and unipolar disorder: Clinical and theoretical implications. *Journal of Psychiatric Research, 41*, 979–990.

Post, R. M., & Leverich, G. S. (2006). The role of psychosocial stress in the onset and progression of bipolar disorder and its comorbidities: The need for earlier and alternative modes of therapeutic intervention. *Development and Psychopathology, 18*, 1181–1211.

Price, J., Sloman, L., Gardner, R., Gilbert, P., & Rohde, P. (1994). The social competition hypothesis of depression. *British Journal of Psychiatry, 164*, 309–315.

Putnam, F. W. (2002). Ten-year research update review: Child sexual abuse. *Journal of the American Academy of Child and Adolescent Psychiatry, 42*(3), 269–278.

Quilty, L. C., Sellbom, M., Tackett, J. L., & Bagby, R. M. (2009). Personality trait predictors of bipolar disorder symptoms. *Psychiatry Research, 169*(2), 159–163.

Raes, F., Hermans, D., Williams, J. M. G., Deymettenaere, S., Sabbe, B., Pieters, G., & Eelen, P. (2006). Is overgeneral autobiographical memory an isolated memory phenomenon in major depression? *Memory, 14*(5), 584–594.

Rao, U., Ryan, N. D., Birmaher, B., Dahl, R. E., Williamson, D. E., et al. (1995). Unipolar depression in adolescents: Clinical outcome in adulthood. *Journal of the American Academy of Child and Adolescent Psychiatry, 34*(5), 566–578.

Regier, D. A., Boyd, J. H., Burke, J. D., Rae, D. S., Myers, J. K., Kramer, M., . . . & Locke, B. Z. (1988). One-month prevalence of mental disorders in the United States. *Archives of General Psychiatry, 45*(11), 977–986.

Rehm, L. P. (1977). A self-control model of depression. *Behavior Therapy, 8*(5), 787–804.

Reinecke, M. A., Ryan, N. E., & DuBois, D. L. (1998). Cognitive-behavioral therapy of depression and depressive symptoms during adolescence: A review and meta-analysis. *Journal of the American Academy of Child and Adolescent Psychiatry, 37*(1), 26–34.

Restifo, K., & Bogels, S. (2009). Family process in the development of youth depression: Translating the evidence to treatment. *Clinical Psychology Review, 29*(4), 294–316.

Reynolds, C. F., Miller, M. D., Pasternak, R. E., Frank, E., Perel, J. M., Cornes, C., et al. (1999). Treatment of bereavement-related major depressive episodes in later life: A controlled study of acute and continuation treatment with nortriptyline and interpersonal psychotherapy. *American Journal of Psychiatry, 156*(2), 202–208.

Rice, F., Harold, G., & Thapar, A. (2002). The genetic aetiology of childhood depression: A review. *Journal of Child Psychology and Psychiatry, 43*(1), 65–79.

Robb, J. C., Young, L. T., Cooke, R. G., & Joffe, R. T. (1998). Gender differences in patients with bipolar disorder influence outcome in the Medical Outcomes Survey (SF-20) subscale score. *Journal of Affective Disorders, 49*(3), 189–193.

Roberts, B. W., & DelVecchio, W. F. (2000). The rank-order consistency of personality traits from childhood to old age: A quantitative review of longitudinal studies. *Psychological Bulletin, 126*(1), 3–25.

Roberts, B. W., Kuncel, N. R., Shiner, R., Caspi, A., & Goldberg, L. R. (2007). The power of personality: The comparative validity of personality traits, socioeconomic status, and cognitive ability for predicting important life outcomes. *Perspectives on Psychological Science, 2*(4), 313–345.

Roberts, B. W., & Mroczek, D. (2008). Personality trait change in adulthood. *Current Directions in Psychological Science, 17*, 31–35.

Roberts, B. W., Walton, K. E., & Viechtbauer, W. (2006). Patterns of mean-level change in personality traits across the life course: A meta-analysis of longitudinal studies. *Psychological Bulletin, 132*(1), 1–25.

Robinson, J. J., Thompson, J. M., Gallagher, P., Goswami, U., Young, A. H., Ferrier, I. N., & Moore, P. B. (2006). A meta-analysis of cognitive deficits in euthymic patients with bipolar disorder. *Journal of Affective Disorders, 93*, 105–115.

Robinson, L. J., & Ferrier, I. N. (2006). Evolution of cognitive impairment in bipolar disorder: A systematic review of cross-sectional evidence. *Bipolar Disorders, 8*, 103–116.

Rohde, P., Clarke, G. N., Mace, D. E., Jorgensen, J. S., & Seeley, J. R. (2004). An efficacy/effectiveness study of cognitive-behavioral treatment for adolescents with comorbid major depression and conduct disorder. *Journal of the American Academy of Child and Adolescent Psychiatry, 43*(6), 660–668.

Rohde, P., Lewinsohn, P. M., Klein, D. N., Seeley, J. R., & Gau, J. M. (2013). Key characteristics of major depression occurring in childhood, adolescence, emerging adulthood, and adulthood. *Clinical Psychological Science, 1*(1), 41–53.

Rose, D., Fleischmann, P., Wykes, T., Leese, M., & Bindman, J. (2003). Patients' perspectives on electroconvulsive therapy: Systematic review. *British Medical Journal, 326*(7403), 1363.

Rosenthal, D. (1963). A suggested conceptual framework. In D. Rosenthal (Ed.), *The Genain quadruplets* (pp. 505–516). New York, NY: Basic Books.

Rothbart, M. K., Ahadi, S. A., Hershey, K. L., & Fisher, P. (2001). Investigations of temperament at three to seven years: The Children's Behavior Questionnaire. *Child Development, 72*(5), 1394–1408.

Roy-Bryne, P., Post, R. M., Uhde, T. W., Porcu, T., & Davis, D. (1985). The longitudinal course of recurrent affective illness: Life chart data from research patients at the NIMH. *Acta Psychiatrica Scandinavica, 71,* 1–33.

Rudolph, K. D., & Klein, D. N. (2009). Exploring depressive personality traits in youth: Origins, correlates, and developmental consequences. *Development and Psychopathology, 21*(4), 1155–1180.

Russo-Neustadt, A. A., Beard, R. C., Huang, Y. M., & Cotman, C. W. (2000). Physical activity and antidepressant treatment potentiate the expression of specific brain-derived neurotrophic factor transcripts in the rat hippocampus. *Neuroscience, 101,* 305–312.

Rutter, M. (1990). Commentary: Some focus and process considerations regarding effects of parental depression on children. *Developmental Psychology, 26*(1), 60–67.

Ryder, A. G., & Chentsova-Dutton, Y. E. (2012). Depression in culture context: "Chinese somatization," revisited. *Psychiatric Clinics of North America, 35*(1), 15–36.

Ryder, A. G., Quilty, L. C., Vachon, D. D., & Bagby, R. M. (2010). Depressive personality and treatment outcome in major depressive disorder. *Journal of Personality Disorders, 24*(3), 392–404.

Sachs, G. S., Nierenberg, A. A., Calabrese, J. R., Marangell, L. B., Wisniewski, S. R., Gyulai, L., et al. (2007). Effectiveness of adjunctive antidepressant treatment for bipolar depression. *New England Journal of Medicine, 356*(17), 1711–1722.

Sajatovic, M., Valenstein, M., Blow, F. C., Ganoczy, D., & Ignacio, R. V. (2006). Treatment adherence with antipsychotic medications in bipolar disorder. *Bipolar Disorders, 8*(3), 232–241.

Salamone, J. D., Aberman, J. E., Sokolowski, J. D., & Cousins, M. S. (1999). Nucleus accumbens dopamine and rate of responding: Neurochemical and behavioral studies. *Psychobiology, 27*(2), 236–247.

Schalet, B. D., Durbin, C. E., & Revelle, W. (2011). Multidimensional structure of the Hypomanic Personality Scale. *Psychological Assessment, 23*(2), 504–522.

Schatzberg, A. F., Rush, A. J., Arnow, B. A., Banks, P. L., Blalock, J. A., Borian, F. E., et al. (2005). Chronic depression: Medication (nefazadone) or psychotherapy (CBASP) is effective when the other is not. *Archives of General Psychiatry, 62*(5), 513–520.

Schildkraut, J. J. (1965). The catecholamine hypothesis of affective disorders: A review of supporting evidence. *American Journal of Psychiatry, 122*(5), 509–522.

Schneider, K. (1958). *Psychopathic personalities* (M. W. Hamilton, Trans.). London, England: Grune & Stratton.

Schumacher, J., Jamra, R. A., Becker, T., Ohlraun, S., Klopps, N., Binder, E. B., et al. (2005). Evidence for a relationship between genetic variants at the brain-derived neurotrophic factor (BDNF) locus and major depression. *Biological Psychiatry, 58*(4), 307–314.

Scott, J. A. N., Paykel, E., Moriss, R., Bentall, R., Kinderman, P., Johnson, T., et al. (2006). Cognitive-behavioural therapy for severe and recurrent bipolar disorders: Randomised controlled trial. *British Journal of Psychiatry, 188*(4), 313–320.

Scourfeld, J., Rice, F., Thapar, A., Harold, G. T., Martin, N., & McGuffin, P. (2003). Depressive symptoms in children and adolescents: Changing aetiological influences with development. *Journal of Child Psychology and Psychiatry, 44*(7), 968–976.

Seamans, J. K., & Yang, C. R. (2004). The principal features and mechanisms of dopamine modulation in the prefrontal cortex. *Progress in Neurobiology, 74*(1), 1–58.

Shea, M. T., Widiger, T. A., & Klein, M. H. (1992). Comorbidity of personality disorders and depression: Implications for treatment. *Journal of Consulting and Clinical Psychology, 60*(6), 857.

Sheline, Y. I., Mittler, B. L., & Mintun, M. A. (2002). The hippocampus and depression. *European Psychiatry, 17*, 300–305.

Sheline, Y. I., Sanghavi, M., Mintun, M. A., & Gado, M. H. (1999). Depression duration but not age predicts hippocampal volume loss in medically healthy women with recurrent major depression. *Journal of Neuroscience, 19*(12), 5034–5043.

Shenk, J. W. (2005). *Lincoln's melancholy: How depression challenged a president and fueled his greatness.* New York, NY: Houghton Mifflin.

Shih, R. A., Belmonte, P. L., & Zandi, P. P. (2004). A review of the evidence from family, twin and adoption studies for a genetic contribution to adult psychiatric disorders. *International Review of Psychiatry, 16*, 260–283.

Siegle, G. J., Ingram, R. E., & Matt, G. E. (2002). Affective interference: An explanation for negative attention biases in dysphoria? *Cognitive Therapy and Research, 26*(1), 73–87.

Siever, L. J., & Davis, K. L. (1985). Toward a dysregulation hypothesis of depression. *American Journal of Psychiatry, 142*, 1017–1031.

Silberg, J. L., Rutter, M., & Eaves, L. (2001). Genetic and environmental influences on the temporal association between early anxiety and later depression in girls. *Biological Psychiatry, 49*(12), 1040–1049.

Simon, G. E., & VonKorff, M. (1992). Reevaluation of secular trends in depression rates. *American Journal of Epidemiology, 135*, 1411–1422.

Simon, G. E., VonKorff, M., & Barlow, W. (1995). Health care costs of primary care patients with recognized depression. *Archives of General Psychiatry, 52*(10), 850–856.

Simon, N. M., Smoller, J. W., McNamara, K. L., Maser, R. S., Zalta, A. K., Pollack, M. H., et al. (2006). Telomere shortening and mood disorders: Preliminary support for a chronic stress model of accelerated aging. *Biological Psychiatry, 60*(5), 432–435.

Simons, A. D., Murphy, G. E., Levine, J. L., & Wetzel, R. D. (1986). Cognitive therapy and pharmacotherapy for depression: Sustained improvement over one year. *Archives of General Psychiatry, 43*(1), 43–48.

Sklar, P., Gabriel, S. B., McInnis, M. G., Bennett, P., Lim, Y. M., Tsan, G., et al. (2002). Family-based association study of 76 candidate genes in bipolar disorder: BDNF is a potential risk locus. *Molecular Psychiatry, 7*(6), 579–593.

Slater, E., Roth, M., & Mayer-Gross, W. (1969). *Clinical psychiatry.* Baltimore, MD: Williams & Wilkins.

Solomon, D. A., Keller, M. B., Leon, A. C., Mueller, T. I., Lavori, P. W., et al. (2000). Multiple recurrences of major depressive disorder. *American Journal of Psychiatry, 157*(2), 229–233.

Spataro, J., Mullen, P. E., Burgess, P. M., Wells, D. L., & Moss, S. A. (2004). Impact of child sexual abuse on mental health: Prospective study in males and females. *British Journal of Psychiatry, 184*, 416–421.

Spijker, J., deGraaf, R., Bijl, R. V., Beekman, A. T. F., Ormel, J., & Nolen, W. A. (2002). Duration of major depressive episodes in the general population: Results from the Netherlands Mental Health Survey and Incidence Study (NEMESIS). *British Journal of Psychiatry, 181*, 208–213.

Squire, L. R., & Slater, P. C. (1983). Electroconvulsive therapy and complaints of memory dysfunction: A prospective three-year follow-up study. *British Journal of Psychiatry, 142*(1), 1–8.

Srivastava, S., John, O. P., Gosling, S. D., & Potter, J. (2003). Development of personality in early and middle adulthood: Set like plaster or persistent change? *Journal of Personality and Social Psychology, 84*(5), 1041–1053.

Stack, S., & Eshelman, J. R. (1998). Marital status and happiness: A 17-nation study. *Journal of Marriage and Family, 60*(2), 527–536.

Sterling, P., & Eyer, J. (1988). Allostasis: A new paradigm to explain arousal pathology. In S. Fisher & J. Reason (Eds.), *Handbook of life stress, cognition, and health* (pp. 629–649). Oxford, England: John Wiley & Sons.

Stice, E., Presnell, K., & Bearman, S. K. (2001). Relation of early menarche to depression, eating disorders, substance abuse, and comorbid psychopathology among adolescent girls. *Developmental Psychology, 37*(5), 608–619.

Stiles, W. B., Barkham, M., Mellor-Clark, J., & Connel, J. (2008). Effectiveness of cognitive-behavioural, person-centered, and psychodynamic therapies in UK primary-care routine practice: Replication in a larger sample. *Psychological Medicine, 38*(5), 677–688.

Stoll, A. L., Renshaw, P. F., Yurgelun-Todd, D. A., & Cohen, B. M. (2000). Neuroimaging in bipolar disorder: What have we learned? *Biological Psychiatry, 48*, 505–517.

Stone, E. A., Lin, Y., & Quartermain, D. (2008). A final common pathway for depression? Progress toward a general conceptual framework. *Neuroscience & Biobehavioral Reviews, 32*(3), 508–524.

Strakowski, S. M., DelBello, M. P., Fleck, D. E., & Arndt, S. (2000). The impact of substance abuse on the course of bipolar disorder. *Biological Psychiatry, 48*(6), 477–485.

Strakowski, S. M., Keck, P. E. Jr., McElroy, S. L., West, S. A., Sax, K. W., Hawkins, J. M., et al. (1998). Twelve-month outcome after a first hospitalization for affective psychosis. *Archives of General Psychiatry, 55*, 49–55.

Stringaris, A., Baroni, A., Haimm, C., Brotman, M., Lowe, C. H., Myers, F., . . . Leibenluft, E. (2010). Pediatric bipolar disorder versus severe mood dysregulation: Risk for manic episodes on follow-up. *Journal of the American Academy of Child and Adolescent Psychiatry, 49*(4), 397–405.

Stroud, C. B., Davila, J., Hammen, C., & Vrshek-Schallhorn, S. (2010). Severe and nonsevere events in first onsets versus recurrences of depression: Evidence for stress sensitization. *Journal of Abnormal Psychology, 120*(1), 142–154.

Styron, W. (1990). *Darkness visible: A memoir of madness.* New York, NY: Random House.

Sullivan, P. F., Neale, M. C., & Kendler, K. S. (2000). Genetic epidemiology of major depression: Review and meta-analysis. *American Journal of Psychiatry, 157*(10), 1552–1562.

Sullivan, P. F., Prescott, C. A., & Kendler, K. S. (2002). The subtypes of major depression in a twin registry. *Journal of Affective Disorders, 68,* 273–284.

Surguladze, S., Brammer, M. J., Keedwell, P., Giampietro, V., Young, A. W., Travis, M. J., et al. (2005). A differential pattern of neural response toward sad versus happy facial expressions in major depressive disorder. *Biological Psychiatry, 57*(3), 201–209.

Swann, A. C., Dougherty, D. M., Pazzaglia, P. J., Pham, M., & Moeller, F. G. (2004). Impulsivity: A link between bipolar disorder and substance abuse. *Bipolar Disorders, 6*(3), 204–212.

Swann, W. B., (1983). Self-verification: Bringing social reality into harmony with the self. In J. Suls & A. G. Greenwald (Eds.), *Social psychological perspectives on the self* (Vol. 2, pp. 33–66). Hillsdale, NJ: Erlbaum.

Swann, W. B., Wenzlaff, R. M., Krull, D. S., & Pelha, B. W. (1992). Allure of negative feedback: Self-verification strivings among depressed persons. *Journal of Abnormal Psychology, 101*(2), 293–306.

Tackett, J. L., Quilty, L. C., Sellbom, M., Rector, N., & Bagby, R. M. (2008). Additional evidence for a quantitative hierarchical model of the mood and anxiety disorders for DSM-V: The context of personality structure. *Journal of Abnormal Psychology, 117,* 812–825.

Tackett, J. L., Waldman, I. D., Van Hulle, C. A., & Lahey, B. B. (2011). Shared genetic influences on negative emotionality and major depression/conduct disorder comorbidity. *Journal of the American Academy of Child & Adolescent Psychiatry, 50*(8), 818–827.

Tang, T. Z., DeRubeis, R. J., Hollon, S. D., Amsterdam, J., Shelton, R., & Schalet, B. (2009). Personality change during depression treatment. *Archives of General Psychiatry, 66*(12), 1322–1330.

Taylor, P. J., Gooding, P., Wood, A. M., & Tarrier, N. (2011). The role of defeat and entrapment in depression, anxiety, and suicide. *Psychological Bulletin, 137*(3), 391–420.

Taylor, S. E., Welch, W. T., Kim, H. S., & Sherman, D. K. (2007). Cultural differences in the impact of social support on psychological and biological stress responses. *Psychological Science, 18*(9), 831–837.

Teasdale, J. D., Segal, Z. V., Mark, J., Williams, G., Ridgeway, V. A., Soulsby, J. M., & Lau, M. A. (2000). Prevention of relapse/recurrence in major depression by mindfulness-based cognitive therapy. *Journal of Consulting and Clinical Psychology, 68*(4), 615–623.

Tellegen, A. (1985). Structures of mood and personality and their relevance to assessing anxiety, with an emphasis on self-report. In A. H. Tuma & J. D. Maser (Eds.), *Anxiety and the anxiety disorders* (pp. 681–706). Hillsdale, NJ: Erlbaum.

Tennant, C., Bebbington, P., & Hurry, J. (1981). The role of life events in depressive illness: Is there a substantial causal relation? *Psychological Medicine, 11*(2), 379–389.

Thase, M. E. (2009). A typical depression: Useful concept, but it's time to revise the *DSM-IV* criteria. *Neuropsychopharmacology, 43*, 2633–2641.

Thase, M. E., & Denko, T. (2008). Pharmacotherapy of mood disorders. *Annual Review of Clinical Psychology, 4*, 53–91.

Thase, M. E., Entsuah, A. R., & Rudolph, R. L. (2001). Remission rates during treatment with venlafaxine or selective serotonin reuptake inhibitors. *The British Journal of Psychiatry, 178*(3), 234–241.

Thase, M. E., & Kupfer, D. J. (1996). Recent developments in the pharmacotherapy of mood disorders: The contribution of psychotherapy and pharmacotherapy to national mental health care. *Journal of Consulting and Clinical Psychology, 64*(4), 646–659.

Tilman, R., & Geller, B. (2007). Definitions of rapid, ultrarapid, and ultradian cycling and of episode duration in pediatric and adult bipolar disorders: A proposal to distinguish episodes from cycles. *Journal of Child and Adolescent Psychopharmacology, 13*(3), 267–271.

Tolin, D. F., & Foa, E. B. (2006). Sex differences in trauma and post-traumatic stress disorder: A quantitative review of 25 years of research. *Psychological Bulletin, 132*(6), 959–992.

Tremblay, L. K., Naranjo, C. A., Cardenas, L., Herrmann, N., & Busto, U. E. (2002). Probing brain reward system function in major depressive disorder: Altered response to dextroamphetamine. *Archives of General Psychiatry, 59*, 409–416.

Tully, E. C., Iacono, W. G., & McGue, M. (2008). An adoption study of parental depression as an environmental liability for adolescent depression and childhood disruptive disorders. *American Journal of Psychiatry, 165*(9), 1148–1154.

Uliaszek, A. A., Zinbarg, R. E., Mineka, S., Craske, M. G., Griffith, J. W., et al. (2012). A longitudinal examination of stress generation in depressive and anxiety disorders. *Journal of Abnormal Psychology, 121*(1), 4–15.

Ustun, T. B., Ayuso-Mateos, J. L., Chatterji, S., Mathers, C., & Murray, C. J. L. (2004). Global burden of depressive disorders in the year 2000. *British Journal of Psychiatry, 18*, 386–392.

Vaidyanathan, U., Patrick, C. J., & Cuthbert, B. N. (2009). Linking dimensional models of internalizing psychopathology to neurobiological systems: Affect-modulated startle as an indicator of fear and distress disorders and affiliated traits. *Psychological Bulletin, 135*, 909–942.

Van Orden, K. A., Witte, T. K., Cukrowicz, K. C., Braithwaite, S., Selby, E. A., & Joiner, T. E. (2010). The interpersonal theory of suicide. *Psychological Review, 117*(2), 575–600.

Van Os, J., & Jones, P. B. (1999). Early risk factors and adult person-environment relationships in affective disorder. *Psychological Medicine, 29*, 1055–1067.

Van Os, J., Jones, P., Lewis, G., Wadsworth, M., & Murray, R. (1997). Developmental precursors of affective illness in a general population birth cohort. *Archives of General Psychiatry, 54*(7), 625–631.

Verona, E., Sachs-Ericsson, N., & Joiner, T. E. (2004). Suicide attempts associated with externalizing psychopathology in an epidemiological sample. *American Journal of Psychiatry, 161*, 444–451.

Victor, T. A., Furey, M. L., Fromm, S. J., Ohman, A., & Drevets, W. C. (2010). Relationship between amygdala responses to masked faces and mood state and treatment in major depressive disorder. *Archives of General Psychiatry, 67*(11), 1128–1138.

Viguera, A., Baldessarini, R., & Tondo, L. (2001). Response to lithium maintenance treatment in bipolar disorders: Comparison of women and men. *Bipolar Disorders, 3*, 245–252.

Vitiello, B., Zuvekas, S. H., & Norquist, G. S. (2006). National estimates of antidepressant medication use among U.S. children, 1997–2002. *Journal of the American Academy of Child and Adolescent Psychiatry, 45*(3), 271–279.

Wakefield, J. C., Schmitz, M. F., First, M. B., & Horwitz, A. V. (2007). Extending the bereavement exclusion for major depression to other losses. *Archives of General Psychiatry, 64*, 433–440.

Wallace, D. F. (1996). *Infinite jest*. New York, NY: Little, Brown.

Wang, P. S., Beck, A. L., Berglund, P., McKenas, D. K., Pronk, N. P., Simon, G. E., & Kessler, R. C. (2004). Effects of major depression on moment-in-time work performance. *American Journal of Psychiatry, 161*(10), 1885–1891.

Warner, V., Wickramaratne, P., & Weissman, M. M. (2008). The role of fear and anxiety in the familial risk for major depression: A three-generation study. *Psychological Medicine, 38,* 1543–1566.

Watson, D. (2009). Differentiating the mood and anxiety disorders: A quadripartite model. *Annual Review of Clinical Psychology, 5,* 221–247.

Watson, D., O'Hara, M. W., Simms, L. J., Kotov, R., & Chmielewski, M. (2007). Development and validation of the Inventory of Depression and Anxiety Symptoms (IDAS). *Psychological Assessment, 19*(3), 253–268.

Watson, P. J., & Andrews, P. W. (2002). Toward a revised evolutionary adaptationist analysis of depression: The social navigation hypothesis. *Journal of Affective Disorders, 72,* 1–14.

Weersing, V. R., Iyengar, S., Kolko, D. J., Birmaher, B., & Brent, D. A. (2006). Effectiveness of cognitive-behavioral therapy for adolescent depression: A benchmarking investigation. *Behavior Therapy, 37,* 36–48.

Weersing, V. R., & Weisz, J. R. (2002). Community clinic treatment of depressed youth: Benchmarking usual care against CBT clinical trials. *Journal of Consulting and Clinical Psychology, 70*(2), 299–310.

Weersing, V. R., Weisz, J. R., & Donenberg, G. R. (2002). Development of the Therapy Procedures Checklist: A therapist-report measure of technique use in child and adolescent treatment. *Journal of Clinical Child and Adolescent Psychology, 31*(2), 168–180.

Wehr, T. A., Duncan, W. C., Sher, L., Aeschbach, D., Schwartz, P. J., Turner, E. H., . . . Rosenthal, N. E. (2001). A circadian signal of change in season in patients with seasonal affective disorder. *Archives of General Psychiatry, 58*(12), 1108–1114.

Weiss, E. L., Longhurst, J. G., & Mazure, C. M. (1999). Childhood sexual abuse as a risk factor for depression in women: Psychosocial and neurobiological correlates. *American Journal of Psychiatry, 156,* 816–828.

Weissman, M. M., Wickramaratne, P., Merikangas, K. R., Leckman, J. G., Prusoff, B. A., et al. (1984). Onset of major depression in early adulthood: Increased familial loading and specificity. *Archives of General Psychiatry, 41,* 1136–1143.

Weissman, M. M., Wolk, S., Goldstein, R. B., Moreau, D., Adams, P. et al. (1999). Depressed adolescents grown up. *Journal of the American Medical Association, 281*(18), 1707–1713.

Weissman, M. W., Bland, R. C., Canino, G. J., Faravelli, C., Greenwald, S., et al. (1996). Cross-national epidemiology of major depression and bipolar disorder. *Journal of the American Medical Association, 276*(4), 293–299.

Weissman, M. W., Bland, R., Joyce, P. R., Newman, S., Wells, J. E., & Wittchen, H.-U. (1993). Sex differences in rates of depression: Cross-national perspectives. *Journal of Affective Disorders, 29*(2/3), 77–84.

Weissman, M. W., & Klerman, G. L. (1977). Sex differences and the epidemiology of depression. *Archives of General Psychiatry, 34*(1), 98–111.

Weisz, J. R., McCarty, C. A., & Valeri, S. M. (2006). Effects of psychotherapy for depression in children and adolescents: A meta-analysis. *Psychological Bulletin, 132*(1), 132–149.

Westen, D., & Morrison, K. (2001). A multidimensional meta-analysis of treatments for depression, panic, and generalized anxiety disorder: An empirical examination of the status of empirically supported therapies. *Journal of Consulting and Clinical Psychology, 69*(6), 875–899.

Whisman, M. A. (2001). In S. R. H. Beach (Ed.), *Marital and family processes in depression: A scientific foundation for clinical practice* (pp. 3–24). Washington, DC: American Psychological Association.

Whisman, M. A. (2007). Marital distress and DSM-IV psychiatric disorders in a population-based national survey. *Journal of Abnormal Psychology, 116*(3), 638.

Whisman, M. A., & Bruce, M. L. (1999). Marital dissatisfaction and incidence of major depressive episode in a community sample. *Journal of Abnormal Psychology, 108*(4), 674.

Wichers, M., Myin-Germeys, I., Jacobs, N., Peeters, F., Kenis, G., Derom, C., et al. (2007). Genetic risk of depression and stress-induced negative affect in daily life. *British Journal of Psychiatry, 191*(3), 218–223.

Wikgren, M., Maripuu, M., Karlsson, T., Nordfjall, K., Bergdahl, J., Hultdin, J., . . . Norrback, K.-F. (2012). Short telomeres in depression and the general population are associated with a hypocortisolemic state. *Biological Psychiatry, 71*(4), 294–300.

Williams, J. M. G., Barnhofer, T., Crane, C., Herman, D., Raes, F., Watkins, E., & Dalgleish, T. (2007). Autobiographical memory specificity and emotional disorder. *Psychological Bulletin, 133*(1), 122.

Williams, J. M. G., Watts, F. N., MacLeod, C., & Mathews, A. (Eds.). (1997). *Cognitive psychology and emotional disorders* (2nd ed.). New York, NY: John Wiley & Sons.

Wilson, D. R. (1998). Evolutionary epidemiology and manic depression. *British Journal of Medical Psychology, 71*, 375–395.

Wilson, S., & Durbin, C. E. (2010). Effects of paternal depression on fathers' parenting behaviors: A meta-analytic review. *Clinical Psychology Review, 30*, 167–180.

Winokur, G., Coryell, W., Endicott, J., & Akiskal, H. (1993). Further distinctions between manic-depressive illness (bipolar disorder) and primary depressive disorder (unipolar depression). *American Journal of Psychiatry, 150*, 1176–1181.

Wittchen, H.-U., Kessler, R. C., Pfister, H., Hofler, H., & Lieb, R. (2000). Why do people with anxiety disorders become depressed? A prospective-longitudinal community study. *Acta Psychiatrica Scandinavica, 102*, 14–23.

Wittchen, H. U., & Pittrow, D. (2002). Prevalence, recognition and management of depression in primary care in Germany: The Depression 2000 study. *Human Psychopharmacology: Clinical and Experimental, 17*(Suppl. 1), 1S–11S.

Woolley, C. S., Gould, E., & McEwen, B. S. (1990). Exposure to excess glucocorticoids alters dendritic morphology of adult hippocampal pyramidal neurons. *Brain Research, 531*(1), 225–231.

World Health Organization. (2005). *ICD-10: International statistical classification of diseases and related health problems* (10th Rev. ed.). Geneva, Switzerland: Author.

Wozniak, J., Biederman, J., Kiely, K., Ablon, J. S., Faraone, S. V., Mundy, E., & Mennin, D. (1995). Mania-like symptoms suggestive of childhood-onset bipolar disorder in clinically referred children. *Journal of the American Academy of Child and Adolescent Psychiatry, 34*(7), 867–876.

Young, J. (1999). *Cognitive therapy for personality disorders: A schema-focused approach* (3rd ed.). Sarasota, FL: Professional Resource Exchange.

Zeiss, A. M., & Lewinsohn, P. M. (1988). Enduring deficits after remissions of depression: A test of the scar hypothesis. *Behaviour Research and Therapy, 26*(2), 151–158.

Zisook, S., Lesser, I., Stewart, J. W., Wisniewski, S. R., Balasubramani, G. K., Fava, M., . . . Rush, A. J. (2007). Effect of age of onset on the course of major depressive disorder. *American Journal of Psychiatry, 164*, 1539–1546.

Zisook, S., & Shuchter, S. R. (2001). Treatment of the depressions of bereavement. *American Behavioral Scientist, 44*(5), 782–797.

Zubenko, G. S., Zubenko, W. N., Spiker, D. G., Giles, D. E., & Kaplan, B. B. (2001). The malignancy of recurrent, early-onset major depression: A family study. *American Journal of Medical Genetics, 106*, 690–699.

Zubin, J., & Spring, B. (1977). Vulnerability: A new view of schizophrenia. *Journal of Abnormal Psychology, 86*(2), 103–126.

Index